The Arnold and Caroline Rose Monograph Series
of the American Sociological Association

The cooperative workplace

For other titles in this series, turn to p. 222.

The cooperative workplace

Potentials and dilemmas of organizational democracy and participation

Joyce Rothschild
University of Toledo

J. Allen Whitt
University of Louisville

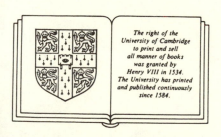

The right of the
University of Cambridge
to print and sell
all manner of books
was granted by
Henry VIII in 1534.
The University has printed
and published continuously
since 1584.

Cambridge University Press

Cambridge

New York   Port Chester   Melbourne   Sydney

Published by the Press Syndicate of the University of Cambridge
The Pitt Building, Trumpington Street, Cambridge CB2 1RP
40 West 20th Street, New York, NY 10011, USA
10 Stamford Road, Oakleigh, Melbourne 3166, Australia

First published 1986
Reprinted 1988
First paperback edition 1989
Reprinted 1990

Printed in the United States of America

Library of Congress Cataloging in Publication Data

Rothschild, Joyce, 1948-
The cooperative workplace.
(The Arnold and Caroline Rose monograph series of the American
Sociological Association)
Bibliography: p.
Includes index
I. Management – Employee participation. 2. Democracy.
3. Political participation. 4. Cooperation.
I. Whitt, J. Allen, 1940-   II. Title
III. Series.
HD5650.R736   1986   658.3′152   86-8310

British Library Cataloguing in Publication Data

Rothschild, Joyce
The cooperative workplace: potentials
and dilemmas of organizational democracy
and participation.–(American Sociological Association
Rose Monograph series)
1. Organization
I. Title   II. Whitt, J. Allen   III. Series
3023′5   HM131

ISBN 0-521-32967-1 hardback
ISBN 0-521-37942-3 paperback

Contents

Acknowledgments

This book was born out of curiosity about how workplaces might be organized without a hierarchy of bosses and workers. But as anyone who has written a book knows, it is a long journey from creative inspiration to final book manuscript. This book represents many years of research, of interpreting and making sense of research observations, of distilling the work of others, and of rethinking and revising conclusions. Many people have contributed to its development along the way.

Long before this project was undertaken, numerous people contributed to our thinking about it. The seeds that later led to a professional interest in democracy were probably planted by Sam and Evelyn Rothschild, who understood the value of a democratic household and self-initiated action. Fellow graduate students at the University of California, Santa Barbara, now sociologists all around the country, provided an abundance of moral support and an ever-present sounding board for ideas not yet polished. Especially to be thanked are Laura Nathan, Tom Koenig, Brad Smith, Rosemary Taylor, and Robert Wolf. This analysis of democratic organizations began as dissertation research and we are grateful to the Department of Sociology at Santa Barbara for providing the kind of intellectually stimulating milieu in which students may learn how to formulate their own questions. Debts are owed especially to Professors Richard Flacks, Bettina Huber, Richard Appelbaum, and Harvey Molotch. Together they combined enthusiasm with considered criticism, and they coupled their high expectations of scholarship with personal autonomy.

In the course of working on this book we have benefited from the ideas of many other people who have given serious attention to the prospects for non-hierarchical forms of organization: Howard Aldrich, Paul Bernstein, Joseph Blasi, Henry Etzkowitz, Art Hochner, Rosabeth Kanter, Frank Lindenfeld, Ray Loveridge, Jane Mansbridge, Patricia Martin, Carole Pateman, Charles Perrow, Corey Rosen, Raymond Russell, Ann Swidler, and William Foote Whyte come especially to mind. Each of these people read one part or another of our manuscript, offered scholarly criticism and innumerable references, and brought a valued sense of professional camaraderie.

A number of institutions provided the time and financial support to pursue different aspects of the work reported in this book: The New Systems of Work and Participation Program at Cornell University's School of Industrial and Labor Relations, supported by funds from the National Institute of Mental Health, and the Program on Non-Profit Organizations at Yale University's Institution for Social and Policy Studies.

This book benefited as well from the rigorous review of Ernest Q. Campbell and the anonymous reviewers he enlisted to review it for the Arnold and Caroline Rose Monograph Series, sponsored by the American Sociological Association.

Finally, this research could literally not have been done were it not for the openness of the participants in the alternative organizations studied. Because the names used in this study are fictitious, they cannot be mentioned by name here, but we sincerely wish to thank them for generously giving of themselves and their time. We hope that this work justifies their many confidences.

Remaining errors are quite obviously our own doing.

J.R., J.A.W.

Introduction

At least since the 1911 publication of Robert Michels's *Political Parties,* the process by which organizational democracy yields to oligarchy has been accepted – however regretfully – as inevitable. Organizations with no bosses and no followers, organizations in which all members have an equal say in running things, have largely escaped the notice of organizational analysts. Though democratic organizations have long existed, detailed study of them has been displaced by the assumption that they are fragile, short-lived structures or that they will eventually come under the control of one or a few leaders, thus losing their defining characteristic. This expectation has become a cornerstone of twentieth-century social science.

Today in the United States we are witnessing the birth and life of scores of grass-roots organizations – organizations calling themselves "collectives," "cooperatives," and "alternative institutions" – that aspire to be radically democratic in purpose and in practice. These organizations provide us with a unique opportunity to take a fresh empirical look at the supposed inevitability of oligarchy and bureaucracy. This book examines the nature, possibilities, and limits of direct democracy in such organizations. We develop a theory of democratic organizations and show how this theory is applicable to a broad range of directly democratic and related organizations.

This subject is relevant to anyone who would hope to live and work in a democratic society; it is relevant also to anyone who has written off the possibility of organizational democracy as utopian. These anomalous organizations reject bureaucracy and attempt to fashion an alternative, providing a natural laboratory for evaluating long-held assumptions about the universality of hierarchy and bureaucracy. To the extent that these organizations succeed, they promise to broaden our theory of organizations and to provide concrete models of alternative organizational practices.

Grounded in empirical observation of collectivist organizations in many different domains, this book has two major theoretical aims. The first is to try to construct a systematic, definitive model of the organizational properties of collectivist or cooperative organizations. *We define a collective or a cooper-*

1

ative as any enterprise in which control rests ultimately and overwhelmingly with the member–employees–owners, regardless of the particular legal framework through which this is achieved.[1] It is the priority given to democratic methods of control that is the essential characteristic of the contemporary cooperative. Since the right to govern rests ultimately with the collectivity of members and delegated authority is accountable to the group as a whole, members also call their enterprises "collectives." In the nineteenth century lexicon, these enterprises would have been called "producers' cooperatives." The term remains technically correct but the participants themselves seldom use this designation.[2] Although the terms *collectives, cooperatives,* and, more recently, *alternative institutions* have been used historically to denote a range of organizational types, we are interested in the central characteristic they all have in common – direct, democratic control by the members. For this reason, we often use these designations interchangeably.

The second theoretical goal of this work is to discover those conditions that undermine or support the most essential characteristic of cooperatives: decision-making procedures based on participatory democracy.

Cooperatives are important organizations. Throughout their long history in the United States and Europe, they have often formed the cutting edge of movements for social change and organizational innovation. They also carry forward and attempt to put into practice long-held dreams of people, dreams with deep roots in the social theory and philosophy of Western society. They are thus organizations that look to both the past and the future. Part I of the book examines the origins of alternative organizations and shows how they are one strand of a broad social movement currently producing several related types of democratically oriented workplaces.

In spite of the historic legacy of cooperatives, they are not organizations of a bygone era. The United States is currently experiencing the largest and most vital burgeoning of cooperatives in its history. Yet, ironically, we know next to nothing about cooperatives, particularly the specifics of their internal structures, processes, and conditions of operation. The case studies that exist are often descriptive and idiosyncratic. Mainstream organizational theory and research have almost entirely ignored these organizational forms. Ecological studies of the distribution and duration of cooperatives reveal general demographic patterns but little of their internal functioning. We are sorely in need of a theoretical model for understanding collectives and cooperatives *as organizations*. In Part II, we attempt to construct a general theory of democratic organizations. Chapter 3 begins the section by detailing the structural features that define the democratic organization.

Nothing is more central in the values of Western society than the ideals of democracy and equality. Visions of direct democracy can be traced back to ancient Greece, resurfacing in many subsequent eras. Yet organizational democracy has been an elusive goal, rarely achieved in practice and chronicled mostly in the breach. The most interesting thing about cooperatives is that they are attempting to achieve something most social science tells us is impossible: viable participatory democracy. Our research on cooperatives convinces us that although they do not always succeed, neither do they always fail. We argue that the creation of organizational democracy is *conditional*. In Chapters 4 and 5 of Part II, we identify specific conditions, some internal to the organization and others external, appearing to favor, or in their absence to undermine, organizational democracy.

In discovering these conditions we hope to advance organizational theory and help to clarify matters for cooperative members. Cooperatives, like all organizations, embrace multiple and often competing goals. The desire for internal democracy, though central, is usually coupled with other legitimate goals. The nexus of these goals places the cooperative in numerous binds. For every condition we identify as supporting democracy, we show the structural dilemma this condition raises for the organization.

We hope this book will help both organizational theorists and practitioners in cooperatives to identify the organizational features essential to the collectivist form, the conditions that promote direct democracy within the organization, and the inherent trade-offs that go with the pursuit of democracy. Identification, however, will not make the necessary choices any easier for members.

Part III draws out the general significance of organizational democracy for the individual and for society. In Chapter 6 we examine not only our own cases, but the existing research literature on worker satisfaction in cooperative-type organizations. Here we reach some unexpected conclusions concerning the effects of democracy on the individual member. Chapter 7 looks at the future of democratic organizations and specifically asks how they perform economically vis-à-vis more conventional forms. We consider what role the government may play in their development, and what kind of evolution and life span we may expect of them in view of historical precedents. The final chapter provides a more philosophical overview of how autonomy and democracy in the workplace may help to transform the relationship between work and play.

As the first step in the analysis, it is necessary to understand the origins and nature of contemporary cooperatives. They are radically different from conventional organizations not only in their form and aims, but also in their unique intellectual and historical roots. For this reason, Chapter 1 begins by

pointing out how certain classical ideas have shaped contemporary cooperatives. Included here are the writings of Rousseau, Bakunin, and Marx. Consciously or unconsciously, members of cooperatives try to put into practice
these venerable ideas. However, according to the work of Weber and Michels
and the considerable body of research and theory following from their tradition, the prospects for organizational democracy are extremely remote. This
tradition forces us to take seriously the forces of bureaucratization, specialization, and oligarchization confronting would-be democratic organizations.
Chapter 1 therefore also examines the Weber/Michels challenge, and then
looks at the cultural and economic forces that have favored the rise of the
recent wave of cooperatives in the United States. Chapter 2 describes the
specific organizations that we have studied and the analytical methods we
have used.

Part I

Origins and types
of alternative organizations

1. Cooperatives in the late twentieth century: the democratic impulse and the challenge of oligarchy

By dinner time that summer afternoon the weekly edition of the *Community News* had been delivered to the racks and newstands and most of the newspaper's staff had gone home for the day. John and Ann remained in the office, sharing the last of the coffee and casually examining the latest issue. For the past several months, John had worked as a reporter covering political affairs in the area. Ann, a photographer, had been in her present job for almost two years. Anyone at the paper, if asked, would have been quick to say both of them had been doing fine work and were well liked. The unusual amount of attention they were giving at that moment to a just-printed edition may have been due to the realization this might be the last time – at least for a good while – they would be doing their present jobs at the paper.

Although he would probably not have admitted it, John was proud to see that the story on the incorporation controversy, into which he had poured so much time and effort, was the week's lead. He didn't want it to be too obvious to Ann, but he was privately admiring his story's prominent position. Ann was more open with her feelings. She had two photos on the front page and another on page 4. She rested her index finger on the photo of the mayor, who was shouting in anger at a contrary City Council member. A slight smile came to her lips.

"This photo really is effective," she said, half to herself. Then her eyes fastened more critically on the page. "But maybe next time a little less back-lighting. . . ."

John said he thought the photo was great as it was.

"Yeah," she brightened, "I love doing photography."

He knew how she felt.

Had anyone been there to ask them, Ann and John would have also agreed they liked working at the *Community News*. It was not like other newspapers. Indeed it was unlike any other organization for which they had ever worked. Here, Ann and John and the others had a real say in how the paper would be run. Instead of having bosses at the top and workers at the bottom, the *News* was run democratically, as a collective. Whatever functional role they might be playing at the time – reporter, photographer, proofreader, ad salesperson – everyone had an opportunity to attend weekly meetings at which all important matters of internal policy, finances, news coverage, and the like were jointly decided by a process of consensus. The meetings were sometimes long and sometimes tedious, but most people left afterward feeling their voices had been heard and they were committed to the decisions that had been reached. It was *their* newspaper in a profound way, and all were proud of what they had accomplished together. Most had never had another job they liked nearly as well, nor a job that seemed so important to the community. Although conflicts and unhappiness occasionally erupted, as in any work group, morale was generally high.

A few weeks before, John and Ann had been at the meeting in which all had agreed jobs at the newspaper should be rotated periodically. This would give everyone a chance to develop new skills, would introduce some variety, would equitably distribute the dull and exciting aspects of specific jobs, and would help everyone to develop a healthy sense of all that is required to operate a newspaper. Just as important, it would prevent the growth of a bureaucratic hierarchy. No one wanted that to happen. So they, along with the others, had heard all the arguments for and against the idea of job rotation, and had agreed it should be done.

There had been considerable talk around the paper about the upcoming rotation, and everyone was curious about what was involved in the various jobs. Most people appeared to be excited about breaking old routines and learning some new skills. John was among these. Even though he liked his reporting job and was good at it, he felt he would like the more technical side of the process as well. Maybe layout or pasteup, things he now knew little about. And that would probably work out fine for the paper since he was aware of three other people who wanted to switch out of production. John did not have any trouble listing his first and second job choices. His sheet of paper was in the box with all the rest, and he had been comparing notes with others and joining in the speculation about who might be moving into what job.

John said he had to be going in order to get home on his bike before the sun went down.

Ann folded the paper.

They noted they would see each other early Saturday morning at the meeting. A yellow piece of paper on the bulletin board above the desk announced that job rotations would be worked out at the meeting.

As he started toward the door, John light-heartedly commented: "Well, I guess we'll soon know what we'll be doing next week!"

He stopped, noticing what he took to be a troubled look cross Ann's face.

"I haven't put down my choices yet," she said softly.

He was surprised.

She said she'd thought about it a long time, but just couldn't come up with anything she thought she would enjoy nearly as much as being a photographer. She took out a cigarette. He had rarely seen her smoke before.

Lowering his backpack and claiming the corner of the desk opposite her, he reminded her of the reasons why it was the best thing to do, and of the careful consensus the group had reached.

As he talked, her cigarette made increasingly frequent trips to the ashtray.

"I'm not saying I don't agree with the principle," she interrupted, "I really do. It's just that I'm not sure what I want to do next. . . ." Her voice trailed off and she was quiet for a while.

Then, as if exploring a new idea, she said, "I guess I've been worried. I'm good at what I do. It's kind of scary to think about giving that up. Photography is a challenge and I'd like to learn to do it even better, not have to start all over again at something else."

Another silence.

She wondered if other people didn't share some of her feelings.

He said he'd not heard any real doubts expressed, but there might be some.

"Well, I know we're all committed to this and everyone wants to see it work, but once in a while I wonder," she added, suddenly rising from the desk and declaring in mock-dramatic humor, "if this is any way to run a newspaper!"

They both laughed.

This vignette, based on actual events at one of the organizations we studied, illustrates several of the general themes this book addresses. We are concerned with understanding what collectives are, how they work, what principles they follow, what possibilities and options they seem to present, what problems and limits they face, and what their impact may be on individuals and the larger society.

What is most unusual about the above story is not the existence of individual doubts and ambivalences. These exist in all organizations. What is most striking is the fact that this particular organization, this collective, was trying to do things that almost no other type of organization even attempts: to conduct itself as a pure democracy, deliberately rotating organizational roles among its members. These are bold steps.

The information contained in the story is suggestive, but incomplete. Where did such ideas and practices originate? Not simply in this particular organization, for it is virtually identical in form with other cooperatives and collectives around the United States. More precisely, then, we need to know the source from which this whole class of organizations draws its inspiration. To find the answer, we must go far beyond the origins of the *Community News*. We must seek the beginnings of the ideas that gave birth to these organizations – and ultimately to dilemmas such as Ann's – in history.

The historical legacy

The idea of workers cooperatively producing goods or services is not new. In the United States, for example, workers' cooperatives have a long history, dating back to the revolutionary period. The historical record from 1790 to 1940 reveals more than 700 producers' cooperatives. These co-ops have not been randomly distributed in time, but have appeared in distinct waves – the 1840s, the 1860s, the 1880s and the 1920s–30s. What is intriguing is that these four historical periods immediately followed major movements for social change; the pattern of these events suggests a connection between social movements and cooperative formation (Aldrich and Stern, 1978).

In part, producers' cooperatives in the nineteenth century represented efforts by workers to retain highly skilled craft production in the face of increasing mechanization and standardization in industry. In addition, they attempted to put into practice the age-old ideals of democracy, equality, and community, turning direct control over the means and the product of production to the producers.

After a 50-year hiatus, a new, fifth wave of cooperatives has arisen in the United States. The thousands of cooperatives created in local communities since 1970 make the current wave larger than any previous one in American history. In fact, the past decade has seen the emergence of more cooperatives than the rest of American history combined. This latest wave, too, comes on the heels of some of the largest and most vigorous social movements in U.S. history: the civil rights, antiwar, environmental, women's, and student movements of the 1960s and 1970s.

Most contemporary cooperatives are involved in high-quality craft production, retail sales, or the provision of human services. They are made up largely of college-educated young people who were active in, or who were influenced by, the social movements of the 1960s and 1970s. Unlike the nineteenth century artisans, they are not trying to maintain a former state of autonomy, but hope to create entirely new (for them) opportunities and conditions of work and community life. The development of cooperatives in the 1970s appears to be the natural outgrowth of counter-cultural values and sentiments developed and expressed in the social movements of the 1960s. It was a short step from insisting that blacks, women, and the Vietnamese be given control over the conditions of their own lives to insisting on the same for oneself. In the 1970s, as the people who had taken part in these social movements graduated from college, they came to focus on the institutions that most touched their day-to-day lives – the community and the workplace. They created community-oriented workplaces such as alternative newspapers, arts and handicrafts shops, food co-ops, publishing houses, restaurants, health clinics, legal collectives, natural foods bakeries, auto repair cooperatives, and retail stores.

These organizations continue to spread at a remarkable rate. A national directory (Gardner, 1976) lists some 5,000 alternative organizations and estimates that about 1,000 new ones are created yearly. A recent estimate (Jackall and Crain, 1984) places the number of producer co-ops at over 1,000, with a median size of 6.5 employees/firm. Other researchers estimate at least 1,300 alternative schools (Moberg, 1979, p. 293), between 5,000 and 10,000 food co-ops (Zwerdling, 1979, p. 90), and several thousand communes (Moberg, 1979, p. 285).

With a few notable exceptions, most of the worker co-ops contain no more than 10 or 20 members, but taken together they account for the employment of thousands of people. Since they often choose to remain small so they can retain their democratic structure, members may create additional co-ops in an area if the market is too large for one. And as each co-op has a demonstration effect, it often spawns another. Most have been organized at the grass-roots level without the aid of government agencies, banks, or other established institutions.

The apparently sudden growth of collectivist organizations in the 1970s is understandable only if we recognize that one such organization spawns another, and that they are manifestations of a social movement. Five thousand alternative organizations do not represent 5,000 isolated, independent social inventions. They derive from, and for the most part they continue to identify with, larger movements seeking societal change.

Since collectivist organizations are oriented toward goals of social or personal change, they can be considered social movement organizations (Zald and Ash, 1966). Their development, however, has not been directed by some centralized leadership with clearly defined means, ends, and dogma. There has been a great deal of spontaneity and experimentation in local cooperative enterprises. And yet, because they are part of a movement, the basic organizational forms that have developed from place to place are virtually identical.

Contemporary co-ops represent attempts to build organizations that are parallel to, but outside of, established institutions and that fulfill social needs (for food, health care, education, etc.) without using bureaucratic authority.

That is, they often produce goods or services currently provided by conventional organizations, but in a manner members consider more responsive and socially progressive. For this reason, participants may refer to their organizations as "alternative institutions." In this sense alternative institutions represent rejection of mainstream organizations and an attempt by members to live out other values. For members, to use the feminist slogan, "the personal is political." They believe their most important political message lies in the very act of doing cooperative work: Insofar as members accomplish the job at hand without resorting to hierarchical patterns of authority, they demonstrate that democratic management can work.

From our observations of alternative organizations of many different types, we attempt to draw out the characteristic features that define and unify these organizations. We hope to identify the specific conditions that facilitate, or conversely, that undermine participatory democracy in individual organizations, and finally, to locate the structural dilemmas in which these cooperatives find themselves.

By any standard, cooperatives are radical organizationally. They struggle to resist the hierarchical and bureaucratic practices that we all take for granted and to establish in their place participatory-democratic practices. This makes them unusual in a society based at the organizational level on bureaucracy and subordinate/superior relations, and at the political level on representative democracy. In order to understand how cooperatives came to exist, we must examine the intellectual roots from which they draw their inspiration.

Intellectual roots

The theories, philosophies, and ideas of one era are the common currency of the next. The intellectual dialogues of earlier ages not only become the conscious heritage of future scholars but also give a diffuse coloration to the larger culture through which they percolate. Members of social institutions are not always aware of the origins of the ideas that gave birth to those institutions. So it is with cooperatives. Members are often unaware of the specific historic roots of their ideas and practices.

Democracy is a much-used term in our society. Members of cooperatives, however, use it to mean something quite different from what is traditionally meant. To understand their meaning, one must grasp the distinction between *participatory* democracy and *representative* democracy.

Participatory democracy.   Participatory democracy has a firm foundation in the intellectual history of Western society. Indeed, some of the major architects of Western political thought, such as Rousseau, J. S. Mill, and twentieth-century theorist G. D. H. Cole argued that direct participation by citizens in government and other institutions is crucial for a democratic society. They were thinking of something more than simple discussion of issues and voting, however. A far more direct and active process is essential to the creation and maintenance of a democratic polity, possessed of the skills and attitudes needed for such a system to work. Participation had an important educational function.

As Carole Pateman puts it, summarizing the views of J. J. Rousseau, J. S. Mill, and Cole: "The existence of representative institutions at [the] national level is not sufficient for democracy; for maximum participation by all the people at that level, socialization, or 'social training,' for democracy must take place in other spheres in order that the necessary individual attitudes and psychological qualities can be developed. This development takes place through the process of participation itself" (Pateman, 1970, p. 42). In short, one learns how to effectively participate only through participation. And, people will not develop such skills and attitudes if opportunities are found at only the national political level. This means that a truly participatory polity can exist only if other social institutions are also participatory. Of particular importance for these writers is industry, where most adults spend the greater part of their working lives. If individuals are to learn to expect and to exercise self-determination and democratic responsibilities in the political arena, then work and other local institutions must be organized in such a way that people can participate directly in decision making. The argument is that if people are given a good taste of self-governance, they will want more, and will come to know how to use it effectively.

Rousseau, J. S. Mill, and Cole, then, developed the classical notion of participatory democracy: self-governance in the workplace as well as in political institutions. These ideas form the intellectual background – conscious or not – of modern cooperatives. Co-ops are motivated both by the desire to build direct participatory democracy at the organizational level in economic enterprises and by the vision of someday achieving a more fully democratic society.

However, in reality most workplaces and other social institutions in the surrounding society are organized hierarchically, and the political system is built on representative democracy. How is it that the heritage of participatory democracy has been lost in society as a whole? Why do scholars and laypeople tend to think of democracy only in its representative rather than its direct form?

Pateman (1970) argues this one-sided thinking is due in part to the long-held myth that there is but one "classical" theory of democracy – that one being representative democracy. On the contrary, her analysis of the work of Rousseau, Mill, and Cole reveals, not one, but two very different theories of democracy. Pateman traces this myth of a single theory primarily to the influential work of Joseph Schumpeter (1942). Schumpeter asserts that the classical theory of democracy rests on the idea of an institutional arrangement for making political decisions through the election of representatives. In order for this system to function, Schumpeter maintains, an unrealistically high level of public rationality, independence, and knowledge would be required of ordinary people. He goes on to charge that classical theory compounds the problem by virtually ignoring the (for him, essential) issue of leadership. Given these – for Schumpeter – unrealistic tenets of classical democracy, he rejects the classical model and constructs his own, presumably more practical, model of democracy. Pateman, however, maintains that Schumpeter misrepresents what the classical theorists had to say and also fails to distinguish the two very different theories about democracy found in those writings (Pateman, 1970, p. 18).

The influence of Schumpeter and others who followed his lead remains strong among contemporary political theorists who base their theories of democracy on the work of such writers as Bentham, Locke, and James Mill. These writers stress representative democracy, in which "participation" of the populace is limited to voting and discussion. For them, as for Schumpeter and most contemporary theorists, participation has a narrow aim: It is designed to protect private interests of citizens and, in that sense, to ensure good government. The educative and self-generating nature of participation is lost; here, participation is merely defensive. Democracy, according to representative democratic theory, rests on the competition of leaders (potential representatives) for votes and office. Thus, as Pateman (1970, p. 20) notes, "theorists who hold this view of the role of participation are, first and foremost, theorists of representative government."

The ascendancy of the ideas of representative democracy in our society obscures the equally rich heritage of participatory democratic theory. Whereas our society and theorists have largely forgotten the legacy of direct democracy, co-ops have not.

Anarchism.   A second intellectual foundation of cooperatives, as strong as that of participatory democracy and perhaps even less known by members, is the philosophy of anarchism. From the anarchistic tradition co-ops have inherited crucial principles of organization, operating strategies, and goals.

The Greek word *anarchos,* the root of anarchism, means "without a ruler."

It signifies the existence of organization without external authority and thus implies social order can be achieved solely by internal discipline.[1] The terms *anarchism* and, more frequently, *anarchy* are unfortunately associated with the idea of chaos and disorder, and with nihilism and terrorism. This widespread misunderstanding, one sympathetic historian suggests, arises in part from the nature of anarchism: "few (doctrines) have presented in their own variety of approach and action so much excuse for confusion" (Woodcock, 1962, p. 9). Because of this tendency toward confusion, and because anarchist principles play a large role in co-ops, we wish to clarify these ideas and resolve the seeming paradox of an anarchist organization.

One caveat should be borne in mind: anarchism does not lend itself to a systematic and determinate social theory.[2] Its libertarian attitude admits a variety of viewpoints and actions. But, in spite of the range of anarchist thinking and its resistance to codification, all forms of anarchism do share common features.

The first premise of anarchist organization is what Colin Ward (1966, p. 389) calls the "theory of spontaneous order": "[G]iven a common need, a collection of people will, by trial and error, by improvisation and experiment, evolve order out of chaos – this order being more durable and more closely related to their needs than any kind of externally imposed order." This belief in a naturally evolving cooperative order can be traced to Kropotkin's (1903) proposal for an extensive network of mutual-aid institutions. With external authority abolished, Kropotkin believed, people's "natural" tendency toward "mutual-aid" would express itself in the evolution of countless local associations granting mutual support to each other.

Mutualism, collectivism, anarchist communism, and anarcho-syndicalism are all closely linked in the history of anarchist thought. Proudhon in the 1840s was the first writer to willingly adopt the term *anarchist,* knowing it to be perjorative, believing it to be otherwise. He used this term in the development of the idea of mutualism. By mutualism he meant a future society of federated communes and workers' cooperatives, with individuals and small groups controlling (not owning) their means of production, and bound by contracts of mutual credit and exchange to ensure each individual the product of his or her own labor. Mutualists established the first French sections of the International in 1865.

Collectivists, following Bakunin in the 1860s, continued to stress the need for federalism and workers' associations, but tried to adapt these ideas to industrialization by arguing that larger voluntary organizations of workers should control the means of production. Bakunin and his collectivist followers challenged Marx's leadership at the congress of the International at the

Hague in 1872. A fierce debate and struggle for power ensued, during which Bakunin's followers charged Marx with being "an authoritarian and centralizing communist." The anarchists lost the fight. So began a split in the history of socialist movements between those who support a central-management model of socialism and those who support a decentralized popular-control model. The outcome of the battle at the International ensured the ascendancy of the former.

In the main, the Marxists and anarchists were divided over the use of state authority. Engels (1959, pp. 481–485) argued bluntly that it was impossible to eliminate authority relations in work and industry. Marxists were unwilling to relinquish the state bureaucracy as an instrument of power and wished to use it to implement socialist authority, whereas anarchists were unwilling to accept hierarchical authority, proletarian or otherwise. Authority relationships were anathema to anarchists because they violated principles of individual liberty. Further, anarchists did not believe Marxian claims of the eventual "withering away of the state." A revolution for the anarchists would consist of dissolving the structure of authority, not merely switching who controls that structure.

Following Bakunin came Kropotkin and his fellow anarchist-communists in the 1870s, and, based in the French trade unions, the anarcho-syndicalists in the 1880s. The latter stressed the trade union as an organ of struggle and as a basis for future social organization.

Although differing in emphasis, all of these strains of anarchist thought have much in common. All would have two basic types of social institutions provide the organizational structure for a future free society: the "commune" or "soviet" and the "syndicate" or "workers' council." Both are seen as relatively small, collectively controlled, local units that would federate with each other to deal with large social and economic affairs and thereby benefit from mutual aid and exchange. Each local unit would retain its own autonomy. The commune or soviet would federate territorially; the syndicate or workers' council would federate industrially. Today, clear examples of a commune structure are found in the kibbutz community assemblies in Israel (Rosner, 1981) and in the syndicates or workers' councils existing throughout Yugoslavia and Western Europe.

Collectives and cooperatives in the United States have several characteristics of anarchistic forms of organization. One is their commitment to decentralized, small, voluntary associations. Another is their support of the anarchist federative principle, inasmuch as many of these groups are committed to the development of full-blown "alternative communities" within their own locales, and form support networks regionally with similar alternative organizations. Furthermore, their goal, which is to create functional organizations without hierarchical authority, is anarchistic, as is their dual emphasis on community control over community functions and workers' control over workplace decisions.

The features mentioned so far relate to anarchist goals. Alternative organizations also utilize many of the methods and tactics of anarchism. A key feature of anarchist strategy is the insistence upon a unity of means and ends:

Anarchism doesn't want different people on top; it wants to destroy the pyramid. In its place it advocates an extended network of individuals and groups, making their own decisions, controlling their own destiny. (Ward, 1972, p. 289)

Anarchist strategies stress the congruence of means and ends, and thus, for example, would not propose mandatory organizations to reeducate people for a free society. They would not advocate violent means to achieve a peaceful society; nor would they choose centralized means to attain a decentralized society. From the congruence of means and ends flows the conception of "direct action." Direct actions are directly relevant to the ends sought and are based on individual decisions as to whether or not to participate in the proposed action. Examples of direct action include the general strike, resistance to the draft, and the creation of food cooperatives, credit unions, and worker-run workplaces.

Members of collectives see themselves as providing working models for a future society. If they succeed, they may constitute what Buber (1960, pp. 44–45) calls "pre-revolutionary structure-making." That this is the political meaning members ascribe to their collectivist organizations is implicit in the words of a person at the alternative newspaper in this study:

What I see that we are doing is trying to create soviets. We're creating organizations of people's power. . . . Capitalism is getting more and more into crisis everyday and in defense of themselves people are organizing . . . creating institutions that fulfill people's needs. . . . The more crisis, the more organization will occur.

By the time the final crisis arrives [alternatives] will be everything. The new society will kind of just grow up through the roots and the old society will just be brushed aside.

Our point is that the decision of cooperators to build and work in organizations in the present embodying what they want to create on a societal level in the future is a political strategy in the anarchist mode. It is politics of function, a unity of means and ends.

Although the political strategy of cooperative enterprises fits well with anarchist principles, members may be unaware of the connections. As in the case of participatory-democratic theory, their anarchist predispositions are largely unschooled and unconscious. It is much more common for people in alternative institutions to pay intellectual tribute to Karl Marx than to Bakunin or Kropotkin.

Marxism.   Marxian ideas are a third foundation of co-ops. Generally, co-ops subscribe to: the critique of private property; the analysis of capitalism as riddled with contradictions; the concepts of alienation and exploitation; the materialist conception of history; and the vision of a future society that is classless and just, and one in which producers control the means of production.

Marx himself was ambivalent toward workers' cooperatives. Avineri (1968, pp. 179–180) points out that Marx saw co-ops as representing revolutionary new forms of property – social property – that would prefigure the coming of socialism. But he also believed cooperatives would have to be developed on a national scale, under public sponsorship, if they were to significantly improve working conditions for the masses or arrest the spread of monopoly in the economy. Most members of contemporary co-ops are probably not aware of Marx's specific ideas about cooperatives, and if they were they would likely prefer grass-roots development rather than centralized government sponsorship of co-ops.

The point at which Bakunin departed from Marx is the point at which the contemporary cooperatives depart from Marxian principles: the seizure of state power versus the dismantling of it. This is really a dispute over political means, not ends, but it has serious repercussions for the ends attained. Marx believed that without the state apparatus at its disposal, the proletariat would not be able to assert its will nor to suppress its capitalist adversaries who might attempt a counterrevolution. Thus, state power had to be invoked, if only temporarily. In opposition to this idea, Bakunin spoke of the dangers of "red bureaucracy" that would prove to be "the most vile and terrible lie that our century has created." He warned that state socialism would produce an overwhelming centralization of property and power, and ultimately a bureaucratic despotism. Instead, he urged the use of direct means of appropriating capital: workers' associations, federated in cooperative relationships with each other.

Although the contemporary collectives tend to attribute more of their intellectual debt to the ideas of Marx than to anarchism or classical participatory-democratic theory, in fact, Marxism offers them little direction in their day-to-day affairs. Their practices, we argue, owe far more to the ideas of anarchism and participatory democracy.

Alternatives to bureaucracy: why now?

Max Weber argued bureaucracy would increasingly come to dominate all aspects of social life, replacing all previous forms of organization in history and perpetuating itself indefinitely. More than almost any prediction in social science, his has stood the test of time. For Weber, "once . . . fully established, bureaucracy is among those social structures which are the hardest to destroy" (1946, p. 228), one reason being that it has a powerful set of beliefs supporting it. Bureaucracy, like the forms of organization preceding it, requires certain "legitimating principles" to sustain it, and it finds this legitimation in the modern belief that, for the sake of efficiency, a hierarchy of expertise and standardized procedures should be followed.

In a Weberian framework, then, it is puzzling that contemporary collectivists, or anyone else, could ever develop antibureaucratic sentiments and practices. If social beliefs support institutional arrangements, and vice versa, then how does change in either begin?

Despite Weber's belief that bureaucracy would prove to be revolution-proof (1946, p. 230), it is possible to ferret out of his work three sources of tension that have the potential to undermine the legitimacy of bureaucratic authority. First, Weber recognized that public officials who blatantly disobey the law would undermine the rule of (formal) law itself. In the post-Watergate era, examples are plentiful. Second, he noted that special laws passed for particular interests would constitute another assault on the universalistic basis of formal law. Most important, he realized that demands for substantive justice and special treatment would likely arise from the underprivileged in a desire to equalize life opportunities (1946, pp. 220–221).

Although a Weberian analysis suggests several general reasons why Americans might begin to question the justice and legitimacy of established institutions, it does not tell us why a particular group of people, American young adults of the 1970s and 1980s, have taken their questioning of the system to greater lengths, attempting to construct organizational embodiments of countervalues. Young American adults in alternative institutions are critical not only of bureaucracy: They also frequently oppose the fundamental principles of our capitalist economic system.

Joseph Schumpeter provided in 1942 perhaps the most cogent analysis and prediction of a coming change in attitudes toward capitalism. In brief, he argued capitalism is the most productive and efficient economic system in history (so far, both Marx and Weber would agree). However, "its very success undermines the social institutions which protect it and 'inevitably' creates conditions in which it will not be able to live" (1942, p. 61). For Schumpeter, the capitalist process creates a critical frame of mind that ultimately turns against private property and bourgeois values. The very logic of capitalist society generates a hostile atmosphere, and creates a special social class of intellectuals who help to articulate and organize this general hostility. The defenses of capitalism are broken down further with the disintegration of the bourgeois family. As rationalization spreads to all domains of society, including private life, it renders children and home irrational in cost accounting terms, and thus removes an important force that had motivated people to save and invest. Without children, people become more present oriented and less willing to sacrifice for the future.

In one institution after the next, Schumpeter argues, the process of capitalism destroys its own institutional framework – its protective strata. The modern bureaucratic corporation narrows the scope of capitalist motivation until it eventually kills its roots. In time, the entrepreneurial model of thrift, hard work, risk taking, and self-denial is replaced by the values and mentality of the salaried bureaucratic worker. A consumption orientation overtakes a production orientation. Ultimately, "the bourgeois order no longer makes any sense to the bourgeoisie itself" (1942, p. 161).

The material well-being generated under a capitalist, bureaucratic system undermines the entire cluster of values that had supported it – what Weber called the Protestant Ethic. That is, from the individual's standpoint it no longer appears rational to be frugal, hard working, or dedicated to the intense pursuit of material wealth. As the Protestant Ethic is weakened, the compelling nature of the capitalist mode of production wanes. Not only does the evolution of capitalism tend to wear away its own socio-cultural bases, but at the same time "it shapes things and souls for socialism" (Schumpeter, 1942, p. 220), thereby clearing the way for (centralized) socialism as the heir apparent. Thus, although Schumpeter reaches Marxian conclusions, his mode of analysis is distinctly non-Marxian. His is an analysis of the contradictions inherent in the culture of capitalism, not in the economics.

If it is the rationalization, the technology, and the affluence generated by a capitalist mode of production that permit freedom from the necessity of human toil and that render the values of the Protestant Ethic obsolete, then we should expect the work ethic to lose its coherence first for people who have grown up under conditions of affluence. This expectation is supported by a variety of analyses of social change in advanced capitalist society (Flacks, 1971; Marcuse, 1962). Following Flacks (1971), we would expect young people who find conventional cultural values so incoherent that they create alternative values, motivation patterns, and life meanings (viz., they become participants in alternative institutions) to be disproportionately from affluent, well-educated, intellectually oriented families. As we will show in the next chapter, the data of this study do fit such a model. Participants in the organizations we studied tend to come from relatively affluent, well-educated families. They have backgrounds and social characteristics quite similar to the social activists of the 1960s and 1970s, and have often taken part in those earlier protest movements. They have high expectations for their jobs and careers, and commonly have been frustrated by perceived and actual possibilities in mainstream organizations, with the result that they have created their own workplaces as an alternative.

A summary to this point

Current economic and cultural conditions have nourished the most recent wave of cooperatives in the United States. The new cooperatives embody the historic themes of anarchism, participatory democracy, and, in part, Marxian thought. Cooperatives thus attempt to be true to ideas with deep intellectual and historical roots, ideas that have lost out in the mainstream of both capitalist and centralized socialist societies.

As we have seen, two distinct models of democracy co-existed in the eighteenth century, but as the Western capitalist societies emerged from their revolutions, it was the ideal of representative democracy that was institutionalized, displacing the notion of participatory democracy. In socialist societies such as the Soviet Union, it was the centralized version of Marxian socialism that won out over the more decentralized, democratic vision of the anarchists. With the ascendancy of representative systems of democracy in the capitalist societies and of state socialism in the socialist societies, there was no system built on decentralized local control of community institutions and of workplaces by the people in them. Cooperatives represent this third road. They are based on principles of economic and political organization that are an alternative to the concentrated corporate power of capitalism and to the centralized state power of socialism. The world has yet to see an entire society based on a system of local, participatory democracy, yet that is the vision of many in cooperatives.

The challenge posed by Weber and Michels

In a modern bureaucratic society, cooperatives are sometimes seen as curious anomalies, inconsequential organizations without serious possibilities for growth or influence. Far from seeing co-ops as models for entire societies, many outside of co-ops are skeptical about the possibility of participatory democracy even at the level of the single organization. In order to appreciate this point of view it is essential to return to the important work of Max Weber and to consider another enormously influential early theorist of organizations, Robert Michels.

For Weber, Bakunin's anarchist ideas were "naive" (Weber, 1946, p. 229). From a Weberian point of view, the anarchist ideal of organization without authority would be revolutionary because it would represent a structural transformation, not a mere change in who controls the state bureaucracy. But to Weber, it is a hopelessly utopian idea. As earlier noted, the requirements of modern society, Weber believed, would make bureaucratic authority a permanent and indispensable feature of the social landscape.

Cooperatives do not fit into the well-known Weberian typology of legitimate authority relations. For in their collectivist mode of organization, they do not grant authority on the grounds of formal legal-rational justifications, nor on the basis of tradition or the charisma of leaders. Instead they conform to a fourth basis of legitimate authority, a type mentioned but not elaborated in Weber's work, that of value-rationality. They are committed first and foremost to substantive goals, to an ethic, even where this overrides commitment to a particular organizational setting.

Weber defined "authority" as the power of command and the duty to obey. He used the term synonymously with "domination" (*Herrschaft*) to refer to situations in which both the ruler(s) and the ruled subjectively accept the legitimacy of commands from the former.[3] Domination, in Weber's view, requires an administrative apparatus to execute commands, and conversely, all administration requires domination.

However, in the alternative organizations studied here no one (ideally) has the right to command, and no one the duty to obey another. There can be no subordinates where there are no superordinates. They strive for the absence of domination. Legal-rational justifications for hierarchical authority have been actively challenged. In collectives, ultimate authority resides not in the individual (by virtue of positional incumbency or technical expertise) but in the collectivity of worker–owner–members as a whole.

The prime goal of collectivist organizations is escape from the Weberian imperatives of domination and hierarchical administration. Central to our analysis, therefore, is an examination of the means they use and an evaluation of how well they succeed.

Weber did acknowledge that under select conditions (e.g., small size, functional simplicity) organizations can avoid structures of domination and can maintain directly democratic forms (Weber, 1968, pp. 289–290). However, since he was primarily interested in the principles that legitimate domination and the corresponding administrative machinery that implements it, he unfortunately did not examine the conditions supportive of genuinely democratic forms of organization, free from *Herrschaft*. It is here we hope to make a contribution.

Weber's insistence on the inevitability of bureaucracy has profoundly shaped later thinking about organizations. The work of his contemporary, Robert Michels, speaks even more directly to the problem of maintaining democracy within organizations. Boldly stated and well remembered as the "Iron Law of Oligarchy," it has had great influence. On the basis of his study of the German socialist party, Michels concluded: "Who says organization, says oligarchy" (Michels, 1962, p. 365). The main subject of Michels's study, the German Social Democratic Party, tried to be internally democratic in a manner consistent with its socialist principles. However, Michels argued, the party evolved a relatively closed and oligarchic structure, controlled by only a few of its central members, and abandoned the interests of its rank and file. He perceived similar situations in other socialist parties and trade unions. In the case of political parties, for example, he attempted to delineate the process of oligarchization: The primary goal of a political party is to attain political power. As the power of a party is largely a function of the size of its membership, growth is of the essence. In search of growth, members are seduced into abandoning their principles. Internal democracy gives way to rule by a small group of elite members who are able, through the control of information and patronage, to make themselves indispensable.

Michels wanted to generalize from his case studies of political parties and trade unions to organizations of other kinds. Indeed, the subtitle of his 1911 book, *Political Parties,* is *A Sociological Study of the Oligarchical Tendencies of Modern Democracy,* which suggests he thought his ideas had broad applicability. Even today, scholars treat Michels's work in just this way: The Iron Law is assumed to apply to all types of organization. Mainstream organizational and management theories typically ignore or dismiss the possibility of internal organizational democracy and, following Weber and Michels, take for granted the presence of hierarchical, superior/subordinate relationships, and oligarchic control.

Although Michels's work has had large and continuing influence in promoting the idea of the inevitablity of oligarchy, it has not stood without challenge. Some scholars of Michels's work, for example, have charged the history of the German Socialist Democratic Party does not fully support Michels's thesis. There is some evidence, too, that Max Weber, mentor to Michels, did not entirely agree with Michels's conclusions. A long correspondence between the two scholars indicates Weber wanted Michels to tone down or qualify his blanket assertions about the inevitability of organizational oligarchy. As Scaff (1981, p. 1282) puts it:

For Weber, the mere appearance of power, leadership or professional specialization in an organizational setting could not in itself eliminate all possibility of democratic rule. . . . Thus, unlike his colleague [Michels] Weber was prepared to see democratization as a typical development in modern societies, just as he was later able to characterize the "often-described organization" of the SPD [Social Democratic Party of Germany] as "strictly disciplined and centralized" but "within democratic forms."

Thus, Weber was somewhat more open to the possibility of organizational democracy than was Michels, but since Weber never really spelled out his own ideas regarding the topic, Michels's more absolute point of view captured the stage. It is thus the work of Michels that poses the most acute theoretical challenge to the direct democracy that cooperatives wish to create and maintain. In the analysis to follow, we assess to what extent cooperatives are able in practice to successfully evade the Iron Law.

2. The organizations studied, the methods used

Sociologists have long recognized and bemoaned "the gap between the character of current theories and the character of much current research" (Merton, 1964, p. 242). Sociologist Robert Merton (1957) suggests that "middle-range" theories, by being more amenable to verification than grand theories, might help to narrow this gap. Responding to this call, Glaser and Strauss (1967) have proposed a specific research approach to close the gap between ungrounded theories and empirical studies unguided by any theory. They urge that theory should be generated from the data, and that theory arrived at in this way, namely "grounded theory," will have more power to predict and to explain the subject at hand than will theory arrived at through only speculation or logical deduction. For Glaser and Strauss, it is the responsibility of sociologists to ground their theoretical categories and propositions firmly in empirical research. Further, they maintain that a comparative method of analysis based on systematic procedures for collecting, codifying, and analyzing data (particularly qualitative data) best lends itself to the discovery of grounded theory.

This study attempts to develop an original and grounded theory of organizational democracy using the qualitative, comparative method of analysis developed by Glaser and Strauss. In so doing, we develop middle-range theoretical propositions about the form, conditions, and dilemmas of democratic organization in modern society.

We base our analysis of collectivist organizations on two sources of data: intensive case studies of five cooperative workplaces we observed, and an extensive and systematic review of the work done by other researchers on similar or related organizations. As we develop our theory in Part II, which is based primarily on our own case studies, we also bring in the empirical observations of other researchers to further support our points. In Part III, however, we turn chiefly to the research of others to indicate the broader applicability of our theory.

The small-scale collectives and cooperatives that are the focus of our study are but one part – albeit an important part – of a much larger movement toward the democratization of work organizations. As we noted in Chapter 1, contemporary cooperatives are motivated by a special set of values and by the desire of people to integrate their values with the need to earn a livelihood. However, for reasons that stretch beyond any new values that may be arising in our society, democratization is proceeding in more conventional sectors too.

The growing international competition for markets and the resulting pressure to improve productivity have led to Quality of Work Life (QWL) programs in a substantial number of *Fortune* 500 corporations (Simmons and Mares, 1983). Such programs typically try to enhance the degree of worker influence in decision making, even if only in an attempt to tap workers' ideas for solving problems. Although the actual level of worker influence or control varies from case to case and is hotly debated, the point is that this very large and vigorous corporate movement *has* appreciated the link between increased worker influence and improved productivity.

Another type of democratization that is proceeding apace can be seen in the thousands of Employee Stock Ownership Plans (ESOPs) that have been created in the last five years. Most of these give only a minority ownership position to the workers, but in an estimated 250 cases workers have acquired a majority of the voting stock. Clearly this new development carries with it the potential for worker control, but researchers have found that the vast majority of these cases do not extend substantial participation rights to workers in the actual process of production (Rothschild-Whitt, 1983, 1984). In general, ESOPs arise in part because the ability of capital to move internationally produces numerous shutdowns of what once were – and could again be – viable plants (Bluestone and Harrison, 1980). The foreseeable devastation to workers and communities produces cooperative efforts to "save" the plant under the terms of worker ownership. Still other ESOPs arise because of the tax advantages allowed in the law, and other material reasons. Again, our point is that this reflects a realization of the connection between worker motivation and productivity.

Other countries, too, have made substantial forays – indeed, they have often led the way – into experiments with various forms of worker control, including workers' councils and codetermination in Europe, self-management in Yugoslavia, cooperatives in Israel, and so on.

Still another kind of organization in which sustaining member interest and participation are often a central problem is the nonprofit, voluntary organization such as a charity or public interest research group. Our hypotheses concerning the conditions and dilemmas of democratic organizations should prove relevant here too.

If one takes the perspective of Karl Marx, one might expect the ownership structure to be the most determinative aspect of any production organization. Following the lead of Max Weber, on the other hand, one might take the bureaucratic control structure to be primary. Looking at the worldwide movement toward the democratization of work, we note that some models provide examples of democratizing ownership, but fail to give actual control to workers. Other models, like QWL, focus on the control structure and neglect the underlying structure of ownership. The "purest" forms of democratization, of course, represented by the cooperatives in this study, attempt to democratize *both* ownership and control.

To emphasize, Part II of the book builds a theory of organizational democracy on the basis of the purest examples of direct democracy we have available, the five cooperatives we observed intensively. Part III draws out the relevance of the theory and the cooperatives' experiences for other, related democratizing organizations.

As theoretical points are made in the chapters to come, we frequently refer to empirical examples from each of the organizations in our study. We therefore need to begin with an overview of these five organizations and of the research methods used to study them.

Research methods

Since the aim of this study is to create a new theory about the factors that nurture organizational democracy, we have selected for study organizations that, on close scrutiny, appear to share a sincere desire for democracy, but that are as varied as possible along several other dimensions: Some are relatively large, others are small; some perform complicated tasks and use a sophisticated technology to do so, others perform more simple tasks requiring little technological support; some produce goods, others provide services; some are self-supporting financially, others receive outside grants from foundations and government agencies. Because we also want to see how well participatory democracy can function in a variety of specific organizational settings, we picked five different kinds of collectivist organizations: a cooperatively run community medical clinic, an alternative high school, a food cooperative, a collective newspaper, and a legal collective. By making systematic comparisons among these organizations, we have tried to isolate for analysis the generic features of cooperative organizations.

Because of the limitations of space, we are able to report only a fraction of the extensive qualitative and quantitative data we have collected. In making a theoretical point, we have tried to select those examples that seem most characteristic of *collectives in general,* not those that occur only rarely or that appear typical of only one or two kinds of organizations. We would argue therefore that the theoretical formulations in this work should prove applicable in a broad range of participatory democratic settings.

A number of research methods were employed, with data from one serving as a check on the other. Participant observation was undertaken in four of the five research settings. Field observations ranged in duration from six months to two years. Meetings were a focus of attention, and the researcher observed an average of 16 meetings per organization. Meetings ranged from a full day in some cases to just an hour or two. Detailed field notes were taken both during and immediately following observed events. The fifth setting, the legal collective, would not permit field observation of routine activities, and so documents (including a diary written by a participant) and interviews with organizational members were used. Although participant observation forms the core of this study, it is amplified in important ways by three other sources of data. First, intensive, semistructured interviews were conducted with a number of members from each of the five groups. Interviews were recorded on tape, and took from 1 to 5 hours, with the mean interview time being 2¼ hours. Second, written documents from each of the groups were examined; these included constitutions and by-laws, funding proposals, agenda and minutes of meetings, personal diaries, internal memoranda, budgets and financial statements, statistics on clients, and newsletters. Finally, observational material was supplemented by questionnaires returned from the members of the free medical clinic, the food cooperative, and the community newspaper. Several sets of questionnaires were used, with individual items worded similarly where appropriate.

The comprehensive questionnaires dealt with the socioeconomic-economic backgrounds of people in alternative organizations, their political attitudes, and their religious backgrounds. In addition, the questionnaires contained items pertaining to members' reasons for joining the organization, their perceptions of their own decision-making influence in the organization, their estimate of the distribution of power and influence in the organization, their sense of an optimal size, the degree of satisfaction and participation in the organization, the responsiveness of the staff and board of directors to members' interests and needs, and a variety of other organizational issues. Further, in each case, the researcher solicited questionnaire items from the members themselves, and added their suggestions – usually items of practical utility to the particular organization – to the final questionnaire.

In sum, we used data from many different sources – direct observation, interviews, organizational documents, and questionnaire surveys – to triangulate on the research problems at hand. This strategy holds the advantage of allowing the researcher to obtain independent confirmation or disconfirmation of any generalization arrived at inductively (see Webb, 1970; Whyte, 1979).

The research settings

The five alternative organizations selected for this study were located in California in a medium-sized metropolitan area. To ensure that some permanence was involved, no organization was included in the study unless it was at least two years old. All organizations have been given fictitious names. The brief descriptions that follow are intended to provide contextual and historical information, so that examples introduced later for analytic purposes will be more meaningful.

Freedom High. The first alternative organization to be examined in this study is a "free" high school, hereafter referred to as Freedom High. This school was not an accredited school and was not part of any public school system. It was a legal alternative day school in the state of California (its students were not considered truant from public school, but they received no official accreditation). The school financed its meager budget from tuition payments, which were based on a sliding scale.

The initial conception of Freedom High emerged in March of 1970. At that time two young adults who were interested in educational reform began to hold weekly coffeehouse discussions with high school students who were disaffected with the public schools; about 20 students attended. Discussions were organized by the student council president of a local high school. Meanwhile, some adults in the community were helping to set up a free school at the elementary level, and a number of contacts existed between these two groups.

On April 6, 1970, the free high school opened with 12 full-time students. Their enthusiasm spread by word of mouth, and by the end of May they had lined up about 50 students who wanted to attend Freedom High in the fall. Since the two nonstudents who were associated with the formation of the school would soon be leaving the area, they convinced two out-of-town friends to direct the high school. Upon arriving, the latter found a nascent organization and 50 eager students.

The high school was able to get on the nonprofit corporation charter of the elementary school and thereby avoid certain legalities. The charter allowed the school to be a legal alternative to the public system. Sharing a charter meant the two schools shared the same board of directors. Although the board had certain policy-making rights and legal responsibilities, it opted from the beginning not to exercise its powers with regard to the high school. The board was made up of a number of wealthy, liberal adults who were instrumental in starting the elementary school. Since they were mainly interested in the elementary school, they did not raise money or make decisions for Freedom High. This left control of the school to the participants.

Freedom High was located in a storefront in a downtown area. It was staffed by a large number of part-time volunteers, most of whom were college students enrolled in a special course for which they received university credit. There were also a handful of full-time but poorly paid staff members. Classes at the school were generally shaped around the interests and the talents of available staff, and so a comprehensive program was not initially possible. As time went on, the school was able to stabilize its staff somewhat and to expand its program. By the second year of operation, it was asking volunteer teachers for a full year's commitment to the school (rather than just 2½ months) and was able to recruit volunteer staff to fill specific gaps in the program in response to students' interests (e.g., in oceanography, women's history, nutrition). In addition, resources in the community began to be utilized extensively for their pedagogic value, and job apprenticeships were arranged for students desiring them, for example, in carpentry and legal aid.

Decisions at Freedom High were made in three types of meetings: plenary "all school" meetings, staff meetings, and coordination meetings. All meetings were open to any staff member or student who wanted to attend, and decisions at all were taken by a process of consensus, not by vote. Meetings tended to be long and frequent, with participation regarded as a right and a responsibility of members. Full-time staff, part-time staff volunteers, and students were all considered "members" with equal rights whose responsiblity it was to participate in shaping the school. Even the usual dichotomy in schools between staff and students was purposefully blurred at the Free School.

The school contained from 27 to 41 enrolled students during the course of this study, which coincided with the school's first three academic years. A slight majority were from upper middle-class families and all were white. The large numbers of part-time volunteers from the university permitted an enviable student-teacher ratio of about 3:1, if part-time teachers are weighted .5. Classes ranged in size from individual tutorials to seven.

Tensions sometimes developed at the Free School between two main sets of goals: those oriented toward personal change and those oriented toward social change. Like many free schools, this one tried to combine these goals by stressing: learning outside the schoolhouse; affective development and its

integration with the cognitive; individualized instruction; no tracking or grad-
ing, though there were some written evaluations; a critical understanding of
institutions in American society; and an activist orientation toward changing
society.

Participant observation at Freedom High took place over a period of two
years and three months, ending at the close of the school's third full year of
operation. At this point, the school was losing its first generation of students,
who had helped to found the school, and its second full generation of staff
members. The need for a local free school no longer seemed so pressing,
since the public high school had liberalized its program. Thus, the school was
considering dissolving itself when a graduate student in education, heretofore
not associated with the school, asked if he could take it over for the next year.
Having no definite plans for the future of the school, the people at the school
agreed. Thus, during its fourth year, Freedom High was the same organization in name only. It experienced a complete turnover in staff, it was able to
recruit only 12 students, and what had been an enthusiastic, self-initiating
student body was replaced by a largely passive student body, eager to escape
the punitive aspects of public school, but uninvolved in creating a positive
alternative. Field observations were not made during this last year, but interview reports indicate it provided a fruitless environment for the students.
After an unsuccessful year, Freedom High closed its doors in June of 1974.

Research on the four other organizations, described below, began shortly
after Freedom High closed and extended over an 11-month period. The same
research methods and sources of data were used (participant observation, interviews, surveys, and documentary analysis), except that only interview and
documentary material could be obtained in the case of the legal collective.

The Free Clinic.   The Free Clinic began as a two-month pilot project in May
1971 under the auspices of a county health department. Originally,the project
was initiated by professionals at the county health department, funded by a
state grant, and targeted to reach three separate communities of youth: blacks,
Chicanos, and the counterculture. Personnel and outreach representatives
from each of these groups were recruited to run the pilot program. Although
it was moderately successful, officials at the county health department decided not to continue a free medical clinic there because, in the words of one
health department professional, "They felt there was too much conflict between the establishment way of operating clinics and this group's way."

The demonstration project did arouse the enthusiasm of the people who had
worked on it, and they decided to launch an autonomous free clinic. Within
two months they had obtained a nonprofit corporation charter for the new

clinic and they opened a few months later. Although this was among the earliest free clinics, its founders were well aware of similar efforts around the country. From the start, they defined their medical goals very broadly, as captured in their motto: "health care for the whole person, mind and body." Unlike many other clinics at the time, they were not devoted solely to providing venereal disease or drug treatment.

The social base of the Free Clinic turned out to be rather narrow. Some of the early organizers learned from their experience in the pilot program that "these three groups [blacks, Chicanos, counterculture] do not interrelate too well," and decided to tailor their services toward the counterculture. That the Free Clinic would have had to design itself differently to appeal to each of these three groups was explained by one founder of the clinic:

The counterculture group is very casual . . . barefoot, casual, wild colors . . . and the Chicano and the Black have grown up with an image of medical care as being – if it's too casual it's second class, and they want the best. . . . They want the doctor in the white coat, everything spic and span, just right. Otherwise we're saying to them we're giving you second-class medicine. That's how they interpreted it to us.

Thus, the early organizers of the Free Clinic instead settled on the strategy of providing a very broad range of medical services to a restricted target population of counterculture youth.

By becoming incorporated, the clinic was forced by law to assemble a board of directors. Like Freedom High, they sought out the most prestigious members of the community they could find to be board members, hoping in this way to lend an air of legitimacy to their alternative institution. But, unlike Freedom High, they endowed this board with organizational power and responsibilities that the board of Freedom High did not have or desire. This set the Free Clinic up for bitter staff-board conflicts that Freedom High never had.

As Sarason (1972) suggests, all the decisions made in the "before the beginning" stage of the Free Clinic – its early relationship to the county health department, its independence from them, its countercultural orientation, the breadth of its conception of health, and its powerful board – significantly influenced later events at the clinic.

When the Free Clinic opened in late 1971, one of the organizers of the pilot project, and later of the clinic itself, became its director. A number of assistants worked with him. Although the clinic was quite participatory in its early days, it was not collectivist. It resembled any human relations organization with a rather horizontal structure of authority. The director, however, was not pleased with this mode of organization, and tried to develop in the clinic a number of "component coordinators" to replace the present director-assistant relationship. After instituting these changes, he realized he would always be regarded as the de facto "director," a common problem in the transition to collectivist organization. He soon left to get a Ph.D. in public health, leaving the clinic with a health education coordinator, a counseling coordinator, and two medical coordinators, arranged in an egalitarian manner. Though it continued to grow, the clinic retained that structure.

At the time of observation, the Free Clinic had six full-time staff coordinators: two on medical, two on administration, and one each on health education and counseling. Each of the four components had a trained staff of volunteers to implement the components' programs: patient advocates, lab technicians, counselors, receptionists, and health education speakers and writers.

Decisions were made at component meetings, at weekly staff meetings, and at monthly board of directors meetings. After the original director left, staff insisted upon a collectivist mode of operation (e.g., equal pay, no "director") over the strong objections of the same prestigious board members the clinic had eagerly sought in the beginning. While staff struggled to retain "collective" control over the clinic (i.e., staff control), the board tried to reassert hierarchy among staff, and board control, by appointing a director accountable to the board. For two years dozens of staff-board conflicts raged over day-to-day concerns involving this issue. Finally, the staff succeeded in gaining the resignations of those members of the board who had wanted to reestablish hierarchy, and filled those vacancies with friends and clinic volunteers who supported collectivism.

The philosophy of the Free Clinic remained progressive. To quote from a position paper written by Free Clinic staff:

We are committed to providing an alternative health care system showing the way health care should be. . . . We believe illness is a social-economic problem, not just biological. . . . We are dedicated to total health care, of mind and body. . . . We believe that prevention is as important as treatment of illness.

The clinic tried to affirm these principles in its everyday practices. In addition, a later philosophical statement reads:

No one should gain excess profit from the sickness, death, or misery of others. . . . Health care workers, patients and community members should determine the priorities of health institutions. . . . The roles and interrelationships of health workers should be redefined to be nonsexist and nonelitist.

At first, the Free Clinic was entirely supported by city and county revenue-sharing grants, private foundation grants, and donations from patients and others. This allowed it to be, as the name implies, entirely free to patients. Even such services as analysis of laboratory tests, dispensing of prescribed drugs, physician examinations, and private counseling sessions were free.

The average patient donation was $1.00 to $2.00 per visit. However, toward the close of its fourth year of operation, the clinic faced the serious probability of not receiving further revenue-sharing funds for the 1975-76 fiscal year. Although the clinic was well regarded, local government officials did have a general rule of not supporting any community organization for more than three years. The threat of losing this base of financial support and the prospect of having to close the clinic jolted the staff into making plans to become more financially self-supporting. They decided to move gradually toward a fee-for-service system. This entailed instituting a liberal sliding scale of nominal fees, and where possible, billing insurance companies and Medi-Cal for services rendered.

The Free Clinic provided an extensive range of services. The medical component had several afternoon and evening medical clinics each week, a weekly dental clinic, and a weekly children's clinic. Clinic hours were staffed by one or two physicians, a medical coordinator (who was also a nurse), and 6 to 8 volunteer patient advocates, lab technicians, and receptionists. The medical component generally had about 50 volunteer "patient advocates" from which to draw at any one time. These people had gone through a two-to three-month training program, and attended component meetings at which they decided issues of relevance to the medical component and were kept abreast of new medical information useful in their jobs. Patient advocates, an innovation of free clinics, took medical histories, tried to ensure that the physician understood the patients' problems and that the patient understood the physicians's diagnosis and treatment, and in general tried to personally give patients health care information that would help them to care for themselves.

The counseling component provided individual psychological counseling with its staff of trained volunteer counselors. In addition, it held evening group sessions on such topics as transactional analysis, verbal self-defense for women, and psychodrama.

The main purpose of the health education component was to "demystify medicine." Following the clinic's belief that "educating people about their health problems is an important and basic part of any treatment process," the clinic's health educators tried to raise public awareness of health care treatment and prevention. Toward this end, they wrote a series of free pamphlets on such topics as Medi-Cal, dental care, herpes, hepatitis, venereal disease, and drugs. These pamphlets were widely respected in the medical community; they were translated into Spanish and were distributed at several community clinics, at general hospitals, and at the county health department. Health education also had a speakers' program in which trained volunteers spoke by invitation to a variety of organizations such as schools, colleges, juvenile hall, and a Lion's Club on such topics as sexuality, venereal disease, birth control, sex roles, drugs, and nutrition. The health education component also put on a regular radio program. Subjects covered in this show included self-healing, nutrition, pre-orgasmic counseling, male sexuality, and child abuse. At any given time, the Free Clinic had 60–100 active volunteers, and each component was to hold meetings with these people.

Over the years the Free Clinic had grown from an average clientele of 130 patients per month by the end of its first year of operation to a mean of 479 patients per month by the close of its third year. Most of the patients (79 percent) were between 15 and 30 years of age and were white (86 percent). Typically, they came to the clinic for venereal disease testing and treatment (23 percent), followed in frequency by treatment for the skin (18 percent), and gynecology (16 percent). In addition, the counseling program reached an average of 69 people per month, and the health education speakers' program reached an estimated 675 people per month. As free clinics go, this one was large in the number of patients it saw and comprehensive in the services it provided.

The Community News.   The alternative newspaper in this study was just that – an alternate – it was neither "underground" nor "establishment." Referring to similar alternative newspapers in Boston, Kopkind (1974) describes them as "sea-level."

The genesis of the *Community News* can be traced to the summer of 1971. At that time a number of student activists who later were to found the paper were working on an underground paper. One member described the group as, "very political, almost to a Weatherman position . . . we were studying self-defense and guerrilla warfare." However, by mid-1971 the group began to reanalyze the political situation:

We came to the realization that the revolution will be a very gradual thing. . . . The collective had thought about the problems of ideological hegemony and how it was maintained by the media. We came to see all media as propaganda . . . toyed with the idea of having an alternative media to present leftist propaganda instead of the usual capitalist propaganda.

What transformed this from a pipe dream into a feasible plan was the coincidental discovery of a fellow West Coaster who had reached the same conclusion and who had just received $5,000 from a wealthy liberal patron to set up an alternative paper in California. All through the summer and fall the group held discussions about the paper they were to launch. In the words of one of the founders:

It was, like all media, to be a political organ, not an impartial voice. We wanted to activate liberals and open them up to a left perspective . . . try to reach a broad base, not just the students and the underground . . . concentrate on local issues. The Left had been associated with national issues, with Vietnam. We would resist being labeled and ignored as "radicals" if we emphasized community issues. Also, we felt it was important to learn to apply a left analysis to local isues and that these issues, being more concrete, would be better able to arouse people . . . if we wanted to reach nonradicals. We really had a commitment to speaking in a language and style that anyone could understand and accept.

These were the consensual goals of the *Community News* when it began publishing in December 1971, and they remained its essential goals.

However, specific points of disagreement existed among the organizers of the *Community News*. For instance, all agreed the paper should appeal to a "broad base," not only students, but some favored a labor orientation, whereas others wanted to cultivate their most "natural audiences" – liberals, professionals, and the middle class.

Evidence seems to indicate the paper did best at attracting the latter. According to a readership survey conducted by the researcher, 52 percent of the readers of the paper identified themselves as professional or as middle class. But the paper had also self-consciously tried to attract the interest of the working class. A content analysis of articles in the paper over a 10-month period reveals that stories about labor were among those most frequently published. Of the respondents to the readership survey, 18.5 percent identified themselves as working class. Since its earliest days, people at the *Community News* sought to develop a broad community-based constituency rather than a student-based one. Consequently, the content analysis shows stories about the university and the student community were among the type least frequently covered. Only 13 percent of the respondents of the readership survey classified themselves as students and, only 21 percent of the readers of the paper were under 23 years of age, but 76 percent were between 18 and 40 years old. The median educational attainment of the readers of the paper was a B.A., but the median income was reported at only $7,500 to $10,000. Thus, the *Community News* did attract an audience wider than the student community.

There is also evidence that the *Community News,* again in line with its objectives, appealed to liberals and perhaps had some impact on their perspectives. Twenty-five percent of the readers of the paper viewed themselves as radicals, 53 percent identified themselves as liberal, and only 4 percent classified themselves as conservative. Twenty-one percent of the readers of the paper thought the paper was radical, while 71 percent believed it was liberal on most issues. Of more importance was the impact the paper had on its readers. Two-thirds of the readers reported that the paper's coverage had changed their opinion about specific local issues. Of the remaining one-third who reported no opinion change, this was usually (in 71 percent of the cases) because the individual already agreed with the paper's opinion, and seldom (in 15 percent of the cases) because the reader was unconvinced by the paper. Fifty-four percent of the readers reported they always or usually followed the endorsements of the *Community News* in voting. The *News* was proud of a variety of liberalizing political changes that had taken place locally since the creation of the newspaper (for example, the election of progressives to city council and county Board of Supervisors positions), although it is difficult to tie such changes directly to the effect of the paper.

When the paper first began publishing it was a biweekly of about 12 pages. As a newly created newspaper, it had to build its circulation and its advertising from a base of zero. Two years later, it was putting out a weekly paper of 28–40 pages, and by its third year it boasted a circulation of 22,000. As a proportion of the local population, the readership of the *Community News* was higher than the 1974 combined readership (150,000) of the *Real Paper* and the *Boston Phoenix* (Kopkind, 1974).

The growth and success of the alternative press came at a time when "straight" community newspapers were folding or shrinking. The Los Angeles metropolitan area alone had more than 300 straight community newspapers. Many were suffering severe financial problems owing to the rapidly rising cost of newsprint, recessionary advertising cutbacks, and a decline in readership of local newspapers (*Los Angeles Times*, pt. I, pp. 1, 25–18, June 22, 1975). However, in marked contrast to the *Community News* and the alternative press in general, most of these papers saw their purpose as covering such traditional community items as the PTA, high school football, and civic clubs. The *News* tried from its inception to emphasize community issues, but this did not mean it covered high school football scores. At the alternative paper, a community orientation meant applying a left perspective to community issues, local investigative reporting, and "advocacy journalism." A member of the paper explained:

People who started [the paper] kept using the words "advocacy journalism" . . . [to suggest] that no media is objective. The mere choice of a headline, what's included and what's excluded, are political judgments. We hoped to be upfront about that and to provide an alternative voice to the [city newspaper]. . . . We didn't like the idea of a one-paper town and wanted to provide the other side of their stories, as well as covering a lot of stories the [city newspaper] wouldn't touch.

The *News* was run by a full-time staff collective of 12 to 18 people at any one time. In addition, the paper had a number of part-time people on the periphery. When the staff collective was unable to find one of its own to do particular tasks (e.g., typesetting), it was forced to hire a few people for wages:

"We've always had marginal people who weren't necessarily in the collective, but they weren't outside either. A distinction was always made though between the hired staff and the collective, who could be expected to work for nothing if need be."

Staff members at the *News* became co-owners of the paper after six months.

At the paper, participatory democracy was taken very seriously. Decisions were made via consensus at weekly meetings of the full staff. All manner of decisions were made at these meetings and they covered both editorial and organizational issues. The job of chairing the meetings was rotated among staff members. As noted in the story about Ann and John in Chapter 1, jobs were also rotated at the paper.

The Food Co-op. The food cooperative began in 1970 as a buying club for about 100 people, mostly students, operating out of members' living rooms. On Wednesdays members would get together to place their orders, on Saturdays they would get their food, and in between they would rotate the tasks of tabulating orders, buying the food, distributing it, bookkeeping, and so forth. Altogether, this came to 10–15 hours per week for each household. As one early member put it, "There weren't enough people with the energy to keep it going. It just took too much time to get your food."

By mid-1973 about 12 core members began to work on plans for a direct-charge food co-op. This meant the co-op would take the form of a grocery store (for members only) that would charge each member a small monthly service fee to cover overhead expenses but would sell the food at cost. Members would each donate at least one hour's work per month toward running the store. In September 1973 a membership drive was launched, and in January 1974 the Food Co-op opened its store. In this new form, the co-op was able to attract 1,102 members after one year of operation. The sales were equally impressive: about $35,000 per month during the academic year. This figure would decline substantially during summers when most student members were out of town.

Food purchases took place in a relatively small storefront located in a student community adjacent to a university. The 1,400-square-foot store was packed with food from top to bottom, had bulletin boards for members' suggestions and messages, and was decorated with contributed plants and artwork with such titles as "exploding orange on desert highway" or "exploding corn in field with Indian family looking on."

Almost all of the Food Co-op's members were young (90 percent between

18 and 23), and 69 percent were college students. Members of the Food Co-op had very little money, at least for the time being: Only 6 percent made $7,000 per year or more, and the vast majority (85 percent) received $3,000 per year or less. Politically, 79 percent of the general membership (and 100 percent of the staff and board members) considered themselves to be between "liberal" and "radical" on the political spectrum. Eighty percent voted in elections, but even more (89 percent) had taken part in demonstrations, and 72 percent reported they had engaged in civil disobedience at some time. People at the Food Co-op tended not to believe solutions to American socioeco-nomic-economic problems would come through more progressive leadership (28 percent), but even fewer believed an armed struggle would be needed to change things (17 percent). Instead, they tended to think solutions to our country's problems would come through massive changes in people's basic values (87 percent), and by organizing self-governing communities and direct democracy (74 percent).

The Food Co-op was incorporated as a nonprofit corporation, meaning it had to have a board of directors. The board was elected by the general membership at quarterly meetings. It was their function to act as a "coordinating committee" to administer the co-op's operations, but major policy changes were reserved for the general membership meetings. In addition to the nine elected board members, any member who wished to attend the weekly board meetings was allowed a full vote there. A paid staff of three to four people ran the store and coordinated the volunteer labor of the 1,100 members.

Any mutual-benefit association must constantly struggle to maintain the interest and participation of its membership (Blau and Scott, 1962, pp. 45–49), and food cooperatives are no exception (see, e.g., Giese, 1974). Because the acquisition of food is not problematic to most members, it may be especially difficult to sustain interests in food cooperatives.

The Food Co-op, like any food cooperative, could not claim the participation of all of its 1,100 members. However, the majority of members did put their hour per month into the store, and most (81 percent) reported working longer. Ninety-eight percent said they read the co-op's newsletter, and 64 percent of the general members thought they had "quite a bit" of say in decisions at the co-op.

Financially, the Food Co-op was self-supporting. At its inception it did receive $6,500 in seed money from the student government of a nearby university, but none thereafter. The capital costs of establishing the store (equipment, initial inventory, remodeling the storefront) were largely covered by members' deposits ($10 per individual or $30 per household). These shares of the co-op were refundable when members left. The operating costs were fully covered by a monthly service charge of $2.50 per member. The food was sold at cost. Individuals reported spending an average of $10 per week at the store. With this financial arrangement, the co-op was able to operate in the black, but several financial problems lingered. Since it was not a profit-making organization, it operated with almost no cushion, leaving sparse savings with which to finance one-time expenses such as the down payment on a mortgage for its store. Also, like many other co-ops (see Zwerdling, 1975), the Food Co-op found it had to pay much higher prices for wholesale food than the supermarkets did. Thus, after one year of operation, the co-op invested a considerable sum as a deposit so it could buy groceries through a major wholesaler, thereby ensuring lower prices for the co-op's members in the future.

The goals of the co-op were "economy, ecology, and community." Its motto stated: "Through economy we are trying to provide the commodity most basic to our survival, food, to co-op members at the lowest possible prices." In addition, the co-op tried to minimize environmental waste in its use of resources, for example, by using reusable containers and trying to sell only food of high nutritional value. Finally, it attempted to develop a sense of community both within the co-op and in the larger community of which it was a part. Its organizers saw the co-op as the first of a series of community development corporations. It supported efforts to create other community-run economic and political institutions in the town where it existed. In members' words:

Part of the reason the [Food Co-op] was formed was so that we in [name of town] might begin to gain control over some of the economic institutions which affect our lives.

The Law Collective.   The legal collective in this study began in 1971. Most of its members first met during a trial stemming from charges against participants in a protest demonstration in 1970. As a result of the trial, some of the defense attorneys and some of the defendants realized there was a need for a legal collective in town and began to make joint plans to form one. The Law Collective defined collective law practices as "experiments in the delivery of legal services to people whose lack of money and power severely limits their access to any form of legal assistance."

Over time, the Law Collective developed from defending oppressed individuals in need of legal aid to defending groups of people, particularly workers. By 1974–75 the latter were a priority, and they were providing legal counsel about labor contracts to a number of established unions. In addition, they had helped cab drivers, waitresses, and sea urchin fishermen to organize.

Before the Law Collective could take on a case for no fee, the case had to be, in its judgment, of political significance. However, most of their cases were more or less routine, and for these they received competitive or somewhat lower fees.

The Law Collective categorically refused to take some types of cases. They would not, for example, defend accused rapists, because the "prime defense tactic in rape cases is to attack the integrity of the prosecutrix" (document, 1974). They also refused to accept the cases of men in contested divorces, or cases for landlords or corporations.

Taken together, the cases the collective considered worthy of free legal attention and the cases they refused to take at any price reflected its political perspective. In fact, the collective spent many hours at meetings deliberately trying to bring its practice in line with its political ideals. In the words of one member of the collective: "We see ourselves as one front in a common struggle against bureaucracy and capitalism."

The Law Collective had 6 to 10 members in it at any one time. Usually 3 or 4 of these were attorneys, and the others were legal workers. The collective managed to pay each member a base salary of $250 per month in 1975 plus an additional amount for any dependents they might have, so a new legal worker who entered with no experience and with one child was paid $325 to start.

Members were very cautious about who was admitted into the collective. As one member put it, they had to be sure "each new person can generate the energy and the money to allow the collective to support one more person." Another criterion they used to decide on potential members was:

They have to have a certain amount of past experience in political work . . . something really good and significant that checks out. We never take anyone in cold. . . . They have to share the same basic assumptions as far as politics goes and they have to be willing . . . to accept the collective way of doing things, which is on the basis of consensus.

This criterion meant the Law Collective was a much more homogeneous group than any of the other organizations in our study. It was also more exclusive. It required that new members undergo a longer initiation period, had definite organizational boundaries, and demanded rather exclusive commitment from the members. (As noted, it did not permit participant observation by researchers.) There was no room here for the part-timers, the hangers-on, and the volunteer labor we saw in abundance at all of the other alternative organizations we studied.

Tasks at the Law Collective were accomplished in a collectivist manner. There was no division of labor between, for instance, typists, receptionists, and lawyers. Although legal workers entered the collective with little or no former training in law, each member was responsible for closing the gaps in knowledge, and was not to perpetuate them by dividing the labor on the basis of such differences. Thus, attorneys and legal workers alike shared the tasks of typing, reception work, cleanup, legal research, writing pleadings, appearing in court, and so forth. The Law Collective apparently had considerable success in developing in its legal workers the skills of effective jurists. A number of these workers later pursued admission to the bar through the alternative means of apprenticing under an experienced attorney (namely, through their work at the Law Collective). After three years, this work experience qualified them for the bar in the state of California.

Overview

Similarities and differences among the organizations.   As a way of summarizing some of the differences among these five organizations, consider their board–staff–member relationships. At the Free Clinic, the board was self-perpetuating; it appointed its own new members to fill vacancies. The board at the clinic had formal powers, but when staff and board interests clashed, the staff tended to prevail. At Freedom High, the board was also originally appointed, but it never changed its composition, and it had no powers, board members being merely figureheads. At both the clinic and the school, the board was made up of prestigious, sometimes wealthy, patrons of the alternative institution. However, at the Food Co-op the board was elected by the membership, and was composed of fellow members of the co-op. It exercised some decision-making authority, but only within parameters carefully circumscribed by the general membership. The most committed participants – those from whom the greatest sacrifices could be expected in the interests of the organization – were the staff at the Free Clinic and the board at the Food Co-op. Staff at the clinic tried to fill many new board positions with more committed members, and the board at the co-op tried to fill new staff positions with more committed members. The *Community News* and the Law Collective did not have to work out a special staff-board relationship because they were completely self-governing staff collectives.

Clients or members of these alternatives also had varying relationships to the organization. Staff at the Free Clinic and the Law Collective tried to be attentive to clients' interests, and, as part of this responsiveness, they often tried to "demystify" medicine or the law in order to make the client less dependent on the organization's continued help. At the Free Clinic, some of their most interested patients underwent training and became volunteers for the clinic. But, at the Law Collective, clients had no place to fit into the internal organization. The *Community News,* of course, had customers rather than clients, and although the paper sought community feedback, it was, by the very nature of a newspaper, more distant from the individuals it served. At Freedom High, the clients (the students) were so integrated into the decision-making structure of the school that they could be considered full-fledged members. As such, they exercised considerable influence over the selection of staff, curriculum, the issue of where the school should locate, and other important decisions. At the Food Co-op, the member-owners were, in a sense, its "clients," and the co-op was constantly aware it had to justify itself in terms of member satisfaction and participation.

Characteristics and backgrounds of participants. Questionnaire data on the social base of alternative institutions were gathered from three of the observed organizations (the Food Co-op, the Free Clinic, and the *Community News*). At the *News,* full-time staff members (of whom there are 14 to 18 at any one time) grew up in families whose mean annual income was about $29,000, a high figure for the times (early 1970s). A random sampling of the general membership at the Food Co-op (consisting of 1,100 people) revealed an average parental income of $19,500 (though these young members themselves are quite poor, if only temporarily, with 85% of them receiving annual incomes below $3,000). The more active members of the co-op, the staff and board, had a mean parental income of approximately $46,000. At the Free Clinic, the part-time volunteers (of whom there are 60 to 100 at any one time) reported an average parental income of about $25,000.

In addition to having rather financially privileged origins, people in grassroots collectives tend to come from well-educated families. In all three organizations, more than half the mothers of members had at least some college education; fathers on the average had acquired some graduate or professional training beyond the B.A., except at the Free Clinic, where fathers had a median education of some college. As these educational levels would suggest, only 14 to 18 percent of the members of each group report family occupations that could be categorized as working class (again, with the notable exception of staff at the Free Clinic).

The social origins of people in alternative institutions correspond strikingly with those of the New Left students. Moreover, it appears members of collectivist enterprises are not only the same types of people that Flacks (1967) and Keniston (1968) found in the social movements of the 1960s, but they are often the very same people, now a few years older.

Almost all of the founders of the collectives we studied had been active in the student-based movements of the 1960s. At the *Community News*, for instance, members had taken part in an average of 14 demonstrations apiece, and all had engaged in acts of civil disobedience at some time. At the Food Co-op, more of the members had utilized demonstrations as a means of political expression (89 percent) than voting (80 percent). Fully 72 percent reported engaging in civil disobedience, such as resistance to arrest or dispersion at demonstrations. Even at the Free Clinic, the least explicitly political of the five organizations studied, 68 percent of its member-volunteers reported participating in some demonstrations. Between 79 and 100 percent of the members of each organization identified themselves as falling between "liberal" and "radical" on the political spectrum. Between 57 and 71 percent of the staff members of each group reported feeling a sense of solidarity with the New Left. Very similar levels of identification with the women's movement and the ecology movement were found in these groups. However, of the general (consumer) members of the Food Co-op, only 30 percent reported feeling a sense of solidarity with the New Left, probably because they are significantly younger than the "political generation" (Zeitlin, 1970) of the 1960s student activists.[1]

These statistics on social origins and political identifications reveal a marked continuity between people in collectivist organizations at present and former New Left students. Activists of the 1970s and 1980s are the same types of people, and often enough, are the very same individuals who participated in social movements in the 1960s, but they have changed their political strategy. They have moved from a strategy of student-based protest and political confrontation to one of building decentralized, community-based, collectivist organizations. This is an important cause of the recent rise of alternative organizations aiming to embody countercultural values, motivations, and work forms.[2]

These data on participants also suggest to us other social and economic causes of the rise of cooperatives in the 1970s. The work of Abraham Maslow (1954) tells us that once people satisfy their basic needs for subsistence and security, they become more concerned with fulfilling higher-order needs for self-esteem and self-actualization. Most of the people in the groups we observed were born and socialized under conditions of relative affluence and security. Not having to worry much about the basics, they began to see future jobs not just as sources of income or necessary drudgery to be endured, but as mainsprings of personal growth, satisfaction, and social meaning. They expected to put a lot into their work and to gain a lot from it. But to many growing up in the 1950s and 1960s, it appeared that the reality of work, as experienced by their parents and peers, would fall short of their own high aspirations.

Unemployment and underemployment hit young people particularly hard. In 1978, almost half of all unemployment was among 16- to 24-year-olds (Thurow, 1980, p. 187). Similarly, Sullivan (1978, p. 89) concludes, after a detailed analysis of marginality among workers, that the young and the old are more likely to be "underutilized" than other workers (i.e., either unemployed, enduring inadequate working hours, subject to low income, or mismatched in terms of occupation and education).

Adding to young adults' difficulties in finding satisfactory employment was the master trend of the past couple of decades toward a more concentrated economy. With the size of both private corporations and public bureaucracies growing, personal control over institutions was becoming increasingly remote. The inflation of educational credentials was pushing career entry requirements higher and higher. Among parents, relatives, and friends, children could see personal evidence of the pervasive "blue-collar blues" and "white-collar woes," as many jobs of both kinds became less autonomous, less skilled, and less satisfying (HEW, 1973; Braverman 1974). A 1977 survey found, for example, that 60 percent of American workers would prefer a job other than the one they presently hold, a rise of 16 percent over 1969 (Quinn and Staines, 1977, p. 210). Compared to workers in general, young workers – along with nonwhites and females – have significantly higher levels of job dissatisfaction (Sullivan, 1978, p. 202). Many young workers would have agreed with a young woman, working as a magazine editor, who said, "I think most of us are looking for a calling, not a job. Most of us . . . have jobs that are too small for our spirit. Jobs are not big enough for people." (Terkel, 1975, p. xxix).

Coupled with a desire for more meaningful and challenging work has been an increased willingness on the part of some young adults to forego traditional life-styles. Often they trade the consumption patterns of their parents for their collectively run workplaces with slimmer incomes, giving up split-level suburban ranch homes for communal living, station wagons for shared old VWs. In addition to being the common currency of much of the new generation, these modes of living give support to – and are sometimes necessitated by – the creation of alternative workplaces. People do not get rich in co-ops. Yet many people apparently do often find work there that they feel is psychically and socially enriching.

In a true participatory democracy, any new member (whether staff, volunteer, or client) with the inclination and the energy to participate in the affairs of the organization, would be able to exercise decision-making influence after only a few months or less. All of the organizations in this study tried to achieve this goal. The degree to which it was attained varied among organizations and within a single organization over time. As we will see in the initial chapter of Part II, the exact nature of participatory democracy departs from bureaucratic forms of organization to such an extent that it must be considered an alternative model of organization.

In closing this chapter, we must reiterate that the above five case studies form only the point of departure, the grounding for our theory. Our analysis is in no way limited to them. The two parts of the book to follow examine many other organizations and organizational forms to broaden and corroborate our theoretical observations.

PART II

A theory of democratic organization

3. The collectivist organization: an alternative to bureaucratic models

For many decades the study of organizations has been, in effect, the study of bureaucracy and its many variations. This decade, however, has given rise to a wide array of organizations that self-consciously reject the norms of bureaucracy and identify themselves as "alternative institutions" or "collectives." In view of the history of cooperatives and the recent emergence of these counterbureaucratic organizations, we need a new model of organization that is able to encompass their alternative practices and aspirations. This chapter attempts to construct such a model. As a first step, it is necessary to distinguish between formal and substantive rationality, using the work of Max Weber.

Weber (1947; 1954) recognized a tension between formal and substantive rationality. For Weber, formal rationality – an emphasis on instrumental activity, formal laws, and procedural regularity – would have its main locus of expression in bureaucracy. But formal rationality would come into inevitable conflict with people's desire to realize their substantive goals and values such as peace or equality or good health, what Weber called substantive or value-rationality. Modern bureaucracy would be built on the procedural regularity of formal law, but in Weber's view it could never eliminate all moral, subjective concerns (Bendix, 1962, pp. 391–438). Nevertheless, in his classic statement on bureaucracy, Weber (1946, pp. 196–244) sets forth the characteristics of bureaucracy as if it could eliminate all substantive, moral considerations.

Taking a historical view, Weber believed virtually all organizations fit into one of three types. In the first and oldest type, authority was inherited and orders were accepted as legitimate and were obeyed because this was the way things had been done since time immemorial. Traditional societies gave rise to a patriarchal mode of organization. In a second type, charismatic leaders could depart from long-held traditions, since their authority rested on their own inspiring or magnetic qualities, their special gifts of grace. This situation gives rise to a communitarian form of organization, whose core consists of the charismatic leader and disciples. To Weber, a third type, legal-rational authority, would eclipse the first two and come to dominate modern society. Here authority is followed because it represents consistently applied rules implemented by those with the appropriate position or expertise. Bureaucracy is the form of organization that implements legal-rational authority. Thus, for Weber, each legitimating principle develops a special mode of organization to implement it.

Weber notes in passing that a fourth type of legitimation and organization, that of substantive rationality, might be possible. Unfortunately, however, he does not elaborate. This chapter attempts to develop Weber's neglected type. The contemporary collectives in our study reject traditional, charismatic, and bureaucratic authority. Decisions are taken to be morally binding only if they reflect the will of the collectivity and are arrived at through a process of democratic consensus. Herein lies the importance of these organizations. They point the way to a fourth type of organization in history that, like the first three, is cohesive and internally consistent, but, unlike them, turns on principles of substantive rationality.

Just as the ideal of bureaucracy, in its monocratic pure type, is probably not attainable (Mouzelis, 1968), so the ideal of democracy, in its pure and complete form, is probably never achieved. In practice, organizations are hybrids.

We seek to develop an ideal-typical model of collectivist–democratic organization by which to delineate the form of authority and the corresponding mode of organization following from value-rational premises. The ideal-typical approach will allow us to understand collectivist democracies, not only in terms of bureaucratic standards they do not share, but in terms of the countervalues they do hold (see Kanter and Zurcher, 1973). Further, the use of an ideal type permits us to classify actual organizations along a continuum, rather than forcing us to place them in discrete categories. There are *degrees* of collectivism.

The collectivist organization: characteristics

Collectivist–democratic organizations can be distinguished from bureaucratic organizations along at least eight dimensions,[1] each of which will be taken up in turn. Table 3.1, at the end of this chapter, summarizes these eight characteristics.

Authority.

When we're talking about collectives, we're talking about an embryonic creation of a new society. . . . Collectives are growing at a phenomenal rate all over this country. The new structures have outgrown the science of analyzing them. Sociology has to catch up with reality. . . . Collectivism is an attempt to supplant old structures of society with new and better structures. And what makes ours superior is that the basis of authority is radically different. (Staff member, *Community News*)

The words of this activist get right to the heart of the matter – authority. Perhaps more than anything else, it is the basis of authority that distinguishes the collectivist organization from any variant of bureaucracy. The collectivist–democratic organization rejects bureaucratic justifications for authority. Here authority rests not with the individual, whether on the basis of incumbency in office or expertise, but resides in the collectivity.

This notion stems from the ancient anarchist ideal of "no authority." It is premised on the belief that social order can be achieved without recourse to authority relations (Guerin, 1970). Thus it presupposes the capacity of individuals for self-disciplined, cooperative behavior. Like the anarchists, collectives seek not the transference of power from one official to another, but the abolition of the pyramid in toto: organization without hierarchy. In his empirical study of decision making in kibbutzim enterprises, Rosner (1981) finds hierarchy in the workplace limits the degree to which people can sit as equals in both community and workplace assemblies. In other words, hierarchy inhibits equality of influence in decision-making bodies.

An organization, of course, cannot be made up of a collection of autonomous wills, each pursuing its own personal ends. Some decisions must be binding on the group. Decisions become authoritative and binding in collectivist organizations to the extent they arise from a process in which all members have the right to full and equal participation. This democratic ideal, however, differs significantly from conceptions of "democratic bureaucracy" (Lipset et al., 1962), "representative bureaucracy" (Gouldner, 1954), or even, as noted earlier, representative democracy. In its directly democratic form, it does not subscribe to the established sets of rules of order and protocol with which we are all acquainted: It does not take formal motions and amendments, it does not usually take votes, majorities don't rule, and there is no two-party system. Instead there is a "consensus process" in which all members participate in the collective formulation of problems and negotiation of decisions.[2] All major policy issues, such as personnel hiring, firing, salaries, division of labor, the distribution of surplus, and the shape of the final product or service, are decided by the collective as a whole. Only decisions that appear to carry the consensus of the group behind them carry the weight of moral authority. Only these decisions, changing as they might with the ebb and flow of sentiments in the group, are taken as binding and legitimate.

Empirically, this consensus process seems to be well suited to the alternative organization. It reveals that the group is not as concerned with simple efficiency as it is with exemplifying in its internal process the values of self-expression and group cohesion. For nothing is ruled out of order, no vote cuts short discussion because a majority are in agreement. Issues are discussed for as long as it may take for a consensus to be negotiated. Further, this process seems appropriate because it does not imply any authority structure; leadership of meetings can be rotated or meetings may not be chaired at all. Thirdly, it reflects, and perhaps serves to instill, cooperation and self-determination, attributes these groups usually want to foster.

In Weberian terms, then, we are concerned with organizations that aspire and claim to be free of *Herrschaft*.[3] They are organizations without domination in that ultimate authority is based in the group as a whole, not in the individual. Individuals, of course, may be delegated carefully circumscribed areas of authority, but authority is delegated and defined by the collectivity and subject to recall by the collectivity.

Rules.   Collectivist organizations challenge too the bureaucratic conception that organizations should be bound by a formally established, written system of rules and regulations. Instead, they seek to use as few rules as possible. But just as the most bureaucratic of organizations cannot anticipate, and therefore cannot circumscribe, every potential behavior in the organization, so the alternative organization cannot reach the theoretical limit of zero rules. Collectivist organizations can, however, reduce drastically the number of spheres of organizational activity subject to explicit rule governance.

The most simple of the collectivist organizations we observed, Freedom High, formulated only one explicit organizational rule: no drugs in school. This rule was agreed upon by a plenary meeting of the school's students and staff primarily because its violation was perceived to threaten the continued existence of the school. Other possible rules were discussed as well, rules that might seem self-evident in ordinary schools, such as "each student should take X number of classes" or "students are required to attend the courses for which they are registered," but these did not receive the consensual backing of the school's members.

In place of the fixed and universalistic rule use that is the trademark of bureaucracy, operations and decisions in alternative organizations tend to be conducted in an ad hoc manner. Decisions generally are settled as the case arises, and are suited to the peculiarities of the individual case. No written manual of rules and procedures exists in most collectives, although norms of participation clearly obtain. Although there is little attempt to account for decisions in terms of literal rules, concerted efforts are made to account for decisions in terms of substantive ethics. This is like Weber's (1968, pp. 976–

978) *Kadi* justice, based on substantive ethics, and is a long distance from the formal justice that guides rational bureaucratic action.

A chief virtue of extensive rule use in bureaucracy is that it allows predictability and the appeal of decisions to higher authority. The lack of universalistic standards in prebureaucratic modes of organization did invite arbitrary and capricious rule. In bureaucracy at least, decisions can be calculated and appealed on the basis of their correspondence to the written law. In collectivist organizations, on the other hand, decisions are not arbitrary. They are based on substantive values (such as equality) applied consistently, if not universally. This permits some calculability on the basis of knowing the substantive ethic that will be invoked in a particular situation.

Despite the desire for minimal rules, some rules may be useful to collectivist organizations. In cooperatives that have a fast turnover of members, written rules may help to communicate to new members the agreements and expectations of former members. For example, in seven housing co-ops studied by Gillespie (1981), those that did incorporate rules were perceived by members to be as democratic, communal, and egalitarian as those that did not. In fact, the use of rules helped the co-ops to rapidly convey their norms to new members; this feature was important since the average length of residence of the members was only 12.7 months (Gillespie, 1981, p. 7). However, because people in most worker co-ops expect to be in the organization for a longer period of time and there is daily social interaction, it is easier to provide each other with an oral history of events and there may be less need for written rules. The fact that turnover is usually more rapid in consumer co-ops than in worker co-ops may increase their need to write down a history and rules with which to socialize new members. But there is still an important difference between collective and bureaucratic rule use. In a collective, rules are always subject to group negotiation and change. They are not carved in stone or ritualized, nor are they passed down from above.

Although collectives tend to be suspicious of rules, rules need not be antidemocratic. Certain rules may actually enhance democratic control. For example, the Food Co-op made a rule that if any member attended three consecutive meetings of the board, then they were allowed to vote as a board member. Clearly, this encouraged member participation.

In comparison with bureaucratic organizations such as a government agency or a corporation, collectives are characterized by the minimal use of formal, written rules. Of course, in no case that we observed or have heard about, have written rules been entirely eliminated. Indeed, collectives do have many informally shared expectations and agreements, as do all organizations. The degree to which collectives commit such understandings to writing may depend upon their turnover rates, needs for rapid socialization, legal requirements, and other practical as well as philosophic concerns. It is important to keep in mind that the extent of rule use is *not* the most fundamental characteristic of collectivist organizations – the locus of authority is.

Social Control.   From a Weberian point of view, organizations are tools, instruments of power for those who head them. But what means does the bureaucracy have of ensuring that lower-level personnel, people who are quite distant from the centers of power, will effectively understand and implement the aims of those at the top? This issue of social control is critical in any bureaucracy. Perrow (1976) examines three types of social control mechanisms in bureaucracies. The first type of control is the most obvious – direct supervision. The second is less obtrusive, but no less effective: standardized rules, procedures, and sanctions. Gouldner (1954) shows that rules can substitute for direct supervision. This allows the organization considerable decentralization of everyday decision making and even the appearance of participation, for the premises of those decisions have been carefully controlled from the top. Decentralized decision making, when decisional premises are handed down from the top via standardized rules, may be functionally equivalent to hierarchical authority (Blau, 1970; Bates, 1970; Perrow, 1976). "Top-down" rules have the same consequence as centralized authority.

   Collectivist organizations generally refuse to legitimate the use of centralized authority or standardized rules to achieve social control. Instead, they rely upon personalistic and moralistic appeals to provide the primary means of control. In addition, the search for a common purpose, a continuing part of the consensus process, is a basis for collective coordination and control. Examining free schools, Swidler (1979, p. 179) finds them "obsessed with the search for common goals" and shows this search to be an important source of social control. For Etzioni (1961), compliance here is chiefly normative. One person appeals to another, "do X for me," "do X in the interest of equality," and so forth. *The more homogeneous the group, the more such appeals can hold sway.* Thus, where personal and moral appeals are the chief means of social control, it is important, perhaps necessary, that the group select a membership sharing their basic values and worldview. An effort was made to do just that in all five of the alternative organizations under study. At the Law Collective, for instance, members were asked how they decide whether to take in a new member. One commented:

They have to have a certain amount of past experience in political work . . . something really good and significant that checks out. . . . same basic assumptions as far as politics goes and they have to be willing to accept the collective way of doing things.

Such recruitment criteria are common in alternative work organizations.

Like Perrow (1976), we might conclude that alternative organizations avoid first- and second-level controls, but accept third-level controls. Third-level controls are the most subtle and indirect of all: selection of personnel for homogeneity. On this level, social control is achieved in traditional bureaucracies by selecting for top managerial positions only people who "fit in" – people who read the right magazines, go to the right clubs, and share the same style of life and worldview. Unless recruitment for homogeneity is considered a device for social control, it is difficult to understand why it so often takes precedence over criteria of competence in the corporate world (Kanter, 1977; Perrow, 1976). And so it is in collectivist organizations. Where people are expected to make major decisions – and this means everyone in a collective, and high-level managers in bureaucracy – consensus is crucial, and people who are likely to challenge basic assumptions are avoided. A person who eagerly reads the *Wall Street Journal* would be as suspect in applying for a position at the Law Collective as a person who avidly reads the *New Left Review* would be at General Motors. Both kinds of organizations utilize selection for homogeneity as a mechanism for social control.

Social relations. Impersonality is a key feature of the bureaucratic model. Personal emotions are to be prevented from distorting rational judgments. Relationships between people are to be role based, segmental, and instrumental. Collectivist organizations, on the other hand, strive toward the ideal of community. Relationships are to be wholistic, affective, and of value in themselves. In the extreme, the search for community may even become an instance of goal displacement, as when, for example, a free school comes to value community so highly that it loses its identity as a school and becomes a commune (see, e.g., Kaye, 1972).

Recruitment and advancement. Bureaucratic criteria for recruitment and advancement are resisted in the collectivist organization. Employment is not based on specialized training or certification, nor on any universalistic standard of competence. Instead, staff are generally recruited and selected on the basis of friendship and social-political values. Personality attributes seen as congruent in the collectivist mode of organization, such as self-direction and collaborative styles, may also be consciously sought in new staff (see, e.g., Torbert, 1973). Further, employment does not constitute the beginning of a career in collectivist organizations in the usual sense, for the organization does not provide a life-long ladder to ever-higher positions. Work may be volunteer or paid, and it may be part-time or full-time (or even 60 hours per week), but it is not thought of as a career. Whereas career advancement in bureaucracy is based on seniority and/or achievement, in collectives it is not a meaningful concept; for where there is no hierarchy of offices, there can be no individual advancement in positional rank (though there may be much change in positions).

How can a collectivist organization recruit competent and skilled personnel if selection criteria explicitly emphasize friendship networks, political values, and personality traits? To illustrate, during the year in which the Free Clinic was observed, four full-time staff positions were filled, and between 9 and 65 applications were received for each position. Yet each of the four positions went to a friend of staff members. The relevant attributes cited most frequently by the staff making these decisions were: articulation skills, ability to organize and mobilize people, political values, self-direction, ability to work under pressure, friendship, commitment to the organization's goals, cooperative style, and relevant experience. These selection criteria are typical of alternative organizations. In spite of their studied neglect of *formal* criteria of competence (e.g., certification), alternative organizations often attract highly qualified and able people.[4] In many ways, their selection criteria are well suited to their needs for multitalented and committed personnel who can serve a variety of administrative and task-oriented functions and who are capable of comanaging the organization.

Incentive structure.   Organizations use different kinds of incentives to motivate participation. Most bureaucratic workplaces emphasize remunerative incentives, and few employees could be expected to donate their services if their paychecks were to stop. Collectivist organizations, on the other hand, rely primarily on a sense of shared purpose, secondarily on friendship ties, and only tertiarily on material incentives (Zald and Ash, 1966). As Etzioni has shown (1961), this kind of normative compliance system tends to generate a high level of moral commitment to the organization. Specific structural mechanisms that produce and sustain organizational commitment are identified by Kanter (1972a). Because collectivist work organizations require a high level of commitment, they tend to utilize some of these mechanisms as well as value-purposive incentives to generate it. Indeed, work in collectives is construed as a labor of love, and members may pay themselves very low salaries and may even expect each other to continue to work during months when the organization is too poor to afford their salaries.

Alternative organizations often appeal to symbolic values to motivate people to join and to participate. The range of these values is considerable. At the Free Clinic, for instance, a member describes motivation:

Our volunteers are do-gooders. . . . They get satisfaction from giving direct and immediate help to people in need. This is why they work here.

In contrast, at the *Community News,* the following was more illustrative:

Our motives were almost entirely political. . . . We wanted to create a base for a mass left. To activate liberals and open them up to left positions. To tell you the truth, the paper was conceived as a political organ.

At the Food Co-op, the value of community was most stressed, and the co-op helped to create other community-owned and controlled institutions in its locale.

However, we should guard against an overly idealistic interpretation of participation in alternative organizations. In these organizations, as much as in any, there exists an important *coalescence of material and ideal interests.* Even volunteers in these organizations, whose motives on the face of it would appear to be wholly idealistic, also have material incentives.

For example, staff members at the Free Clinic suspected that some volunteers donated their time to the clinic "only to look good on their applications to medical school." Likewise, some of the college students who volunteered to teach at Freedom High believed that in a tight market, this would improve their chances of obtaining a paid teaching job. And, for all the talk of community at the Food Co-op, many members undoubtedly joined simply because the food was cheaper. Because material gain is not part of the acceptable vocabulary of motives in these organizations, public discussion of such motives is suppressed.

Nonetheless, for staff members, as well as for volunteers, both moral and material incentives operate. At the Law Collective, for instance, legal workers often used their experience there to pursue the bar, since California law allows eligibility for the bar through the alternative means of apprenticing under an attorney for three years. At the *Community News,* a few staff members confided they had entered the paper to gain journalistic experience.

Yet members of alternative institutions often deny the existence of material considerations and accept only idealistic motivations. In the opinion of one long-time staffer at the *Community News:*

I don't think anyone came for purely journalistic purposes, unless they're masochists. I mean it doesn't pay, the hours are lousy, and the people are weird. If you want professional journalistic experience you go to a straight paper.

In many ways, she is right: Alternative institutions generally provide woefully inadequate levels of remuneration by the standards of our society. But, it does not impugn the motives of participants to recognize that these organizations must provide some material base for their members if they are to be alternative places of employment at all.

At the Free Clinic, for illustration, full-time staff were all paid $500 per month during 1974–75; at the Law Collective they were paid a base of $250 per month plus a substantial supplement for dependents; and at the *Community News* they received between $150 and $300 per month, in accordance with individual "needs." These pay levels were negotiated in open discussion by all members, as were decisions regarding the entire labor process. Thus, if these wage levels appear exploitative, it is a case of self-exploitation. It is these subsistence wage levels that permit the young organization to accumulate capital and to reinvest this surplus in the organization rather than pay it out in wages. This facilitates the growth of the organization, and hastens the day when it may be able to pay high salaries.

Many collectives have found ways to help compensate for meager salaries. The Law Collective stocked a refrigerator with food so members could eat at least a free meal or two per day at the office. The collective also maintained a number of cars its members could share, thereby eliminating the need for private automobile ownership. Free Clinic staff decided to allow themselves certain fringe benefits to compensate for what they regarded as underpaid work: two weeks of paid vacation each year, plus two additional weeks of unpaid vacation, if desired; one day off every other week; and the expectation that staff would regularly work 28–30 rather than 40 hours a week. These are compensations or supplements for a generally poor income, and like income, they do not motivate people to work in alternative organizations; they only make work there possible.

The main reason people come to work in an alternative organization is because it offers them substantial control over their work. Collective control means members can structure both the product of their work and the work process itself. Hence, the work is purposeful to them. It is frequently contrasted with alienating jobs they have had, or imagine, in bureaucracies:

A straight paper would have spent a third of a million dollars getting to where we are now and still wouldn't be breaking even. We've gotten where we are on the sweat of our workers. They've taken next to no money when they could have had $8,000 to $15,000 in straight papers doing this sort of job. . . . They do it so they can be their own boss. So they can own and control the organization they work in. So they can make the paper what *they* want it to be. (Member of *Community News*)

Social stratification.   In the ideal-typical bureaucracy, the dimensions of social stratification are consistent with one another. Specifically, social prestige and material privilege are to be commensurate with one's positional rank, and the latter is the basis of authority in the organization. Thus, a hierarchical arrangement of offices implies an isomorphic distribution of privilege and prestige. In this way, hierarchy institutionalizes and justifies inequality.

In contrast, egalitarianism is a central feature of the collectivist–democratic organization. Large differences in social prestige or privilege, even where they are commensurate with level of skill or authority in bureaucracy, would violate this sense of equity. At the Free Clinic, for instance, all full-time staff members were paid equally, no matter what skills or experience they brought to the clinic. At the Law Collective and the *Community News* pay levels were set "for each according to his or her need." Here salaries took account of dependents and other special circumstances contributing to need, but explicitly excluded considerations of the worth of the individual to the organization. In no case that we observed was the ratio between the highest pay and the lowest pay greater than two to one.

In larger, more complex democratic organizations wages are still set, and wage differentials strictly limited, by the collectivity. For example, in the 65 production cooperatives that constitute the Mondragon system in Spain, pay differentials are limited to a ratio of 3:1 in each firm (Johnson and Whyte, 1977). In the worker-owned and managed refuse collection firms in San Francisco, the differential is only 2:1, or less (Russell, 1982a). Schumacher (1973, p. 276) reports a 7:1 ratio between the highest and the lowest pay in the Scott Bader Co., a collectively owned firm in England. The cooperatively owned plywood mills in the Pacific Northwest pay their members an equal wage (Bernstein, 1976, pp. 20–21). By comparison, the wage differential tolerated today in Chinese work organizations is 4:1; in the United States it is about 100:1 (Eckstein, 1977).

Prestige, of course, is not easily equalized, as is pay. Nonetheless, collectivist organizations try in a variety of ways to indicate they are a fraternity of peers. Through dress, informal relations, task sharing, job rotation, the physical structure of the workplace, equal pay, and the collective decision-making process itself, collectives convey an equality of status. As Mansbridge observes (1977), reducing the sources of status inequality does not necessarily lead to the magnification of trivial differences. Likewise, decreasing the material differentials between individuals in a collectivist organization does not ordinarily produce a greater emphasis on status distinctions.

Differentiation. A complex network of specialized, segmental roles marks any bureaucracy. Where the rules of Taylorism hold sway, the division of labor is maximized: Jobs are subdivided as far as possible. Specialized jobs require technical expertise. Thus, bureaucracy ushers in the ideal of the specialist-expert and defeats the cultivated, renaissance man of an earlier era (Weber, 1946, pp. 240–244).

In contrast, differentiation is minimized in the collectivist organization. Work roles are purposefully kept as general and wholistic as possible. The aim is to eliminate the bureaucratic division of labor that separates intellectual worker from manual worker, administrative tasks from performance tasks. Three means are commonly utilized toward this end: role rotation, task sharing, and the diffusion, or "demystification," of specialized knowledge.

Ideally, universal competence of the collective's members would be achieved in the tasks of the organization. It is the *amateur-factotum* who is ideally suited for the collectivist organization. In the completely democratized organization, everyone manages and everyone works. This may be the most fundamental way in which the collectivist mode of organization alters the social relations of production.[5]

This alteration in the division of labor is perhaps best illustrated by Freedom High, an organization in which administrative functions were quite simple and undifferentiated. Freedom High had no separate set of managers to administer the school. Whenever administrative tasks were recognized, "coordination meetings" were called to attend to them, but these were open to all interested teachers and students.

"Coordinators" were those who were willing to take responsibility for a particular administrative task, such as planning the curriculum, writing a press release, organizing a fund-raiser. A coordinator for one activity was not necessarily a coordinator for another project, though a few core members were involved in many. Further, since administrative tasks were assumed to be part-time, these would be done alongside of one's other responsibilities. Coordinators, then, were self-selected, rotated, and part-time. No one was allowed to perform administrative tasks exclusively. By explaining and simplifying administration and opening it up to the membership at large, the basis and pretense of special expertise were eliminated.

The school even attempted to break down the basic differentiation between students and staff, regarding students not as clients but as members, with decision-making rights and responsibilities. Few organizations can allow their clients so full a participatory role as Freedom High, but all of the alternative service organizations in this study did try to integrate their clients into the organization. The Free Clinic created spaces on its board of directors for consumers of medical care, and recruited many of its volunteers from the ranks of its patients.

Most alternative organizations are more complex than Freedom High. They cannot assume that everyone in the organization knows how (or would want to know how) to do everything. Thus, they must develop explicit procedures to achieve universal competence. Such procedures, in effect, attack the conventional wisdom of specialized division of labor and seek to create more integrated, multifaceted work roles.

The *Community News*, for example, utilized task sharing (or team work), apprenticeships, and job rotations. Instead of assigning one full-time person to a task requiring one person, it would more likely assign a couple of people to the task part-time. Individuals' allocations of work often combined diverse tasks, such as 20 hours of selling advertisements with 20 hours of writing. In this way, the distribution of labor combined satisfying tasks with more tedious tasks and manual work with intellectual work. People did not enter the paper knowing how to do all of these jobs, but the emphasis on task sharing allowed the less experienced to learn from the more experienced. Likewise, if a task had few people who knew how to perform it well, a person might be allocated to apprentice with the incumbent. Internal education was further facilitated by occasional job rotations. Thus, although the *News* had to perform the same tasks as any newspaper, it attempted to do so without permitting the usual division of labor into specialties or its concomitant monopolization of expertise.

Minimizing differentiation is difficult and time-consuming. The *Community News* spent 1 hour and 40 minutes of regular meeting time deciding when and how the staff should do a complete role rotation, another 8 hours and 40 minutes at a special Sunday meeting called for that purpose, and not having finished, they spent an additional 5 hours and 20 minutes at the following regular staff meeting. Attendance at these meetings was 100 percent. This particular job rotation, then, absorbed 15 hours and 40 minutes of formal meeting time and countless hours of informal discussion. The time and priority typically devoted to internal education in collectivist organizations make sense only if they are understood to be part of a struggle against the division of labor. The creation of an equitable distribution of labor and wholistic work roles is an essential feature of the collectivist organization.

We have developed an ideal-type model of collectivist-democracy that is analogous to Weber's ideal-type characterization of bureaucracy.[6] Table 3.1 summarizes the ideal-type differences between the collectivist mode of organization and the bureaucratic. The eight dimensions discussed are not all equal. The basis of authority and the type of division of labor are plainly the most essential. Democratic control is the foremost characteristic of collectivist organization, just as hierarchical control is the defining characteristic of bureaucracy. For this reason, collectivist organizations transform the social

Table 3.1. *Comparisons of two ideal types of organization*

Dimensions	Bureaucratic organization	Collectivist–democratic organization
1. Authority	1. Authority resides in individuals by virtue of incumbency in office and/or expertise; hierarchal organization of offices. Compliance is to universal fixed rules as these are implemented by office incumbents.	1. Authority resides in the collectivity as a whole; delegated, if at all, only temporarily and subject to recall. Compliance is to the consensus of the collective, which is always fluid and open to negotiation.
2. Rules	2. Formalization of fixed and universalistic rules; calculability and appeal of decisions on the basis of correspondence to the formal, written law.	2. Minimal stipulated rules; primacy of ad hoc, individuated decisions; some calculability possible on the basis of knowing the substantive ethics involved in the situation.
3. Social control	3. Organizational behavior is subject to social control, primarily through direct supervision or standardized rules and sanctions, tertiarily through the selection of homogeneous personnel, especially at top levels.	3. Social controls are primarily based on personalistic or moralistic appeals and the selection of homogeneous personnel.
4. Social relations	4. Ideals of impersonality. Relations are to be role based, segmental, and instrumental.	4. Ideal of community. Relations are to be wholistic, personal, of value in themselves.
5. Recruitment and advancement	5a. Employment based on specialized training and formal certification.	5a. Employment based on friends, social-political values, personality attributes, and informally assessed knowledge and skills.
	5b. Employment constitutes a career; advancement based on seniority or achievement.	5b. Concept of career advancement not meaningful; no hierarchy of positions.
6. Incentive structure	6. Remunerative incentives are primary.	6. Normative and solidarity incentives are primary; material incentives are secondary.

7. Social stratification	7. Isomorphic distribution of prestige, privilege, and power (i.e., differential rewards by office); hierarchy justifies inequality.	7. Egalitarian; reward differentials, if any, are strictly limited by the collectivity.
8. Differentiation	8a. Maximal division of labor: dichotomy between intellectual work and manual work and between administrative tasks and performance tasks.	8a. Minimal division of labor: administration is combined with performance tasks; division between intellectual and manual work is reduced.
	8b. Maximal specialization of jobs and functions; segmental roles. Technical expertise is exclusively held: ideal of the specialist-expert.	8b. Generalization of jobs and functions; wholistic roles. Demystification of expertise: ideal of the amateur factotum.

relations of production. Bureaucracy maximizes formal rationality precisely by centralizing control at the top of the organization; collectivist organizations decentralize control in such a way that it may be organized around the alternative logic of substantive rationality.

Constraints on organizational democracy

Research and observation over the years have pointed out that many factors limit the actualization of the ideal features of bureaucracy as drawn by Weber. Similarly, we have found that various factors limit the actual attainment of organizational democracy. In practice, collectivist democracy, like bureaucracy, can be approximated, but not perfectly attained. This section outlines some of the more important of these constraints.

Judgments about the relative importance of the following constraints are intricately tied to cultural values. Alternative organizations may be assessed incorrectly when seen through the prism of the norms and values of the surrounding bureaucratic society. As in anthropology, one must seek to understand a different culture on its own terms.

Time.   Democracy takes time. This is one of its major constraints. Two-way communication structures may encourage higher morale, innovative ideas, and more adaptive solutions to complex problems, but they are undeniably slow (Leavitt, 1964, pp. 141–150). Quite simply, a boss can hand down a bureaucratic order in a fraction of the time it would take a group to decide the issue democratically.

The time absorbed by meetings can be extreme in democratic groups. During the early stages of the *News,* three days out of a week were taken up with meetings. Between business meetings, political meetings, and "people meetings," very little time remained to do the tasks of the organization. Members quickly learn that this arrangement is unsatisfactory. Meetings are streamlined. Tasks are given a higher priority. Even so, constructing an arrangement that both saves time and ensures effective collective control may prove difficult. Exactly which meetings are dispensable? What sorts of decisions can be safely delegated? How can individuals be held accountable to the collectivity as a whole? These sorts of questions come with the realization that there are only 24 hours in a day.

Even under the best of circumstances, however, there is a limit to how streamlined collectivist meetings can be. It is true that with practice, planning, and self-discipline, groups can learn to accomplish more during their meeting time. Nevertheless, once experience is gained in conducting meetings, the time given to them appears to be directly correlated with level of democratic control. The Free Clinic, for instance, could keep its weekly staff meetings down to an average of 1 hour and 15 minutes only by permitting individual decision making outside the meeting to a degree that would have been unacceptable to members of the *Community News,* where a mean of 4 hours was given over to the weekly staff meeting.

Time spent at meetings is not wasted, however, because participation in considering options and making decisions appears to breed commitment to the outcome. When people have had input into a decision, its implementation may be expected to go smoother. Unilateral decisions, albeit quicker, would not be seen as binding or legitimate in collectives, and there would be no enthusiasm for implementation. In bureaucracies, too, the nonparticipatory nature of decisions may contribute to the blocking or sabotage of organizational action. In his study of kibbutzim enterprises, Rosner (1981) has found that the frequency of meetings and the importance of issues raised are strongly correlated with a more equal distribution of influence. In turn, the greater a person's sense of influence, the more that individual will feel personally committed to the organization and the more trust he or she will have in its management. In this way, time spent on democratically deciding things at meetings may enhance commitment and implementation.

Emotional intensity. The familial, face-to-face relationships in collectivist organizations may be more satisfying than the impersonal relations of bureaucracy, but they are also more emotionally threatening. Intense emotions may constrain participatory organization.

Interpersonal tension is probably endemic in the directly democratic situation, and, for better or worse, members often perceive their workplaces to be emotionally intense. At the Law Collective, a member warned that "plants die here from the heavy vibes." And at the *Community News,* people reported headaches and dread before meetings in which divisive issues were to be raised. A study of the New England town meetings (Mansbridge, 1973a) found citizens reporting headaches, trembling, and even fear for one's heart as a result of the meetings. Altogether, a quarter of the people in a random sample of the town spontaneously suggested that the conflictive character of the meetings disturbed them.

To allay these fears of conflict, townspeople utilize a variety of protective devices: Criticism is concealed or at least softened with praise, differences of opinion are minimized in the formulation of a consensus, private jokes and intimate communications are used to give personal support during the meetings. Such avoidance patterns have the unintended consequence of excluding the not fully integrated member, withholding information from the group, and violating the norms of open participation. Further, these same avoidance patterns and fears of conflict are in evidence even in groups that are highly sensitive to these issues and in which many members have been trained in group process (Mansbridge, 1982).

The existence of such feelings in all of the groups we observed in California, in the Boston area alternatives discussed by the Vocations for Social Change collective (1976), and in Mansbridge's democratic organizations suggests that these feelings are rooted in the very structure of collectivist decision making. Although participants generally attribute conflict to the stubborn, wrongheaded, or otherwise faulty character of others, we maintain that it is a structurally induced, inherent cost of participatory democracy.

First, the norm of consensual decision making makes the possibility of conflict all the more threatening because unanimity is required. In contrast, because majoritarian systems are based on voting, they can institutionalize and absorb conflicting opinions. In collectivist organizations, the existence of conflict means the discussion must continue. Second, the intimacy of face-to-face decision making personalizes the ideas that people espouse and thereby makes the rejection of those ideas harder to bear. A formal bureaucratic system, to the extent that it disassociates an idea from its proponent, makes the criticism of ideas less interpersonally risky.

Non-democratic habits and values.   Because of the nature of their prior experience, many people are not very well prepared for participatory democracy. They have not learned the attitudes and behaviors that will be required in cooperative enterprises. This, too, is an important constraint on the development of such organizations.

It is a fundamental premise of sociology that people's behavior, attitudes, and personalities are to a great extent shaped by their environment. If work encourages, or sometimes requires, people to be competitive, narrowly specialized, obedient to authority from above, and willing to give orders below, then it should not be surprising that people accurately receive and act on these messages. Indeed, Kanter (1977) argues that it is the structural features of the modern corporation, much more than individual attributes, that determine the organizational behavior of men and women. In the educational sphere, Jules Henry (1965) poignantly shows how the norms of capitalist culture become the hidden curriculum of the school system. Even at the preschool level, the qualities of the bureaucratic personality are unconsciously, but relentlessly conveyed to children (Kanter, 1972b). Bowles and Gintis (1976) argue that the chief function of the entire educational apparatus is to reproduce the division of labor and hierarchical authority of capitalism.

In the face of these pervasive behavior-shaping institutions, it is difficult to sustain collectivist personalities. It is asking, in effect, that people in collectivist organizations constantly shift gears, that they learn to act one way inside their collectives and another way outside. The difficulty of creating and sustaining collectivist attributes and behavior patterns reflects a cultural disjunction, deriving from the fact that alternative organizations are as yet isolated examples of collectivism in an otherwise capitalist–bureaucratic context. Where collectives are not isolated, that is, where they are part of a network of cooperative organizations, such as the Mondragon system in Spain (Johnson and Whyte, 1977), this problem is mitigated.

One owner of a small graphics firm, himself a convert to democratic management, was dismayed to discover, when he first tried to implement participation, that "the group voted that management was going a good job and that they didn't want to be held accountable for any failures or take on other management responsibilities" (Hendricks, 1973). Slowly, progress has been made in this particular workplace, but as Hendricks says, "it would be easy just to gather up people who could comprehend simplicity and equality and eliminate any consciousness-raising problems, but that doesn't really lead to a new society." What the experience of the alternative institutions has shown is that even handpicking people with collectivist attitudes does not guarantee that these attitudes will be effectively translated into cooperative behavior (see, for example, Swidler, 1976; Taylor, 1976; Torbert, 1973).

Nevertheless, a number of recent case studies of democratic workplaces reveal that the experience of democratic participation can alter people's values, the quality of their work, and ultimately, their identities (Perry, 1978; Jackall, 1976; Bart, 1981). In a comparative examination of many cases of workers' participation, Bernstein (1976, pp. 91–107) finds democratic consciousness to be a necessary element for effective workers' control.

Fortunately for collectives, the solution to this problem of creating democratic consciousness and behavior may be found in the democratic method itself. As was noted in Chapter 1, Pateman has amassed a considerable body of evidence from research on political socialization in support of the classical arguments of Rousseau, Mill, and Cole. She concludes:

We do learn to participate by participating and . . . feelings of political efficacy are more likely to be developed in a participatory environment. . . . The experience of a participatory authority structure might also be effective in diminishing tendencies toward non-democratic attitudes in the individual. (Pateman, 1970, p. 105)

Recent research provides further empirical support for Pateman's position that participation helps to develop feelings of political efficacy (Elden, 1976). Similarly, Gillespie (1981) finds that housing co-ops are able to rapidly socialize new members to accept participatory norms. It is evident that collectivist organization requires that people be cooperative, self-directing, participatory, and open and responsive to the ideas of others. It is equally evident that the condition of relative powerlessness, the experience of most people in hierarchical organizations, thwarts the sense of efficacy needed for participation elsewhere (see Blumberg, 1973, pp. 70–138). Thus, if collectivist–democratic organizations are to expand beyond their currently limited social base, they must, in addition to getting a job done, serve an important educative function.

Indeed, for Pateman (1970) the theory of participatory democracy rises or falls on this educative function. But other social scientists (see especially Argyris, 1974) remain unconvinced that participation in collectivist–democratic processes of organization can produce the desired changes in people's behavior. For Argyris, unilateral, defensive, closed, mutually protective, non-risk-taking behavior, what he calls Model I behavior, is nearly universal: It permeates not only Western bureaucracies but also counterbureaucracies such as alternative schools as well as collectivist organizations in contemporary China and Yugoslavia. Change in organizational behavior, then, cannot be expected to follow from fundamental change in the mode of production, for Model I behavior is rooted in the pyramidal values of industrial culture and in the finiteness of the human mind as an information-processing machine in the face of environmental complexity.

Contrarily, we argue that where people do not have participatory habits, it is because they have not generally been allowed any substantive control over important decisions. Nondemocratic (pyramidal) habits are indeed a problem for democratic groups, but they are not a problem that a redistribution of power could not resolve. Admittedly, the evidence is not yet entirely in on this issue, but much of it does indicate that the practice of democracy itself develops the capacity for democratic behavior among its participants (Blumberg, 1973; Pateman, 1970).

Environmental constraints.   Alternative organizations, like all organizations, are subject to external pressures. Because they often occupy an adversary position vis-à-vis mainstream institutions, such pressures may be more intense. Extra-organizational constraints on the development of collectivist organizations may be legal, economic, political, or cultural.

It is generally agreed among free-schoolers, for instance, that municipal building and fire codes are most strictly enforced for them (Kozol, 1972; Graubard, 1972). This is usually only a minor irritant, but in extreme cases it may involve a major disruption of the organization in that the organization may be forced to move or close down. One small, collectively run solar power firm was forced to move its headquarters several times through this sort of legal harassment. At one site, the local authorities charged it with more than a hundred building "violations" (Etzkowitz and Schaflander, 1978). An even more far-reaching legal obstacle is the lack of a suitable legal statute for incorporating cooperatively owned and controlled firms. The *Community News,* for example, had to ask an attorney to put together corporate law in novel ways in order to ensure collective control over the paper.[7]

The law can be changed, but the more ubiquitous forces against collectivism are social, cultural, and economic. Alternative organizations often find that bureaucratic practices are thrust on them willy-nilly by established institutions. Freedom High, for example, began with an emphatic policy of no evaluative records of students. In time, however, it found that in order to help students transfer back into the public schools or gain entrance into college, it had to begin keeping some records. The preoccupation of other organizations with records and documents may thus force record keeping on a reluctant free school. In another free school, the presence of a steady stream of government communications and inspectors (health, building, etc.) pushed the organization into creating a special job to handle correspondence and personal visits of officials (Lindenfeld, 1982).

Economically, alternative organizations strive to be self-sustaining and autonomous, but, without a federated network of other cooperative organizations to support them, they often cannot. Usually they must rely on established organizations for financial support. This acts as a constraint on the achievement of their collectivist principles. In order to provide free services, the Free Clinic needed, and received, financial backing from private foundations, as well as from county revenue-sharing funds. This forced the staff to keep detailed records on expenditures and patient visits, and to justify their activities in terms of outsiders' criteria of cost-effectiveness.

In less fortunate cases, fledging democratic enterprises may not even get off the ground because they cannot raise sufficient capital. Attempts by employee groups to purchase and collectively manage their firms reveal the reluctance of banks to loan money to collectivist enterprises, even where these loans would be guaranteed by the government.[8] From the point of view of private investors, collective ownership and management may appear, at best, an unproven method of organizing production, and at worst, a high-risk method.

For a consistent source of capital, collectivist enterprises may need to develop cooperative credit unions as the Mondragon system has done (Johnson and Whyte, 1977) or an alternative investment fund. In March 1980 the National Consumer Cooperative Bank began providing loans, mostly to consumer cooperatives. In many worker cooperatives, the poorly paid labor of the founders forms the initial "sweat equity" of the organization that makes possible some measure of financial autonomy. In any case, the larger issue of organization-environment relations remains problematic, particularly when we are considering collectivist organizations in a capitalist context.[9]

Individual differences. All organizations contain persons with very different talents, skills, knowledge, and personality attributes. Bureaucracies try to capitalize on these individual differences, so that ideally people with a particular expertise or personality type will be given a job, rewards, and authority commensurate with it. In collectives, such individual differences may constrain the organization's ability to realize its egalitarian ideals.

Inequalities in influence persist in the most egalitarian of organizations. In bureaucracies the existence of inequality is taken for granted. In collectivist organizations, however, this is less true. Because authority resides in the collectivity as a unit, the exercise of influence depends less on position and more on the personal attributes of the individual. Members who are more articulate, responsible, energetic, glamorous, fair-minded, or committed carry more weight in the group.[10] John Rice, a teacher and leader of Black Mountain, an educational succession that anticipated the free school movement, argued that Black Mountain came as close to democracy as possible: The economic status of the individual had nothing to do with community standing. Beyond rare cases, however, "the differences show up . . . the test is made all day and every day as to who is the person to listen to" (Duberman, 1972, p. 37).

Some individual differences are accepted in the collectivist organization, but not all, particularly not differences in knowledge. In bureaucracy, differences of skill and knowledge are honored. Specialized jobs accompany expertise, and people are expected to protect their expertise. Indeed, this is a sign of professionalism, and it is well known that the monopolization of knowledge is an effective instrument of power in organizations (Weber, 1968; Crozier, 1964). Collectivist organizations, being aware of this, make every attempt to eliminate differentials in knowledge. Expertise is considered not the property of the individual, but an organizational resource. Individually held knowledge is diffused and critical skills are redistributed through internal education, job rotation, task sharing, apprenticeships, or any plan seen as serving this end. Bart (1981) shows how the skills needed to provide abortion services were shared with all of the members of a feminist health collective, despite the fact that such medical procedures are ordinarily reserved for physicians.

The diffusion or "demystification" of knowledge, although essential to help

Figure 3.1. Range of organizational forms

equalize patterns of influence, involves certain trade-offs. Allowing new persons to learn to do task X by rotating them to that job may be good for their growth and development, but, as in the case of Ann at the *Community News,* it may displace an experienced person who had received a sense of satisfaction and accomplishment in job X. Further, encouraging novices to learn by doing may be an effective form of pedagogy, but it may detract from the quality of goods or services that the organization provides, at least until members achieve general competence in the tasks.

Even in the organization that might achieve universal competence, other sources of unequal influence would persist, such as commitment level, verbal fluency, and social skills.[11] The most a democratic organization can do is to remove the bureaucratic bases of authority: positional rank and expertise. The task of any collective workplace – and it is no easy task – is to eliminate all bases of individual power and authority, save those that individuals carry in their own persons.

Conclusion

The organizations in this study are uncommon ones. For this reason they are of great theoretical significance. By approaching the polar opposite of bureaucracy, they allow us to establish the parameters or limits of organizational reality. These parameters appear to be wider than students of organizations generally have imagined. Once the parameters of the organizational field have been defined, concrete cases can be put into broader perspective. Professional organizations, for example, although considerably more horizontal than the strictly hierarchical bureaucracy (Litwak, 1961), are still far more hierarchical than the collectivist–democratic organization. Thus, we may conceive of the range of organizational possibilities illustrated in Figure 3.1.

By contrasting collectivist democracy and monocratic bureaucracy along eight continuous dimensions, this chapter has emphasized the quantitative differences between the two. In many ways, this understates the difference. At some point differences of degree produce differences of kind. Fundamentally, bureaucracy and collectivism are oriented to qualitatively different principles. Whereas bureaucracy is organized around the calculus of formal rationality, collectivist democracy turns on the logic of substantive rationality.

If, in the Weberian tradition, we take the basis of authority as the central feature of any mode of organization, then organizations on the right half of Figure 1 empower the *individual* with authority (on the basis of office or expertise), whereas organizations on the left side grant ultimate authority only to the *collectivity* as a unit. Moreover, if, following Marx's lead, we take the division of labor as the key to the social relations of production, organizations on the right side of Figure 1 maintain a sharp division between managers and workers, whereas organizations on the left side are integrative: *Those who work also manage.* We take both – collectivist authority and the dedifferentiation of labor – to be essential defining characteristics of collectivist democracy. The other six features, although important, clearly are not as fundamental as these two.

As a dramatic departure from established modes of organization, the collectivist organization may be considered a major "social invention" (Coleman, 1970) deserving far more attention than it has yet received. Organization theory has for the most part considered only the right half of this spectrum, and, indeed, the majority of organizations in our society do fall on the right side of the continuum. Still, we gain perspective on all organizations by putting them into a broader frame of reference. With the proliferation of collectivist organizations both in this society and in others such as China, Spain, Yugoslavia, and Israel, we need an alternative model of organization – one toward which they themselves aspire – by which to assess their impact and success. Emphatically, collectivist organizations should be assessed not as failures to achieve bureaucratic standards, but as efforts to realize wholly different values. It is in the conceptualization of alternative forms of organization that organizational theory has been weakest, and it is here that the experimentation of collectives will broaden our understanding.

4. Internal conditions that facilitate collectivist–democratic organizations

It is not easy to maintain participatory–democratic organizations in a bureaucratic society. The surrounding sea of hierarchical organizations, market relationships, and traditions of representative democracy threatens to inundate brave islands of direct democracy. There are, however, defenses that collectives can erect to help them survive and even flourish as democracies. Members have a lot of choice in creating internal conditions, and some choice in creating external conditions, which assist them in maintaining direct democracy. These internal and external conditions are identified in this chapter and the next (see Table 5.1, at the end of Chapter 5 for a summary of all of these conditions).

To Weber, modernity meant that every aspect of life would become more impersonal, rule-bound, and bureaucratic. Today this idea arouses little controversy. It has become a coin of the sociological realm. For Weber, the inexorable process of bureaucratization is based on the technical superiority of bureaucracy vis-à-vis all other modes of organization in history (Weber, 1968, pp. 973–980) and on bureaucracy's indispensability as an instrument of power for those who head it. For this reason, bureaucracy, once firmly entrenched, renders revolution (i.e., a fundamental change in the structure of authority) impossible, and replaces it with mere changes in who controls the bureaucratic apparatus (1968, pp. 987–989). At the same time, the permanence and growth of bureaucracy hold potentially grave consequences. Scholars as diverse as Weber (1968), Jacques Ellul (1964), and C. Wright Mills (1959) have warned that as bureaucracy spreads, control over organizations will become more centralized and remote, thereby abridging individual freedom and control.

This belief in the inevitability of bureaucratic domination can be seen as a "metaphysical pathos," a pessimistic turn of mind not subject to proof or disproof (Gouldner, 1955). Instead, Gouldner urges sociologists to focus on the possibility of nonoppressive bureaucracy. Studying a gypsum mine, he finds that representative democracy, via labor unions, is possible (1954). His case is amplified by other students of organizations who have searched for the social-historical conditions that encourage democratic processes, as in the International Typographical Union (Lipset, Trow, and Coleman, 1962) and in other unions (Edelstein, 1967).

But the quest for conditions that would permit democratic organizations to exist stops short here, for most sociologists of organizations have found patently non-democratic situations wherever they have looked. Firmly rooted in the work of Weber and Michels, the literature on social movement organizations is replete with case studies that indicate the fragility of participatory democratic systems and their tendency to develop oligarchies that displace original goals.

Various explanations for such a conservatizing process of goal displacement and the attendant process of oligarchization have been adduced: (1) Organizational goals may become increasingly accommodated to contrary values in the surrounding community, as in the Tennessee Valley Authority (Selznick, 1949); (2) organizations, such as the March of Dimes, may essentially accomplish their original goals and then shift to more diffuse ones in order to maintain the organization per se (Sills, 1957); (3) organizations, such as the Women's Christian Temperance Union, may find it impossible to realize their original goals and may then develop more diffuse ones (Gusfield, 1955); (4) procedural regulations and rules (means to attain goals) may become so rigid that they are converted into ends in themselves (Merton, 1957); and (5) organization maintenance and growth may be transformed into ends in themselves, as in the German Socialist Party, because it is in the interest of those at the top of the organization to preserve their positions of power and privilege within it (Michels, 1962). These processes of oligarchization and goal displacement – taken as they are to be near constants – represent substantial problems for the social movement organization, for they may destroy the raison d'être for which it was created.

The theoretical model introduced by Zald and Ash (1966), however, views these transformation processes as conditional. Zald and Ash suggest that transformation processes may run counter to those predicted by the Weber-Michels model. For example, increased rather than decreased radicalism may occur (Jenkins, 1977) or organizational coalition rather than factionalism may take place.

More recently, the question of whether democracy is possible within bureaucratic organizations has been approached from a different direction (Bennis and Slater, 1968; Toffler, 1970). Bennis argues that democratic organizations are not only possible but inevitable if organizations wish to survive in a society experiencing rapid technological change. Organizations will have the intellectual resources to adapt to changing and complex technological problems only if they direct the talents of specialists from many disciplines into project groups that are run democratically, groups that are dissolved upon completion of the project at hand.

To conclude, the literature on the prospects of democratic organization has come full circle. It begins with the tradition of Weber and Michels, which stresses that democratic control over bureaucracies is not possible, and ends with the Bennis forecast that democracy is inevitable in the bureaucracy of the future.

Our view is that democratic modes of organization are neither impossible, nor inevitable. They are conditional. Since grass-roots cooperatives aspire to be directly democratic, they are ideal vehicles in which to investigate the conditions under which democratic aspirations are realized or undermined. We seek to identify the structural conditions that allow at least some organizations to maintain democratic forms instead of yielding to oligarchy, and to adhere to their original goals instead of experiencing goal displacement.

The capacity of a cooperative, or any organization, to be directly democratic is conditioned by both internal and external factors. If our hypothesized conditions are correct, these factors should aid in the achievement of a nonauthoritarian, collectivist structure. The absence of any of these conditions should constitute a source of tension or contradiction for the collectivist organization. These hypothetical conditions may be seen as antidotes to specific problems long thought to be endemic in organizations: conservatism of organizational purpose (through goal displacement, succession, or accommodation), rigidification of rules and ossification, oligarchization of power, and maintenance of the organization as an end in itself.

Practitioners in alternative institutions seldom if ever articulate their everyday problems in the sociologists' terms of "goal displacement," "oligarchization," "ossification," and the like. They do, however, constantly wrestle with those problems as conceived in a more specific way: "We're all supposed to be equal, right? So why does ——— have more say than the rest of us?" "How can we keep our commitment to total health care for mind and body, if we don't have the money to support our counseling component?" "With all this talk about promotional campaigns, we sometimes forget that we need a good newspaper to promote." "How do we stop ——— from usurping power for himself?" The hypothesized conditions speak directly to these concerns of participants, though they are necessarily posed on a more general level.

Although we hope practitioners will find this chapter and the next relevant to their concerns, this work is not intended to constitute a handbook in the field. Much as we have tried to identify the organizational conditions that support the participatory ideal, these conditions are not a recipe for organizational success. Each carries with it important trade-offs and raises perplexing dilemmas for the would-be collectivist organization. In the abstract it may be easy to commit one's newly forming group to a democratic course, but in the concrete practice of everyday life, continued commitment to democracy is neither obvious nor easy. For each condition that we identify, we ascertain the corresponding dilemma that follows.

The *conditions* that we identify and examine are organizational features over which members have *some control*. The *constraints* discussed in Chapter 3 refer to received situations or facts of life about which the collective has *little choice*. Hence, the conditions are given a more extensive treatment.

Each of the following propositions has been generated and supported by the evidence of our comparative studies in a wide variety of collectivist organizations. In addition to its empirical grounding, each proposition is logically tied to the processes of oligarchization and goal displacement. This chapter, then, attempts to demonstrate, logically and empirically, that (1) the hypothesized organizational conditions facilitate participatory-democratic modes of organization, (2) that their absence undermines the desired collectivist form of organization, and (3) that the concrete choices participants must make about the conditions pose critical dilemmas for any attempted alternative to bureaucracy.

Provisional orientation

Just as fish are not aware of the water, students of organizations are sometimes unaware of their own most fundamental assumptions. One such assumption, as basic as it is unexamined, is that organizations desire to be permanent. Even research on alternative communal organizations assumes that longevity is desirable (Kanter, 1972a). Because this is assumed in nearly all of the literature on organizations, temporal orientation is rarely treated as an organizational variable (Palisi, 1970). Attitudes toward time can range from the expectation that the organization will be of limited duration to the expectation that it will last indefinitely. By treating such attitudes as an independent dimension of organizations, we can explore organizational consequences. The effect of temporal orientation on the organization can be profound.

One of the most notable features of collectivist organizations is that their members tend to reject the dominant cultural belief in the possibility, or even the desirability, of permanence. As a result, members tend to be oriented to the present. What distinguishes collectives from bureaucratic organizations is not the actual time they span – which may be short or long – but their members' *attitudes* toward time.

Members of collectives are not unique in their relatively short time horizons. Other researchers have pointed out that a rapidly changing environment requires, and brings into being, more adaptive organizations. Temporary organizations or subdivisions within organizations such as project teams are seen as best able to develop innovative solutions to complex problems, and in this way, to meet the challenges of a turbulent environment. For this reason, some scholars believe that such organizations will become increasingly prevalent in modern society (Bennis and Slater, 1968; Toffler, 1970).

Although this makes temporary systems sound like a very futuristic concept, temporary organizations have existed since antiquity. Yet they have received little study. Examples of organizations that are established with the intention of being short-lived include presidential commissions, task forces, theatrical productions, construction projects, negotiating committees, and campaign election organizations. The frequent adaptation required of participants in temporary systems may produce more personal stress and role strain (Bennis and Slater, 1968; Toffler, 1970; Keith, 1978). On the other hand, researchers of theatrical production companies have found that their temporary nature enhances professional growth and innovation (Goodman and Goodman, 1976). Our purpose here is not to address the meaning for the individual (a subject we take up in Chapter 6) but to draw out the meaning of a transitory orientation for organizational transformation.

Taking the long view, we can say all organizations are transitory and the idea of permanence is an illusion. Here we are concerned not with organizational longevity as such, but with members' subjective understandings of the appropriate lifetime of the organization. Many organizations in our society last a short time. For example, 50 percent of the small businesses in the United States go out of business within two years. Yet, insofar as the entrepreneurs desire growth and permanence, these closures are regarded as failures. In this section we focus on organizations that may come to associate the disbanding of the organization not with failure, but with achievement of goals.

Why has this provisional orientation come to be the rule, rather than the exception, in contemporary collectivist enterprises? There are at least three reasons. First, many members come to these collectives from social movements like the New Left. Their overriding commitments are to the broad goals of that movement. They are attracted to particular collectivist organizations as instruments for the achievement of movement subgoals. When the organization fails to live up to its promise, or conversely, when it attains all its goals, it may be considered to have outlived its usefulness. In either case individuals may choose to drop out of the organization or even to dismantle it, turning their energies to other alternative organizations. Where members' paramount commitment is to higher-order movement goals, then provisional attitudes toward particular organizations, and somewhat transitory associations with them may follow.

Second, a provisional orientation may be rooted in the very act of creating a cooperative organization from scratch. The act of creating an organization where none existed before carries with it the implicit recognition that alternatives, as well as established organizations, can in fact also be dissolved.

Third, the provisional orientation may be a reflection of the values of the counterculture from which many collectives have sprung. Observers of the counterculture have depicted it as very present-oriented (Cavan, 1972; Hall 1978). Many participants seem to expect and desire an accelerated pace of social, psychological, and physical change in their lives, and this feeling is generalized to their relationships to organizations. They expect them to be relatively temporary.

History too provides examples of worker cooperatives with relatively short time horizons. During the nineteenth century, workers would sometimes create their own cooperative workplaces as a strategy to counter employer lockouts in a labor dispute. By setting up their own firms, craftsmen hoped to strengthen their bargaining powers and to get their employer to take them back under more favorable terms. Here the cooperative was conceived as a temporary solution to a problem, and its disappearance meant, in effect, that the workers had been successful in their efforts (Rothschild-Whitt, 1979b).

Provisional attitudes carry with them both positive and negative consequences for the organization. Evidence from our study of grass-roots collectives suggests that a *transitory orientation makes organizational maintenance and goal diffusion less likely,* but (as will be discussed) organizational *dilemmas* also arise from such an orientation.

In the Weber-Michels model of organizations, inertia and apathy among members create a situation in which a few are able to take control (i.e., oligarchization) and seek to perpetuate the organization as an end in itself. Much evidence shows that when an organization is either unable to achieve its original goal or when it fully accomplishes its goal, it will attempt to maintain itself by creating new, more diffuse goals (Gusfield, 1955; Sills, 1957).

A transitory orientation breaks these patterns. In the face of membership apathy or inability to move toward its original goals, a collective may simply disband. In the more unusual case of complete accomplishment of its original goals, a collectivist organization would also be more likely to dissolve than to create diffuse new goals.

Organizational ephemerality is expected, and even preferred in some cir-

cumstances, in collectivist organizations. For instance, the Food Co-op periodically encountered inadequate attendance at general membership meetings.
This was reason enough, even in a time of growth and expansion, to provoke
the most serious discussion of the age-old problem of member apathy. On
such an occasion, Daniel, a highly respected staff member and founder of the
co-op, urged that its by-laws be amended to include the following:

If we do not get a quorum for three general membership meetings in a row, then the
board should be required to start procedures for the dissolution of the co-op.

To this proposal, another member quickly retorted:

Don't you think you're being a bit radical, I mean drastic? After all, the co-op still
provides a valuable service, even if its members don't all participate enough.

Daniel replied:

I don't consider this a radical proposal. After all, we started the [Food Co-op] to be
a community owned and controlled economic institution. If its members don't care
enough about it to come to periodic meetings, then control will naturally fall in the
hands of the few interested people. If and when that happens, the [Food Co-op] will
be nothing more than a cheap Safeway . . . and it would be better to close down than
to continue without real member participation.

Ray, a newly elected member of the board objected vehemently:

No, this is coercive. If some people don't want to participate, you can't make them
conform to your ideals of participation. . . . You can't make people come to meetings if they don't want to.

This led to a heated two-hour discussion of how to maximize participation,
with the major point of consensus summarized by Anne, a member of the
board and founder of the co-op:

It's true that [the proposed by-law] would give the board a strong incentive for in-
forming the members about the general meetings and encouraging their participation.
Otherwise, it *is* too easy for an organization to become controlled by a small group,
and we have to guard against that. . . . And it's true that the board didn't try very
hard to get the membership out to this meeting. We'll have to do a lot more information spreading for the next one . . . because from the beginning [the co-op] has
been based on the premise of members' control. Without that, we wouldn't be a true
co-op. . . . They [the members] . . . have the last and final say about everything.
The board always knew that it could impose the 2 percent surcharge. But since this
represents a major policy change from selling at cost, we wanted to let the members
decide.

The decision reached by the board was to refrain from immediate implementation of the 2 percent surcharge and to accept a time delay in the interest of
getting wider participation at a subsequent general membership meeting.

The problem of membership apathy is not unique to the Food Co-op. It is a perennial problem in all mutual-benefit associations (Blau and Scott, 1962, pp. 45–49) and is often a prelude to oligarchization (Michels, 1962). What is novel in the situation described above is the *response* to the problem of apathy. Although it could have been used as a justification for concentrating more power in the hands of board and staff members in the name of speeding up the decision-making process, it was not. Instead, members considered this an occasion to remind themselves that rank-and-file participation was central to the co-op's original goals – and that should the co-op be extensively eroded, it would be left without a legitimate basis for existence. The founders would rather dissolve the co-op than let it operate, however successful in financial terms, as "a cheap Safeway."

A comparable preference for self-dissolution over goal displacement was voiced at the Free Clinic. Fearing that their revenue-sharing grant would not be renewed for the coming fiscal year, staff members at the clinic began to explore the prospect of becoming a fee-for-servic agency, no longer free to patients. At a 1½-hour meeting on the subject, Nancy, the staff financial adviser, described how the budget would have to be altered. The six full-time staff positions would probably have to be cut to three, and counseling and health education programs would have to go in order to make room to hire doctors for more hours, as well as a secretary. Regarding the latter, Leah argued:

Fee-for-service will mean billing and billing means paperwork. But no one can be a full-time paper-pusher without starting to hate the job. It's not fair to lay that on anyone.

Responding to the need for more doctor hours, Andrea pointed out:

If we go fee-for-service we'll need to have the doctor's signature on lots of stuff and we'll need many more clinic hours to raise enough money to run on. We can't expect this level of commitment from a doctor who is a volunteer or is outside our decision-making structure, as is now the case. We'll need at least one doctor to be a part of the collective. And we must consider the impact that may have on our collective structure. The doctor might have a tendency to dominate decision making, to think his professionalism makes him superior.

After much despairing talk about how the clinic might be reorganized to accommodate fee-for-service, Rita pinpointed the tone of the meeting:

What I feel is a death knell in the air. The more we think about the negative changes fee-for-service would bring, the more it seems pointless to continue at all. If we drastically change our collective structure – having doctors running things and cutting our staff size, I have to wonder why we should even continue. At that point we're no longer a collective. We're no longer a free medical service.

Leah poignantly agreed:

I don't want the [Free Clinic] to go on a heart-lung machine. There's such a thing as letting a good thing die, of dying with dignity. . . . That's what I want for the [Free Clinic].

Rita continued on the same track:

When the fiber is dead, you realize that the fiber was not the essence. . . . We must realize that it is the spirit that the [Free Clinic] represents that is important and that lives in all of us and that will be reflected in what we do with our lives. The organizational shell is not so important a thing.

Nancy was strident, but alone, in her objection to the growing "death knell in the air":

I don't give up so easily . . . I'm a fighter. I'll put morals aside and finagle and weasel and do anything to keep the [Free Clinic] going. I'm not going to give up just because there are obstacles.

At this point, Nancy's motives were questioned by several of the staff members. She was accused of wanting to maintain the clinic because it represented a secure job to her. The meeting ended on that note of hostility.

Two points need to be made. First, when faced with an apparent inability to accomplish organizational goals – the clinic could not provide a free medical service if its grant was not renewed – most of the paid staff members would rather have dissolved the organization than water down its original goals. This is in sharp contrast with the many conventional cases where inability to accomplish goals is met with staff efforts to maintain the organization and their jobs (see, e.g., Gusfield, 1955; Messinger, 1955; Helfgot, 1974).

Second, this illustration sheds light on the dilemma arising from a provisional or transitory orientation. It is of course difficult for members to know at exactly what point an organization has outlived its usefulness. At what point is self-dissolution a needless sacrifice of an organization, a premature giving up of a difficult, but worthwhile struggle for survival? In concrete instances, the line between a sensible disbanding and a premature giving up may be devilishly difficult to perceive.

In the case described above, Nancy, the lone "fighter," proved to be correct. The clinic did manage to get the bulk of its grant proposals funded, it was able to maintain its counseling and health education components, it was able to sustain all of its staff positions, and it was able to continue to provide free medical care to financially needy patients. The uncertainty of the situation did shock the staff into realizing that "outside grants cannot last forever," and several months later they instituted measures designed to move toward greater financial self-sufficiency. They hired two doctors for longer hours and integrated them more into the collective decision-making structure. More doctor hours allowed the clinic to stay open for more hours each week and allowed for a greater number of patients to be served. A sliding scale, fee-for-service system was instituted that still allowed many, though not all, patients to be treated for no charge, and the clinic began to charge those patients who had state or private insurance benefits to cover their medical expenses. Had the staff members who wanted the clinic to "die with dignity" moved immediately to dismantle the clinic, it would have proved premature. Their predictions about the loss of grant support proved false, and substantial goal displacement did not occur.

Another case in point is that of an artists' collective studied by Etzkowitz and Raiken (1982). Here two warring factions evolved: those who put organizational permanence above all else (the "Survivors") and those who put democratic process and other goals first (the "Innovators"). In this case, the latter prevailed, leading *not* to the end of the organization, but to different organizational choices and actions that laid the groundwork for the *continuation* of the organization on a more participatory footing (Etzkowitz and Raiken, 1982, pp. 29–31). This case, too, suggests that things are not always as they may seem to participants, and choices about organizational survival and goals often take place in a context of considerable ambiguity.

Sometimes external circumstances make it easier for people in the organization to tell whether it is time to disband. "Jane," a feminist abortion collective that provided thousands of safe abortions to women when the procedure was still illegal in the United States, was a cohesive and thriving organization as long as the members perceived an urgent public need for their service. After the Supreme Court decision in 1973 legalized abortion, the members of Jane saw that the need for safe and clean abortions could be met in hospitals, and, however regretfully, they decided to disband (Bart, 1981, p. 24).

Given the amount of energy that it takes to launch a new organization, participants have reason to be cautious about dissolving an ongoing enterprise. Their choices to support or to dismantle the organization are fraught with uncertainty. To the extent that participants wish to lower the chance that their original goals will be abandoned and that oligarchic control will develop, they raise the risk of needlessly ending the organization. To the extent that participants are more cautious about self-dissolution, they increase the risks of oligarchization and goal displacement.

The point here is not that a provisional orientation is in itself either good or bad, nor, as others have argued, that it will soon pervade many bureaucratic organizations (Bennis and Slater, 1968). Rather, it carries with it important consequences for the organization: at just those times that other organizations would displace goals and develop an oligarchy, these organizations may opt for self-dissolution. The question of organizational life or death, however, is set in a context of ambiguity and dilemma.

This expectation that the organization as a whole may be more or less fleeting holds as well for the programs and operations within it. Members tend to regard organizational operations as experimental or tentative. Procedures and rules often are seen by members as ad hoc and flexible. Programs and operations are experimental, and if they don't work, they are altered. The sentiment that all operations and programs in an organization ought to be tentative militates against the usual ritualization of rule use that turns means into ends.

Concerning rules and procedures, the following quotation is typical:

Don't worry, if there are major objections to our new ID card system, we'll drop it. All our policies and procedures are experiments, in the sense that if they don't work, we change them – fast.

A provisional, experimental attitude toward rules and procedures may have considerable adaptive value for the organization. As Biggart (1977) points out in her study of the reorganization of the U.S. Post Office, old methods must be dismantled before new ones can take their place. In this way a transitory attitude provides a barrier against ossification and the ritualization of rule use. Nancy expressed this value in her advice to a new trainee at the Free Clinic:

I told her to start out using the systems I've worked out, but that when she feels comfortable enough in the job, to go ahead and modify my procedures [of accounting, recordkeeping, statistics, etc.]. It wasn't the hand of God that wrote those procedures down. We did what needed to be done at the time. I told her that as times change, she should change the procedures. . . . We're always in need of creative, new ways of doing things.

Staff members themselves, as well as programs and procedures, are often viewed as relatively short-term elements in these organizations. In the groups we studied, when we asked members, "How long is a long time to be here?" they tended to reply nine months to a year. Anything over two years was often considered "too long":

[Sally] probably shouldn't be staying here any longer. Not that she isn't good at what she does, it's just that the [Free Clinic] needs the enthusiasm of new people and fresh ideas.

Sense of time duration is, after all, relative, as noted by a staff member at the *Community News:*

Four years out of my 26-year life is a long, long time. . . . I just feel like I've outgrown the paper and want to go on and do something else.

Reinharz (1984, p. 37) cites the case of Ozone House, an alternative counseling service in Ann Arbor, Michigan, that provides emergency food, temporary foster care, and other services. In part, she attributes the organization's long existence – 15 years so far – to the fact that the collective has an explicit rule that no staff member may work there more than one year.

In bureaucracies, people strive to develop careers. They are provided a long-term ladder that they hope to climb. In collectivist organizations, as noted in Chapter 3, there is no hierarchy of positions and so there is no ladder to ascend. The lack of the possibility of career advancement contributes to people's short time expectations in these groups. For example, Bart notes (1981, p. 34) that the illegal nature of "Jane" meant that staff members could not use it to further their careers. This fact fostered a present-time orientation in contrast with the future/careerist orientation of bureaucracy.

In sum, bureaucracies are characterized by an orientation toward career-building, the future, and permanence. These are actually quite special attitudes toward time. Though they go without question in bureaucratic society, they are generally not shared by people in collectivist organizations. Equally plausible is an orientation toward the present, a view of the organization itself as provisional, or of one's own commitment to the organization as shorter term and contingent on the organization's ability to fulfill higher-order needs. Such a provisional attitude appears, logically and empirically, to help guard against oligarchization, rigidification of rule use, and goal displacement.

Mutual and self-criticism

The process of mutual and self-criticism is another internal feature that appears to support the egalitarian and participatory character of collectivist organizations. Collectives in as diverse societies as America, China (Hinton, 1966), and the Basque region of Spain (Johnson and Whyte, 1977) have tried to create settings that encourage constructive self-criticism. This often includes assessment of one's own behavior, of others in the group, and of the organization as a whole.

Where it is a systematic and accepted process, criticism helps to level these inequalities. Thus, *a regular and sanctioned process of mutual and self-criticism reduces tendencies toward oligarchization.* The leveling effect of one criticism session may be quite visible, but short-lived. However, when criticism sessions are institutionalized, the knowledge that one is subject to group criticism helps to curb the assertion of individual power.

Although criticism sessions seem to have positive, latent consequences for the organization, the participants themselves are likely to justify mutual criticism in terms of its presumed benefits for the *individual* member:

We need a place to give feedback. . . . If a person is not doing well at their job there should be a time for criticism, so they can grow into their job. A collective should help people become better, more able people. (*Community News*)

This call for group criticism was amplified by other staff members at the *News:*

There's a need for criticism, but there's also a need for praise between us. Too often we forget the praise side of criticism. . . . People need to feel appreciated when they do a good job on something.

Writing for the [*News*] is like writing for a void. There's no feedback at all from staff.

Ironically, however, no regular criticism sessions were instituted at the newspaper. Repeated requests for them were acceded to in principle at general staff meetings, but blocked in practice by claims that "there's not enough time for another meeting." However, in a private interview with an informally recognized leader at the paper, other bases for resistance appeared:

Everyone who really puts work in on that paper gets my positive respect day in and day out. Not just a mechanical thing, but a true deep emotional love. . . . They work their fucking asses off. I feel so strongly about those people and they know it. And I need the same positive reinforcement from them. The whole question of not praising and not criticizing enough are from those people who don't have that respect. For the people who are carrying out their responsibilities, criticism/self-criticism exists. It's such a natural thing, it isn't even criticism. It's discussion.

The feeling that mutual and self-criticism should remain an informal and supposedly "natural" process, rather than being made into a regular and sanctioned one, was also expressed by a leader at the Free Clinic:

Some groups find it necessary to institute sanctioned spaces where they can criticize each other because they don't dare do it otherwise. . . . The [Free Clinic] has a very healthy emotional climate. People feel free to express their anger and emotions on the spot. They needn't let them accumulate while waiting for a meeting.

Even though they may appear to agree with the principle, leaders in collectives often resist instituting regular and public forums for criticism. This is interesting for a number of reasons. First, regardless of leaders' vocabularies of motives, we found that organizations without a regular and agreed upon process for criticism were subject to explosive and sometimes destructive bouts of criticism unbound by any rules of fair play. Alternative organizations that did institute regular forums for criticism appeared to receive more considered and constructive forms of criticism. Secondly, leaders may object –

often covertly – to regular criticism sessions because they fear that they themselves may become the chief targets of the criticism.

Let us illustrate what the absence of a formal criticism system led to at the
Community News. One member commented bitterly on the role of a former
member, Tom:

Mostly it was very insidious, behind-the-back stuff, or slap-across-the-face insults.
That was all left to [Tom]. He was very good at that sort of thing. . . . [Tom] had an
incredibly sharp wit and he would turn other people's ideas into jokes with his wit.
Sometimes he would go on and on compiling one crack on top of another until the
idea was lost somewhere in his snide humor.

And, concerning the "healthy emotional climate" said to prevail at the Free
Clinic, the following example provides a counterpoint:

[Leah] was up-front about her anger with [Sally] for not helping on the winter events
mailing. . . . When [Sally] started crying, Leah accused her of trying to manipulate
the situation.

Asked about the outcome, Leah said that she "felt great about it. We
worked out each of our requirements for personal space, so we won't intrude
on each other's space in the future." But for Sally, this event, and others like
it, took on another meaning, as expressed in a private interview: "I've learned
not to cross [Leah's] path. . . . Her personality has a lot of power over me.
I'll do anything to avoid her wrath."

These two examples suggest that the buildup of destructive hostility and
the growth of unequal influence may occur more readily in groups without a
formal and sanctioned process of criticism. Those organizations that do institute a regular forum for criticism tend to collectively negotiate informal rules
of fair play that define what sorts of criticism are legitimate. Social pressures
are brought to bear on those who violate this sense of fairness.

People at the Law Collective arrived at the following written guidelines for
their criticism meetings:

We feel criticism should be carefully considered and thought out before it is voiced.
We try to be gentle and objective, rather than abrasive, and we attempt to avoid
personal attacks. In receiving criticism, we strive to consider each statement carefully, regardless of its nature or source. (Documents)

Members of the Law Collective spoke of working on their ability to criticize effectively, and thought that over the years they had made progress on
this count. They would not, however, let any outsiders observe their criticism
meetings because of their personal nature.

The only collective in this study in which sanctioned group criticism was
observed was at the Food Co-op. There, the collective – in this case, of board
members – agreed to have self-criticism sessions after each meeting. Some of

the criticism was directed at the group as a whole, rather than at individual members:

Our energy has been too scattered tonight trying to do a meeting and inventory at the same time. In the future we should separate them and be more focused on each.

When an individual's ideas were subject to criticism, great pains were taken to critique and reject that person's proposal without rejecting the person. Criticisms were often balanced with praise. For instance, David, an active member of the co-op, came to a board meeting to propose picture identification cards for co-op usage. All of the costs of the cards had been figured, and the thoroughness of the proposal suggested that David had invested a fair amount of time and energy in the idea. "Picture IDs turn my stomach" was the quick response of a non-board member who happened to be present. Although board members, too, did not favor David's idea, they were obviously embarrassed by this tactless violation of their norms of how criticism should be presented. Board members tried to repair possible damage to David's ego by carefully explaining their objections to picture ID cards in terms of the co-op's honor system, technical difficulties with implementation, costs, and so forth. They ended by commending David on the benefit concert he was planning for the co-op and by stressing all the good things they had been hearing about it. Although the board firmly rejected his ID plan, they attempted to support him personally.

A similar sense of fair play and ego protection was voiced by a lawyer at the Law Collective:

If it's criticism, it's not shattering. If people are laid low by it, it's trashing. There's a difference.

At the Free Clinic and the *Community News,* when criticism erupted it was not contained in special sessions set aside for that purpose, it generally was not thought out beforehand, it was not bound by collective rules of fairness, and it therefore tended to be harsh and global. Personal attacks and bitterness often were the result.

In sum, where the process of criticism is collectively sanctioned, it may serve a constructive function for the organization. By making the leaders or core members publicly and legitimately subject to members' criticisms, such forums tend to reduce the inequalities of influence and to check potential abuses of power. As a result, informal leaders generally resist calls to institute criticism forums. The tendency of leaders to become a major target of criticism in collectivist organizations may be related to the consistent research finding that task leaders are often not particularly well-liked members of groups (Bales, 1950).

But, feelings toward leaders may run deeper than that. Collectives have contradictory feelings about leadership. They need informal leaders for a variety of reasons. However, the very presence of leaders signifies that inequalities in influence exist in an organization where such inequalities are not freely admitted. Prominent leadership is antithetical to the ethos of egalitarian control. If an individual, by virtue of some set of personal qualities, holds extraordinary sway with the group and is able to manipulate the "consensual" outcome of the decision-making process, this influence undercuts the basis of collective legitimacy. In the extreme, strong, individualistic leadership can render the consensual decision-making process a sham.

Collectivist organizations are therefore intensely ambivalent concerning leadership. On the one hand, they recognize the need for leaders or core members:

You always need a few people to take up the slack. If that doesn't happen, if no one comes in to fill the void, the Food Co-op has big trouble.

On the other hand, they prefer to deny the existence of leaders:

Everyone is equal at the Paper!

The whole theory of the collective is that you don't have a leader. You have leaders, the whole group. Everyone is strong and aggressive.

What follows from this ambivalence is an extremely cautious view of the very kind of people who, in conventional organizations, would be regarded as strong, effective, or even charismatic leaders.[1] As in any organization, articulate, talented, inventive people may have magnetic appeal in co-ops, but to the extent that they can single-handedly influence the outcome of decisions, they are seen to threaten collective control over the organization. People in collectivist organizations continuously seek to reconcile the reality of individual differences with the ideal of collective control. According to a *Community News* member:

There *is* a need for leadership. But that leadership must come from everyone; it must be mass leadership. If the leaders are individuals, that is a major flaw in the collective. Leadership by a clique is a perversion of the collective process. . . . We need an editor who can make people meet deadlines, but that position rotates, and who is the editor is chosen by the collective. The *basis* of anyone's authority is the collective, and authority can be taken away by the collective.

Despite serious attempts to articulate the meaning of collectivism, as in the above statement, and sincere attempts to abide by the collective will, individuals do sometimes assert personal authority. This generally is seen as illegitimate by the group, and if the violation is flagrant, the group may try to reassert the legitimacy of collective authority over individual authority. One of the prime mechanisms for this purpose is the process of group criticism.

This point is best illustrated through an extended example. At a regular staff meeting of the *Community News,* two influential members of the paper, Jake and Karl, came in for sharp criticism. Apparently, they had taken aside a reporter, recently assigned to city hall, and informally advised him on how they thought city hall should be covered. They suggested he treat gingerly certain progressives on the city council whose election the paper had supported. Even when in the reporter's view such progressives appeared inarticulate, stupid, or unprepared at council meetings, he was advised to "go easy" on them, for they had "good politics." The reporter objected. He wanted to "cover city hall as it is, showing fools to be fools." Members of the paper all lined up on one side: that of the reporter. One by one, they took the opportunity to remind Jake and Karl that:

Reporters have the right to write stories as they see them. . . . People of influence shouldn't pressure reporters to take their perspectives.

With that said, the tone of the meeting quickly changed. Members singled out perhaps the most influential person at the *News,* Karl, the managing editor, and launched a general attack on him. All aspects of his personality were suddenly fair game: One person rebuked him for being "unapproachable," another for being "intimidating." He was accused of "lacking trust in staff judgments" and of "guarding expertise jealously." Jake, a partner in the misdeed involving the advice to the reporter, eluded all personal criticism, probably because he was not a very powerful person at the paper.

Members then affirmed the following general principle:

Advice giving will and must informally go on, but reporters should assume this advice is from equals. They can throw it out if they want. The only [individual] authority that exists must be specifically delegated by the group.

With that action completed, the meeting took still another tack. Implicit criticism was directed at a new target, Clark, the city editor. This was not for any wrongdoing in this particular case – indeed, he had been instrumental in helping the reporter to bring the case out in the open – but for *potential* abuses of power based on his position at the paper:

Decisions about the politics of stories must come out of the Thursday staff meetings, not out of some dialogue between the city editor and the reporter. . . . Editors should not be policy makers, they should just do editorial style. . . . The line between political judgments and editorial judgments is thin.

Karl, obviously shaken and near tears from the earlier severe criticism of himself, interrupted these thinly veiled warnings to Clark, to defend himself:

[P]eople seem to be assuming, as Ronnie said, that "everyone is equal" except me. That I have to be watched because I'll pressure people and exert power. . . . I consider myself very principled. I've never pressured anyone to do something, I've never made a decision outside of a staff meeting, I've never engaged in intrigue, and now my principles get questioned.

This led to a third dramatic reversal in the tone of the meeting. The reporter who originally raised this case as an instance of abuse of power apologized for generating "this major misunderstanding." The member who had earlier charged Karl with intimidation now affirmed her respect for him and his contribution to the collective. Nearly every member tried to qualify and in some cases to retract their previous criticism of Karl. The earlier criticisms were now coupled with strong praise:

If [Karl] has more influence at the paper it's due to his history of showing good judgment and responsibility in everything he does. People learn from their experience here who is worth listening to and who can be relied upon.

The issue was finally closed, 3 hours and 15 minutes after it was opened, on this note of unity and warm feelings.

Group criticism was used in this instance as a tool to check the actual exercise of individual power as well as its *potential* exercise. It was aimed specifically at those who were perceived to be the most influential members of the collective. Criticism need not be as harsh as it was in this case to have a leveling effect. As argued earlier, it is in groups that have avoided instituting regular forums for criticism (such as the paper), and therefore where no collectively held rules of fairness have been negotiated, that criticism is most unbridled and negative when it does occur.

A study of free high schools by Ann Swidler (1979, p. 81) finds a similarly erratic treatment of leaders. In Swidler's words, "[L]eaders . . . are always treading a dangerous path. Although the organization may temporarily encourage them, it is always ready to turn upon them." For this reason, she finds that the free high schools she studied had a hard time filling their directorship positions.

Similarly, Sandkull's study (1982) of six worker collectives in Oregon found peer pressure and collective self-criticism to be the main means of social control in the groups. In some of the co-ops, group self-criticism was used, in effect, to inhibit the development of leadership. In other groups, neutral outside mediators, trained in group process, were called in to facilitate and teach more constructive communication processes.

A study by Reinharz (1984, pp. 51–64) illustrates the role that a social scientist may play as a consultant to these groups. In this case, Reinharz consulted for a collective bakery that, while deeply committed to democracy on ideological grounds, had no regular forum for group feedback. As a result, interpersonal resentments had simmered for a long time. As an outside consultant, Dr. Reinharz was able to introduce "feelings meetings" as a part of the decision-making process. These meetings functioned in part as the equivalent of the group self-criticism sessions we have described in other organizations. Once introduced, feelings meetings became a regular event in the collective, continuing for years with perfect attendance. Through these sessions, the group was able to clarify its goals, priorities, and organizational boundaries. Moreover, members were able to come to better decisions to put the co-op on a more secure footing, and – particularly – to open lines of communications and improve interpersonal relations in the group. The collective attributes its survival (10 years so far) and its success as a democracy to the innovation of the feelings meetings.

Contemporary collectivist enterprises often use criticism/reevaluation sessions of one type or another – consciously or not – to level inequalities of influence, to express their ambivalent feelings about leaders, and to nip in the bud leadership ambitions. In contrast, many historic communes used a more extreme version of public confession and self-criticism, but made their leaders exempt from such criticism. Where leaders are immune from criticism, as in some of the nineteenth century communes described by Kanter (1972a, p. 119), group criticism cannot check the assertion of power by charismatic leaders, nor is it intended to do so. In such cases, it serves other purposes.

Whether we are observing the extreme versions of self-scrutiny and public confession evidenced in Kanter's (1972a, pp. 106–107) nineteenth century communities and in the Bruderhof (Zablocki, 1971), or the milder process of reevaluation in the light of group ideology and goals that can be seen in the contemporary collectives (Swidler, 1979, pp. 92–95), public criticism functions as a powerful mechanism to regulate group behavior and to build commitment to organizational goals.

To emphasize, group criticism or reevaluation is often used in a context of ambivalence and dilemma. When the group both needs and resents the target of their criticism, it must be delicate in finding fault. It must walk a fine line between criticizing enough so as to level "undue" influence (enough to reassert collective authority over individual authority) but not so much as to lose a deeply committed and competent member.

Limits to size and alternative growth patterns

The face-to-face relationships and directly democratic forms that characterize *the collectivist organization probably cannot be maintained if the organization grows beyond a certain size.*

Rousseau (1950, p. 65) wrote that the upper limit for participatory democracy would be groups in which "each citizen can with ease know all the rest." Weber (1968, pp. 280–290), too, acknowledged the importance of small size for democratic organization. Recent empirical work offers general support for this proposition. In a study of the effects of industrial plant size, Ingham (1970) finds that increasing size is associated with lowered cohesion of the work group, less worker satisfaction, and reduced identification with the plant. Rosner (1981, pp. 32–35) in a study of kibbutz settings, discovers that participation in both the plant and the community declines as the assembly size increases. Confirming Ingham's findings, Rosner also reports that the negative relation between size and participation is most pronounced where the motivation of members is based on identification with system goals rather than on individual material rewards, a circumstance with clear relevance for collectivist organizations of the kind we have studied.

Although it is certainly reasonable to suppose that some large number would be too cumbersome for democratic groups, it may be impossible to determine a particular threshold beyond which democratic control yields to oligarchic control. Over the centuries philosophers and political theorists have posited an upper limit, yet no consistent number has emerged from the record. Likewise, our own study suggests no particular cutoff point, since our sample of organizations is too small and their size varies widely – from approximately 10 members (at the Law Collective) to more than 100 members (at the Free Clinic) to 1,100 members (at the Food Co-op). This leads us to believe that there may be no single cutoff point concerning size but only a curve of diminishing returns – a slow erosion of democracy rather than a sudden break.

Researchers of cooperatives in communist societies have made similar observations. Kowalak (1981), having examined 30 years of postwar experience with worker cooperatives in Poland, concludes, "[D]emocracy is inversely proportional to the size of the cooperative, and it seems to be a rule in spite of several experiments being made to avoid the consequences of that rule." He therefore urges that cooperatives not exceed a size compatible with a general meeting of all of the members. Limits to cooperative size seem also to be acknowledged in China, where the mean cooperative firm size is 78, while the average size of state-owned firms is 850 (Lockett, 1981). Rather than speculate about an upper limit, it seems to us that a more fruitful question would be whether an *optimal* size exists for democratic enterprises, and if so, what it might be.

We decided to put the question of optimal size to the members themselves. Our survey turned up some interesting results. Of those who say that there *is* an optimal size for collectives in *general,* almost all locate this size at the number of persons currently in their particular collective, give or take a few. That is, beliefs about an optimal size are quite consistent within groups, and quite disparate among groups. This may merely reflect positive bias toward one's own group. On the other hand, it may suggest that the actual optimum size for each collective is contingent upon a variety of other organizational factors, such as technology, and thus may not be generalizable. Indeed, most of the members themselves (55 percent at the Food Co-op, 71.5 percent at the Free Clinic, and 67 percent at the *Community News*) believe that there is no single optimal size for collectivist organizations in general. The best size for a collective newspaper may be quite different from the best size for a health clinic. Chickering (1972, pp. 241–227) for instance, proposes that the ideal size of organizations varies according to the task they seek to accomplish. For each organization, the main criterion would be, in Chickering's view, the avoidance of "redundancy" of personnel, that is having more people than are needed to do the job.

Complex as the issue of optimum size may be, there are undoubtedly some limits to size beyond which the familial and collectivist nature of alternative organizations is undone. In practice, members of collectives do indeed act as if they believe that size makes a difference. They often place size limits on their organizations and search for novel alternatives to conventional patterns of organizational growth.

Growth may be inhibited in direct and self-conscious ways. The following quotation from Rita, who six weeks earlier had taken over from Edward the full-time post of health education coordinator at the Free Clinic, reflects this direct approach:

Now that I've got the health ed section organized and I'm almost done training these 20 new volunteers, I find myself making things to do in my job. Like the women's center project – things that aren't really required by the job itself. . . . Parkinson's Law sets in and the job keeps expanding to fill the time I have for it. Edward exaggerated the time demands of the job. Health ed never did require a full-time person. . . . Once I finish training the new volunteers, I'd like to cut down to half-time. I believe that the job can be done better and without all these needless elaborations and diversions as a half-time slot.

Here Rita was asking not only that she be cut to half-time and half-salary, but that the job position itself be permanently cut to a half-time one. Her request was granted. This sort of admission that less money and slots are needed to do a job would be rare indeed in a conventional, growth-seeking bureaucracy.

Sometimes, by self-consciously limiting the usual pattern of organizational growth (gaining more clients and personnel), collectives develop creative alternatives to actual growth. Freedom High, unable to attract any Chicano students and unable to absorb more students than it already had, decided to form a coalition with a Chicano community cultural center. This coalition promised to broaden the school's resource base (library, art room, and so forth were now shared and enlarged) and to give its students some measure of contact with the Chicano community. Freedom High, then, acquired some of the benefits of growth without actually growing.

Building a wider network of cooperative relationships with other small, collectivist organizations is one substitute for growth that some organizations utilize. This federative principle grows out of anarchist thought (Kropotkin, 1902). Some of the most successful instances of cooperative development such as the Mondragon system in Spain attribute a good part of their success to having built a federation of mutually supportive cooperative firms and auxiliary organizations such as cooperative banks, schools, and research and development enterprises (Johnson and Whyte, 1977).

The spin-off of new, autonomous collectivist organizations is another alternative to growth. At the *Community News,* for instance, some of the staff envisioned taking about half of the collective and creating a second collectively run newspaper in another city when this one became "stable enough." Expansion in the form of a larger paper or a larger staff was not contemplated.

The Food Co-op, another case in point, planned to double its store size of 1,400 square feet because:

We already have way too many members for the size store we have. . . . Twenty-eight hundred feet would be a good size for a store – large enough to allow for a good selection of foods and certain economies of scale, but still small enough to be a real community store.

But after this initial expansion, they envisioned no more, preferring instead to "start wholly new and independent co-ops with the additional people who want to be members." In fact, the Food Co-op did help start several other food co-ops, deliberately curtailing membership growth beyond 1,100. A separate study of food co-ops found that more than 20 percent were created as spinoffs from larger co-ops (Nagy, 1980).

The *Community News* and the Food Co-op were not unique in their concept of spinning-off parallel, collectivist organizations as an alternative to internal growth. Schumacher (1973) describes a cooperatively owned manufacturing firm in Britain, the Scott Bader Company, which requires in its by-laws the spin-off of new, autonomous cooperatives when it reaches 350 in size. Kanter (1972a, pp. 227–231) points to a similar phenomenon in some of the nineteenth-century communal ventures, such as those of the Hutterites. Johnson and Whyte (1977) too have observed spin-offs in the Mondragon system of workers' cooperatives in Spain. The search for alternatives to organizational growth may be part of a broader reevaluation of large size in modern society (see, e.g., Molotch, 1976; Appelbaum, 1976; Schumacher, 1973; Sale, 1980).

Members of cooperatives generally do not view small size as a problem. Indeed, as just indicated, they often feel that it contains a number of advantages. Nevertheless, the limited size of such organizations may reduce their impact on the surrounding society and their value as demonstrations of alternative organizational principles. Mainstream attitudes and conventional organizations value large size far more than do people in co-ops. All other things being equal, a large organization will have more real political and economic clout than a small one. A cultural bias toward large size also makes it relatively easy for skeptics to dismiss collectives and cooperatives as trivial organizations espousing principles that would never work in large organizations. In choosing a democratically manageable size, therefore, co-ops may have to face the dilemma of trading off a degree of impact on the larger society.

Homogeneity

Consensus, an essential component of collectivist decision making, may require from the outset substantial homogeneity among members. Participants must bring to the process similar life experiences, outlooks and values if they are to arrive at agreements. The absence of a fundamental similarity in values makes reaching and abiding by a consensus much more difficult.

Bureaucracy may not require much homogeneity, partly because it does not need the moral commitment of its employees. Since it depends chiefly on remunerative incentives to motivate work and since in the end it can command obedience to authority, it is able to unite the energies of diverse people toward organizational goals. But, in collectives where the primary incentives for participation are based on shared purposes and values and where the subordinate-superordinate relation has been delegitimated, moral commitment becomes necessary. Unified action is possible only if individuals substantially agree with the goals and processes of the collective. This implies a level of homogeneity in terms of values unaccustomed and unnecessary in bureaucracy.[2]

Anyone who has participated in democratic meetings can appreciate how disruptive the contrarian can be. The holdout, while perhaps not swaying the group's eventual decision, can surely protract the decision-making process and generate frustration. In observing consumer cooperatives, Gamson and Levin (1980, pp. 9–10) find that, when an admissions policy is overly open, common cultural values tend to be lacking and thus problems arise for the organization. For this reason, as cited in Chapter 3, many worker collectives tend to seek new members who agree from the start with their fundamental values. The Law Collective, for example, after initially selecting new staff who appeared to have congruent political values, additionally instituted a six-month probationary period to make sure that members' assessments proved correct before further committing themselves to the individual.

Consequently, collectivist organizations tend to attract a homogeneous population. In the cooperatives reported in our study (Rothschild-Whitt, 1976a) as well as in those surveyed by Crain (1978) members were disproportionately from economically and educationally advantaged backgrounds. As described in Chapter 2, they also tend to draw members with similar political views, experiences, and identification with social movements.

Homogeneity has also been a salient feature of worker cooperatives in the past. In the 1920s, Italian immigrants in San Francisco came together to form garbage collection co-ops. These cooperatives have endured over the years, have paid their worker-owners well, have succeeded in dignifying what would otherwise be considered "dirty work," and have continued to provide high-quality service at low price. Today several have become large waste-management conglomerates. The point is that these cooperatives originally came together out of economic necessity and the glue of a common cultural background. This generated feelings of trust and a sense of being social equals – the basis for any cooperative. Decades later, when new workers who wished to join the cooperatives were from other racial and minority groups, the Italian founder-owners felt no sense of kinship with them, and in addition had little desire to dilute the value of their own equity. Therefore they did not offer ownership rights to the new workers. As a result, the co-op ironically devolved into a two-class system of owner-members on the one hand, and hired workers on the other (Perry, 1978; Russell, 1982b). Similar ethnic and cultural bonds, in the case of Soviet Jewish immigrants, have united new taxi driver cooperatives in Los Angeles (Russell, 1982b).

In other successful examples of cooperative development, such as the Mondragon cooperatives, cultural homogeneity has played an equally important role in knitting the groups together. The Mondragon cooperatives have not devolved into a two-class system over time, perhaps because they are all Basques (Johnson and Whyte, 1977). In the kibbutzim cooperatives in Israel, members' common Jewish identity bonds the groups together, but separates them from their Arab hired laborers (Ben-Ner, 1982).

Efforts to develop democratic workplaces often run into difficulties if they have a very heterogenous work force. For example, the president and owner of IGP, a multimillion dollar insurance firm, decided to give half of the stock to the workers and to set up democratic committees of workers to manage the firm. Some workers, now worker-owners, took to the new system as an opportunity and a challenge; for others, democratic decision making brought more headaches and responsibilities than they wanted. These attitudes toward democracy mirror the range of attitudes one can expect to find in the larger society. The contemporary cooperatives often avoid confronting such a range by selectively recruiting and attracting only individuals who desire participation and influence in their work. Selectivity is necessary since participatory values and habits of behavior are not widespread in our society. Bernstein (1976) suggests that a democratic ideology is essential in cooperative workplaces.

Though homogeneity eases consensus decision making and promotes group cohesion and friendship, it does present the organization with a dilemma. At a minimum, it narrows the membership base of the collective and it makes it less representative of the surrounding community. Participants in the contemporary collectives often regret the restricted nature of their constituency, especially in the light of their desire to be integrated into the community and to change it in some fashion. In the extreme, as in the garbage collection co-ops in San Francisco, the natural desire for homogeneity may exclude "outsiders" and lead to the degeneration of the co-op form.

The overrepresentation of young adults with upper middle-class origins in contemporary collectives in the United States probably results from the changing values, social movement orientations, reduced employment prospects for this group, and other factors detailed earlier. In addition, certain organizational features of collectives may have the consequence, however unintended, of further narrowing the social base. Specifically, the compensation system of the contemporary collectives, with its formally egalitarian pay principles in the context of low pay levels, may have different meanings to different individuals.

In those worker cooperatives where the pay is low and much less than it would be in comparable jobs in the outside world, collectives may have a difficult time getting and keeping members of working class origin. As a working class staff member of the *Community News* ruefully observed:

You can't ask people who have no option of a rich family to fall back on to make a long-term commitment to the [*News*], if you can't commit the paper to supporting those people and their families.

In a private interview, another working class staff member, soon to leave the *News,* lamented:

Part of the reason I've been bummed out at the paper is a class thing. I think a lot of the people there have a lot more life options that I do. And I think those options account for their rather haphazard attitude about things. I think growing up rich makes a real difference. It allows people to be dilettantes and not to take things that seriously. At first I thought it was California, that people here don't take things seriously. But that's not it. . . . Being from a rich family lets people take their future for granted. Money isn't that important because there's always mom and dad.

In short, working class members of alternative organizations often feel that the members from more privileged backgrounds, while willing to live a very simple life-style now, can always fall back on their parents for money should times get rough, whereas those of more modest means have no such insurance available. This may lead committed working class members to leave collectives in search of more secure, if less inspired, work. In group discussions, this private uneasiness of working class members was never publicly acknowledged in the observed organizations.

The meager pay levels that characterize the contemporary collectives appear to stem from two causes. First, collectives sometimes generate little surplus to distribute among their members. The problem of undercapitalization in cooperatives has long been recognized (Blumberg, 1973). Second, on a more subtle level, cooperatives may continue to pay meager salaries even when they can afford more, because they fear the development of "careerism." People in collectives expect work there to be a labor of love. Some suspect that should the work become too well remunerated, it will degenerate – from their point of view – into merely a career, with attachment to one's position taking priority over organizational goals. For this reason, collectivists often want to avoid the sorts of economic incentives that might encourage people to seek a career in them.[3]

Lean salaries may assure the organization that its workers are committed by nonmonetary values, but for some members it may also mean that the collective is not a viable place of employment. The egalitarian nature of the compensation system (which is an essential feature of the collectivist organization) and the typically low pay levels (which are *not* an inherent feature) combine to take an uneven toll on members.

At the *Community News,* for example, staff members (whose average education level was a B.A.) earned an average of $160.00 per month in November of 1974. Three months earlier they had averaged $125.00 per month. Salaries at the paper were determined by the collective in plenary meetings and given out "to each according to his need." Some staff at the *News* (including some of its most helpful people) were paid nothing; the highest pay was $300.00 per month to a person with a family. Regardless of pay, full-time staff were expected to work a 40- to 60-hour week.[4]

At the Free Clinic, salaries were also collectively determined. However, here it was decided that they would each take salaries of $500.00 per month (in 1974) and that each would be paid equally. This meant that all full-time staff members, whether a 17-year-old doing secretarial work or a Ph.D. co-ordinating the health education program, were paid equally (the average education was a B.A.). Later, unable to find the funds with which to raise salaries and to compensate for what they perceived to be inadequate pay for the job at hand, the staff collectively decided to lower their expectations of work hours from 40 to 28–35 hours per week and to add a number of paid vacations for themselves.

In both organizations, the salary was augmented by the nonmonetary "fringe benefits" of working in a collectivist organization, namely more autonomy and control than could ordinarily be attained in a bureaucratic or even in a professional organization.

The consequences of these two financial situations differed decidedly. At the *Community News* some of the staff lived at a less than adequate standard and a number of capable and dedicated members felt compelled to leave in search of greener pastures. Two of them soon found jobs in journalism for more than $800 per month.

At the *Community News,* staff generally made about 18–25 percent of the salary they could draw at comparable, but established, journalism jobs. At the Free Clinic, some staff people made about 50 percent of what they would draw at comparable nursing or counseling jobs for which they were qualified. The equality principle by which salaries were distributed meant that others such as secretaries made as much as 83–100 percent of what they would be paid in comparable outside jobs.

In the context of a society that grants highly unequal pay, the more or less equal compensation within collectives brings great differentials in relative sacrifice. This implies a kind of de facto inequity built into the equity principle of collectives. Most cooperative organizations tend to pay people according to both their skills and their needs, while strictly limiting the amount of differential allowed. In our observation, it is among those who perceive that they are making the greatest sacrifice by remaining in the co-op that attrition is highest.

The data on social composition in the contemporary collectivist organizations are consistent in this study and in others: Members tend to be drawn from relatively privileged backgrounds and do not have family responsibilities. Members commonly feel uneasy about their restricted social base. In the abortion collective studied by Bart (1981, pp. 25–26), members worried over their homogeneity, but Bart concludes that it was probably a "blessing in disguise," enabling members to stick together and to achieve consensus.

This outlines an important and as yet unresolved dilemma that many collectives face. If pay scales are "too high," there is the risk of engendering careerism, with the attendant problem of organizational maintenance. The need to ensure a value-committed staff suggests relatively low and equal salaries, and the need for cohesion and consensus may require substantial homogeneity, but these structural facts seem to preclude many people, particularly of working class origin, from joining collectives – hardly an ideal situation for those who are trying to broaden the base of a social movement.

Dependence on internal support base

Those people with which an organization comes into regular, direct contact – that is, its members, customers, and clients – constitute that organization's internal support base. Their support, moral and financial, of the organization is crucial. We hypothesize that *the more a collective organization depends on its internal support base, the more likely it is that democratic ideals will be maintained. In addition, there is less chance of displacement of original goals.*[5] Conversely, when a collective acquires an external base of financial support (such as a foundation or government grant) its leaders tend to lose interest in the sentiments and goals of its members and clients, and thereby the likelihood of goal displacement is increased.

When collectivist organizations come to extensively rely on external financing, members typically find themselves more and more caught up in seeking such funding. In turn, they often shape the character of the organization to suit funding agencies. The Free Clinic, for example, depended on external sources for 83 percent of its budget. As a consequence, paid staff at the clinic reported spending an average of three-quarters of their time seeking continued outside revenue. After writing grant proposals and cultivating the sensitivities of those officials who award financial grants, they had little time left to attend to the volunteers and clients. In fact, when the position of health education coordinator opened up (a job whose formal responsibilities required writing health education pamphlets, speaking on health-related topics, and training and organizing a group of volunteers to do the same), the skills that the staff sought in a replacement had mostly to do with one's willingness to "hobnob with politicians," and the "ability to impress government types." Moreover, in the thick of grantsmanship, two of the staff coordinators temporarily suspended their "component meetings," the only formal arena for decision-making input that the volunteers had.

Dependence on external financial support at the Free Clinic resulted in a decline in participation levels and appeared to reduce leaders' sensitivity to volunteers' interests. It also led to more direct forms of goal displacement.

As part of the health education program at the Free Clinic, pamphlets aimed at "demystifying" health care (regarding drugs, herpes, venereal disease, and so on) were produced for public distribution. One day an important county official charged that one pamphlet that described plainly how to qualify for California's Medi-Cal program was "too political." Staff members thought that the pamphlet was valuable for patients, and its widespread use seemed to confirm that assessment. Fearing, however, that continued grant support might be jeopardized, the staff removed the pamphlet from the shelves of the clinic.

These sorts of compromises are difficult to avoid when the organization cannot pay its rent without external help. Such cooptations result not only from direct outside pressures to alter the course of the organization. Members themselves begin to monitor and structure the activities of the organization in terms of their presumed acceptability to money-rendering outsiders.

External agencies need not threaten to withdraw funds from a collective to achieve accommodations. Not uncommonly, the agency will insist on certain conditions before funding will be considered. Money often comes with strings attached. Foundations generally choose which part of a budget they wish to fund, if they choose to give at all. One private foundation decided, among many possibilities, to fund a children's clinic. This was not considered a high priority by the staff at the Free Clinic because there was another children's clinic in town, and the community need for a second one was perceived to be slight. Yet, as one staff member explained: "We're not going to let the $5,000 go to waste. We'll sure as hell do a children's clinic now." That this source of funding made the Free Clinic susceptible to an external ordering of priorities, not subject to collective control, was lamented, but not challenged, by a staff member at the clinic:

What's "in" right now is pediatrics and geriatrics. Nothing for anybody in between. And what these foundations support goes in and out with the fads. What can you do?

In another instance, a private foundation granted the Free Clinic funds for capital expenditures. This led the staff to create pseudoneeds for an elaborate typewriter, acoustic ceiling, and a photocopy machine where other more pressing health care needs existed. Again, clinic members could not challenge the right of the foundation to earmark funds in this way.

Similarly, in recent cases where workers faced with corporate shutdowns and the prospect of personal unemployment have been able to buy their firms, they have been heavily dependent on external sources of financing. They have had to go to private banks and government agencies for loans. Banks have often insisted, as a condition for loaning the capital, that the fledging worker-owned enterprise have "responsible management." In some cases, bank-approved managers had to be installed, with the result that the new worker-owners participated little in managerial decision making. Additionally, the worker-owners have tended to look positively upon the bank or other agency that aided the survival of their firm. These worker-owned organizations are still quite young, and it is too soon to tell what the long-term effects of this external dependency will be.[6] The situation may also be modified by the creation in 1980 of the National Consumer Cooperative Bank, which now loans money to cooperative enterprises.

The proposal of a direct relationship between dependence on external support and lessened regard for members' and clients' goals needs to be qualified. Some sources of external funding appear to be less potentially cooptative than others. The Food Co-op made a point of pursuing grants that appeared to be unconditional. For instance, they sought grants from two wealthy young heirs whose philanthropy was considered to be "radical." Like the Food Co-op, the *Community News* was mainly self-sufficient, but when it did seek grants, it sought them from rich individuals who were known for liberal causes. In fact, a new type of alternative institution has appeared, namely, the "alternative foundation."[7]

In the case of the Free Clinic, the only organization we studied that depended heavily on external funding, we saw an alternative organization that spent much of its staff time seeking continued outside revenue, compromised member participation, watered down some of its projects to accommodate outside pressures, and forfeited some measure of collective control over priorities to external foundations.

The converse of this process seems to hold as well. In service organizations that depend on the goodwill of their members and clients for financial support, as did the Free School and the Food Co-op, leaders tend to remain much more responsive to the goals and sentiments of the membership. We found in a survey of the general membership of the Food Co-op that 74 percent of the members considered their elected board of directors to be either "very" or "reasonably" responsive to their needs. In contrast, only 29 percent of the volunteer-members at the Free Clinic believed that their board was either "very" or "reasonably" responsive.

Likewise, in her study of "Jane," Bart notes that because there was a fee charged for the abortion service, leaders remained sensitive to client needs and expended no time in searching for grants (1981, pp. 20–22). A recent survey of 236 community self-help organizations also confirms our hypothesis. Milofsky and Romo (1981) find that such organizations tend to receive funds from a single type of source, rather than from some random combination of sources. They argue that is true because the sort of organization that is able to attract a specific source of money may be unsuited to attracting an alternative source. The authors find that the most participatory organizations are those that rely on internal funding from their clients and customers.

Two of the most impressive international examples of successful cooperative development are built on internal financing. The founders of the Mondragon system of worker cooperatives in Spain recognized that independence from the state and from private banks would be crucial. They set up their own internal bank through which the co-ops' earnings could be retained and used to sponsor further cooperative development. Mondragon owes its exponential growth from a handful of people to more than 18,000 worker-owners in 25 years to this internal financing mechanism (Logan, 1981; Johnson and Whyte, 1977). Similarly, a system of 12 self-managed enterprises has enjoyed rapid growth in the Netherlands by developing its own internal bank to provide investment capital (Rothschild-Whitt, 1981).

However, in worker collectives, or more broadly in social movement organizations – especially where the clients have low incomes – the organization is faced with a difficult choice of whether to turn to internal or external funding. For example, in his study of 132 community and tenants-rights organizations, Lawson (1981) finds that without external funding these organizations have few resources and must depend on volunteer and part-time labor. When some of these community organizations do receive government funding, morale rises and staff tend to work very hard, providing services (now on salary) that they had formerly provided for no money. After a time, new staff enter, not out of deeply held conviction, but because they need a job, and the organization begins to lose its commitment and focus. In some cases, where government agencies prefer to fund multi-objective organizations, community organizations may find themselves completely shifting in focus and goals from, for example, tenants rights to youth unemployment. Further, the lessened commitment of the second generation of staff may set the organization on a course of steady grantsmanship and lowered volunteer participation (Lawson, 1981; Helfgot, 1974). In groups that rely on volunteer work, such as the Free Clinic, the external grants with which professional staff members are paid undercut the willingness of people to volunteer. Indeed, Lawson (1981: 23) concludes that "the vast majority of externally funded social movement organizations [which have developed a professional paid staff] no longer have either volunteer workers or members as such."

An intensive case study of a women's health center in New England by Sandy Morgan reveals some of the organizational consequences of accepting government funding. As at the Free Clinic, government grants here, too, brought with them project guidelines. In effect, this meant that outside government agencies shaped the internal priorities and programs of the collective as, for example, by curtailing funds for abortion services. In addition, government grants required specific forms to be filled out. In time, the health center ceased soliciting client feedback, concentrating instead on Comprehensive Employment and Training Act (CETA) forms and review.[8]

The dilemma for collectives posed by outside sources of funding is easy to appreciate. When such organizations lead a rather hand-to-mouth financial existence, the possibility of obtaining a foundation or government grant holds considerable attraction for members. Although there may be some reluctance to pursue outside funding because of what such a fostered dependency might do to the organization, some cooperatives eagerly seek external funding.[9] As in the case of the Free Clinic, these organizations are likely to discover that dependency on external money is a two-edged sword. External funds may allow the organization to provide a free or below-cost service to clients, but funding possibilities also seduce the energies of leaders, diverting them from devotion to organizational democracy, and in some cases, from the original aims of the organization.

Technology and the diffusion of knowledge

The egalitarian and participatory ideals of the collectivist organization probably cannot be realized where great differences exist in members' abilities to perform organizational tasks. Put more specifically, *collectivist forms of organization are undermined to the extent that the knowledge and skills needed to perform the organization's tasks* (be they medical knowledge, legal know-how, or whatever) *are unevenly distributed*.

Diffusion of knowledge and skills, crucial as it may be for effective collective control, is difficult to accomplish. It seems to require that *one* of the two following technological conditions obtain.

Either:

1. Tasks involved in the administration of the collective organization must be relatively simple so that everyone readily knows how to do them, or they must involve a relatively undeveloped technology applied in relatively nonroutine situations (Perrow, 1970, pp. 75–85). An example is Freedom High. Since knowledge about the teaching process is more of an art than a science, and since every student at Freedom High was supposed to be treated uniquely, the issue of knowledge diffusion was not prominent. There was no systematic body of reliable knowledge to be communicated or monopolized. The technology employed in most organizations can be exclusively held, however.

Or:

2. If the members of the collective are of sufficiently homogeneous ability and interest to be able to learn the skills involved fairly rapidly, then the technology involved in the organization may be relatively sophisticated and may be applied in more uniform circumstances. In cooperatives that employ a more sophisticated technology, the distribution of knowledge becomes problematic, because scientific, specialized knowledge does lend itself to monopolization. Democratic organizations that utilize a more sophisticated or routine technology must therefore institute a systematic process of knowledge diffusion or risk defeating their egalitarian and collectivist principles.[10]

Sociologists of organizations have long understood that the holding of "official secrets," that is, the monopolization of knowledge, is a prime source of power in bureaucracy (Weber, 1968; Crozier, 1964). It is also an important source of power in organizations in which power differentials are not freely admitted. When knowledge inequalities are not acknowledged by the participants, as in the case below, the consequences are most frustrating and painful for members.

In another collectivist medical clinic, which we will call Southside Clinic, angry conflicts between the doctors and the paramedical staff erupted frequently. Members were confounded by the paradox of doctors who endorsed egalitarian principles in concept, but who seemed in practice to usurp decision-making power. In response, members charged the doctors with being guilty of "elitism," "authoritarianism," and "professionalism." One staff member at the Free Clinic who was in contact with the paramedical personnel at Southside Clinic, described Southside from her perspective:

Sure they [the doctors] will let you have a collective, they'll let you talk things out, as long as you end up agreeing with them. But the minute you don't, it doesn't take long before they remind you of who's bringing in the bread and whose skills are really needed. That's the situation at [Southside] and you have no idea how toxic it is. [Southside] exists not because a collective got together and found two doctors to help them, but because two doctors decided they wanted to be hip, to come white, and they found a group to help them. . . . They have the power ultimately and it can never be a true collective.

Another staff member at the Free Clinic agreed with this analysis of Southside Clinic. She did not believe, however, that the Free Clinic would follow the same route, were it to allow a doctor "into the collective":

You're right – a doctor may have a tendency to dominate the decision making. But [Andy] is a real possibility. *He's not like that.* He's said that he'd like to be more active in the clinic. (Emphasis added)

As the above quotations indicate, participants themselves tend to interpret conflicts as *personality* defects in the people involved. We believe, however, that the conflicts are often *structural* – and not psychological – in origin. The persistent conflicts at Southside Clinic were not due to the doctors being particularly authoritarian. Like all other members of Southside, the doctors endorsed nonelitist, egalitarian principles, yet the distribution of relevant knowledge was vastly unequal. Such disparities in knowledge are structural features of the organization, not a matter of personal idiosyncrasies, and they severely undercut the likelihood of developing or maintaining a directly democratic form of organization.

Collectivist organizations that employ a more sophisticated technology in their operations must focus on the process of knowledge diffusion if they are to avoid the tension and inequality that riddled the medical clinic described above. Toward this end, some of the organizations we observed devoted a great deal of energy to cultivating in their members a general knowledge about overall operations of the organization instead of specialized expertise. This was accomplished primarily through extensive job rotation, task sharing, and most broadly, by attempts to "demystify" normally exclusive or esoteric bodies of knowledge. Members use the word *demystification* to refer to efforts to simplify, explicate, and make available to the membership at large formerly exclusive knowledge.

The process of knowledge diffusion may take a variety of forms. When an attorney at the Law Collective, for example, was asked in an interview how the collective deals with inequalities in influence that arise as a result of differences in knowledge, he responded:

The first thing has been to read some of the basic things that Chairman Mao has written . . . analyzing professionalism as a contradiction. . . . The main problem with professionalism is with the attitude of attorneys. That's the main thing that has to change. Attorneys have to take legal workers more seriously. The other aspect is the legal workers learning more, developing their skills. That's the rising aspect.

In practice, the Law Collective could not divide the labor completely evenly because the law prohibits nonattorneys from performing such tasks as appearing in court, giving legal advice, and visiting people in prison. All other tasks, however, were assigned without regard to professional certification. As members explained, "legal workers have to learn from doing." No regular classes were instituted to teach the newer legal workers the law, but occasionally one of the experienced attorneys would give a "shop talk" on one aspect of the law (e.g., on judicial procedures, sentencing procedures). In spite of this lack of systematic law seminars or courses, people at the Law Collective were very proud of the extent to which their legal workers, people with little or no previous law training, learned to fulfill most of the functions commonly reserved for practicing attorneys. They happily reported the case of one legal worker who, after being a member of the Law Collective for only a month, wrote a writ of mandate to the California Supreme Court that succeeded in overturning local residency requirements for holding city office.

Personal learning through job rotation and team work is found in many innovative workplaces. In Sweden, some automobile plants use work teams and job rotation in the assembly of cars (Gyllenhammar, 1977). A unique auto repair collective in Washington, D.C., provides the means for members to teach themselves the skills of auto mechanics while repairing cars in the shop (*Syracuse Herald-American,* June 18, 1978, p. 13). Member-owners of a collective bakery in Oregon combine a number of tasks on the job (e.g., baking, bookkeeping, purchasing); at a collectivist construction firm in the same state, special efforts are made to teach building trades skills to women (Sandkull, 1982).

A particularly comprehensive and dramatic example of knowledge diffusion is found in the Mondragon worker cooperatives. For many years they have operated their own schools to train young people in technical skills they can later use in the cooperatives, and to teach cooperative values (Logan, 1981; Johnson and Whyte, 1977).

The diffusion of knowledge and skills is widely lauded and practiced in cooperatives because it is a precondition for the diffusion of influence. It is intriguing to note, however, that there are instances, too, in which knowledge diffusion comes about in more bureaucratic settings in an unplanned manner, and with no prior ideological commitment. This suggests that at least some of the features of collectivist organization, particularly the process of knowledge diffusion, may generalize to special subunits of service bureaucracies.[11]

Staff members of collectivist enterprises may try to demystify expertise not only for their worker-members, but for their clients as well. The Free Clinic, for instance, had a large number of "patient advocates," trained volunteers whose job it was to clarify medical knowledge to patients. The explicit aim was to maximize patients' knowledge about healing so that they could better care for themselves and thereby reduce their continued dependence on doctors. In the same vein, the Law Collective wrote:

We view our clients as our brothers and sisters. We attempt to demystify the law so that when they come to us for help, they not only have their specific problems resolved, but they also learn something about the operation of the "system" and what they might do the next time a problem arises.

The Law Collective tried to implement this goal through encounters with individual clients and through efforts to help organize a "people's law school."[12]

The laywomen in the abortion collective (Bart, 1982) reportedly performed some 11,000 successful (though illegal) abortions without the aid of physicians and with an excellent record for safety. After the members learned the necessary medical procedures, they dismissed the physicians. Bart argues that demystification helped the organization to develop and retain its egalitarian form and to provide a high-quality service.

Law or medicine, or any relevant base of knowledge, may be demystified to clients not only as a result of verbal efforts, but also by removing conventional symbols of authority from the organizational setting. For example, the Free Clinic – like most free health clinics in this respect – painted the walls vivid colors, brought noninstitutional furniture into the waiting room, oriented all of its personnel to convey a casual, first-name atmosphere, and replaced the standard white smock with blue jeans and the like for doctors, nurses, lab technicians, and patient advocates alike. These changes represent more than mere style; they have symbolic meaning. They remove important cultural symbols of authority from the setting in which alternative services are to be provided. The removal of culturally accepted props of authority signals to clients that the doctors and other medical personnel are human, and accordingly, that their professional judgments are open to question. The Milgram (1973) experiments on obedience suggest the potency of symbols of professional authority. In effect, the removal of symbols of authority may subtly encourage clients and members to respect the lessons of their own experience over the judgments of an authority figure.

In collectivist organizations that do not have clients, as the *Community News,* the demystification or diffusion of knowledge is directed at the worker-owners. Here the technology is relatively sophisticated and routine, and task sharing is the main method of skills diffusion.

At the *News,* job assignments often combine seemingly unrelated tasks such as 20 hours on editing, 10 on writing, and 10 on production. Such task distributions reflect collectivist principles, meaning that no one is stuck doing tedious work full-time, and no one is allowed to do choice work full-time. Jobs considered to be the most boring or undesirable, such as the production tasks of layout, pasteup, and so on are shared by many, from editors to advertising people. No one at the *News* argued that having people change their job activity practically every other day would be the most efficient way to put out a paper, but they did argue that task sharing was an equitable system that allowed all members to gain experience and knowledge in all aspects of the paper.

The sharing of knowledge may be further accomplished through job rotation. Job rotation at the *News* is planned and comprehensive. It arises out of principle. In reality, however, systematic job rotations are a difficult course to follow. In planning, they are time-consuming, and in implementation, they present a great deal of change for the organization to absorb. Sometimes preparations for a coming rotation have to be laid well in advance, as when people are assigned to train for a particular job by apprenticing under its incumbent. Because job rotations require periodic retraining, they take a good deal of time. In many co-ops, the training of members in new jobs thus may be given inadequate attention, with the result that the performance of newly acquired tasks may be poor (Gamson and Levin, 1980: 30).

Plans for the first rotation at the *Community News* began months prior to its implementation, and discussion related to it (e.g., who should do what) absorbed countless hours of formal staff meeting time. This expenditure of time and energy is only comprehensible if one understands the extent to which members of the *News* prize democratic control. If we fail to identify this ultimate goal of job rotation, we miss its essential meaning to the members, and it may appear to consume time and energy far out of proportion to its organizational utility.

Job rotation at the *News* was not without its rough edges. The story of Ann and John, with which we began Chapter 1, is a case in point. Ann was a good photographer who greatly enjoyed her work at the *News*. She agreed in principle with the idea of job rotation, but didn't want to give up photography. She agonized over it, but could not think of any other job at the paper that she would want to do. Encouragement and appeals by others didn't seem to help resolve her quandary. Finally, after hours of meetings of the collective, she was assigned a new job in advertising. It didn't work out. Shortly after she started her new assignment, she unhappily confided in an interview:

Rotation is a neat thing and I agree with the reasons we're committed to it and all that, but in practice I'm a casualty of the rotation system. . . . I can't go on much longer in the advertising section. Going to look for a waitressing job soon. I'm terrible at advertising, just terrible . . . I go into stores and ask managers to take out ads and try to act like it doesn't matter to me when they say no. No sooner than I'm out of the store, I start crying. . . . I know it's my turn to do other work besides writing, but I just don't know if I'm willing to go through six miserable months trying to sell ads.

Mismatched as Ann was in her new job, she did not question the legitimacy or the morality of the collective's assignment of her new tasks. And neither did anyone else, as reflected in this comment by one of Ann's closest friends at the *News:*

People know [Ann's] unhappy in advertising, but she *did* offer to switch to advertising in the beginning and she hasn't suggested another job at the paper that she'd be willing to do. No one, not even her best friends could accept it if she came out and said "Look, all I ever want to do at the paper is to write and do photography." A switch could be worked out if she would show some willingness to learn another task. But she can't ask for special privileges. . . . She has to be willing to rotate and to do the more fun jobs as well as some of the more tedious jobs, like everyone else.

Soon thereafter, Ann left the *Community News* for good. John, happy with his new job, remained as did the rest of the members. The staff of the *News* are willing to accept occasional casualties of the rotation system such as Ann because they see rotation as instrumental in the process of knowledge diffusion, and knowledge diffusion gets at the heart of collective control over the organization. Sophisticated technologies lend themselves to monopolization, and if such monopolies of knowledge are not diffused or demystified, members fear that democratic control will yield to oligarchic control. This fear is often implied in the justifications that members give for having rotation and task-sharing systems:

Expertise can become a hammer, a jealousy. If it is allowed to grow and grow, it can give some people an undue amount of power and influence in the group. . . . They can block other people from learning their expertise.

Part of the reason of having a collective is to grow and learn things. . . . People learn by doing. Rotation is part of the process of helping people to learn. The drawback to it is after a while people get very good at the tasks they've been doing. When you rotate tasks, it takes new people longer to do things and they may not be done as well as with the old people, at least until the new people grow into the new jobs.

Serious efforts, such as those at the *Community News,* to demystify knowledge also raise an important *dilemma* for the collectivist organization. Substantial diffusion of knowledge seems to entail a loss in organizational efficiency and productivity, at least in the short run. This by no means went unnoticed by staff at the *News:*

We know that ——— won't be as good a writer as ——— was, and that ——— won't be that good at selling ads at first, . . . but people get tired of what they're doing after a while. . . . You can't keep a person on a job as alienating as advertising forever. . . . We think that the long-term benefits of everyone understanding all aspects of the paper, and the kind of equality that comes from that, outweigh the short-run inefficiencies that are involved.

Clearly, people at the *News* realize that by collectively rotating tasks, some productivity might be lost. Nevertheless, all things considered, they are willing to trade off a certain measure of efficiency in order to try to make sure that knowledge about particular operations at the *News* will not be monopolized.

The Law Collective also takes pains to share or to rotate the most menial tasks, such as reception and cleanup. Like those at the *News,* members try to avoid relying on bureaucratic criteria for dividing the labor and instead try to focus on who stands to learn the most from a particular case assignment. They assign cases to pairs rather than individuals so that members can educate each other in specific areas of law. Although they do pay serious attention to the demystification process, they tend, unlike the *Community News,* to gloss over the problems associated with it:

Our biggest fear of an office without traditional divisions of labor was that work would not be done as quickly or as well as necessary. Since attorneys do their own typing, some individual pleadings take twice as long to prepare. But having non-attorneys in the office who also prepare pleadings helps to offset this time loss. The overall effect, we feel, is that everyone develops his or her legal skills, and as a group we become more effective and efficient than if the more menial jobs were left to the nonlawyers.

Whether or not an organization candidly faces the issues involved, a structural dilemma persists. Cooperatives employing relatively developed forms of technology must pay serious attention to sharing knowledge or risk eventual control by the experts. Sharing tasks, rotating jobs, creating apprenticeship systems and other means of demystifying knowledge enhance personal learning and perhaps member satisfaction, but time spent learning is time away from the production tasks of the organization. To the extent that tasks are distributed by criteria other than who is most experienced or talented for the job at hand, some measure of organizational productivity is sacrificed. This is a weighty dilemma for the cooperative that wishes to accomplish its tasks as expeditiously as possible while sustaining an egalitarian organization.

Nevertheless, this observation must be qualified on three counts. First, these organizations have a theoretic goal of universal competence of members in the tasks of the organization. If an organization actually approached universal competence, then it would not have to continue to invest large amounts of time and energy in the learning process, and it might be expected to be exceedingly flexible and productive. Second, in service-oriented organizations it is extremely difficult to gauge efficiency. It makes more sense to assess the *quality* of the services provided and of the decisions taken by the group. The benefits to morale of knowledge sharing may well improve the quality of services and decisions. Third, maximizing efficiency is, of course, not the most important goal to collectivist organizations.

In recent years, evidence has been mounting that small-scale, decentralized, participatory, and labor-intensive organizations may be just as productive and efficient – and by some criteria, more so – as large-scale, hierarchical, and capital-intensive modes of organization. This evidence calls into question a widely accepted tenet of economics and organizations theory.[13] Our data unfortunately, do not permit us to add to this line of argument. In the organizations we studied, schemes that broke down the conventional patterns of differentiation did strengthen collective control, but they also entailed at least short-term losses in organizational efficiency. It is possible that these losses represent only the startup costs of any new arrangement and that they would subside in the long run. In the absence of longer-term observations, conclusions cannot be drawn. However, given the rapid turnover of personnel in collectivist organizations and the fact that rotation systems are not one-time occurrences but are repeated periodically, it is difficult to see how the "startup costs" could ever disappear.

All organizations – democratic ones notwithstanding – encounter a "free rider" problem, the tendency for individuals to avoid taking on added responsibilities or costs where the benefits of such action would accrue to everyone (Olson, 1971). Collectivist organizations may be especially prone to this problem precisely because their egalitarian structure means that individuals will receive few extra rewards for whatever extra work they may do.

Members of collectives seldom, if ever, speak in terms of a "free rider problem," but they do wrestle with the problem in more concrete terms, asking frequently what they should do about "people who don't carry their weight" in the organization. Calhoun (1980) maintains that to have a full flow of all information to everyone in an organization would be prohibitively expensive in terms of transaction costs, making democratic organizations impractical.

However, collectives may operate in such a manner as to challenge Calhoun's assumptions. Abell argues that members may *democratically* decide to permit a certain level of differentiation of information, a decision consistent with democratic principles (Abell, 1981). On the basis of empirical observation, Mansbridge (1980) notes that consensual democratic groups need not share all information and decisions when there is a commonality of interests. Our observations, too, indicate that it is not equally important that all kinds of information be shared, and members realize this. Thus, a partial solution to the free rider problem may be built into the very structure of consensus decision making. The time consumed by the decision-making process has costs, but in the process of giving input and reaching common understandings, loyalty to the group and commitment to carrying out its objectives are being built.

Data from this study generally support the Weberian notion that the decisive reason for the advance of bureaucracy has been its purely technical superiority, its efficiency vis-à-vis all other forms of organization in history. Weber states this proposition clearly:

Precision, speed, unambiguity, knowledge of the files, continuity, discretion, unity, strict subordination, reduction of friction and of material and personal costs – these are raised to the optimum point in the strictly bureaucratic administration, and especially in its monocratic form. (Weber, 1946, p. 214)

For several decades, this proposition has been challenged by researchers in the Human Relations school of organizations. They have tried to demonstrate that more participatory organizations oriented to human relations stimulate greater worker satisfaction and thereby produce goods and services more efficiently.

In contrast, serious and thoroughgoing resistance to bureaucracy in collectives is based on other grounds. Although the Weberian adherent would defend bureaucracy as the most efficient and unambiguous mode of organization, the Human Relationist might retort, "No, more *satisfying* modes of organization are more productive and efficient." On the other hand, members of cooperatives might reply, "Yes, perhaps bureaucracies are more efficient, but who *wants* to maximize mere efficiency, precision, speed, continuity, and so on, anyway?" Where Human Relationists have attempted to challenge the *scientific* basis of the Weberian proposition, members of alternative institutions have generally challenged its *moral* basis.

Yet Weber might not have been so surprised had he seen the alternative, collectivist organizations develop in modern America. As he wrote: "[I]t is primarily the capitalist market economy which demands that the official business of the administration be discharged precisely, unambiguously, continuously, and with as much speed as possible" (Weber, 1946, p. 215). Since people in collectivist organizations generally have little interest in the success of the capitalist market economy, it follows that they would have low regard for its rationalistic basis.

Further, Weber might not have been altogether unprepared for a political strategy of building collectivist organizations. He recognized that parallel, autonomous, small-scale organizations, improbable as they seemed to him, were the *only* theoretical alternative to bureaucratic domination in modern society. This follows logically from his belief that once bureaucracy is firmly established, it makes a fundamental change in the structure of authority impossible, replacing it with mere changes in who controls the bureaucratic apparatus. Thus, from a Weberian perspective, the Marxist proletarian class strategy of seizing the capitalists' bureaucratic machinery is possible, but is not revolutionary. It is only a coup d'etat (Weber, 1968, pp. 987–989). The later Marxian stage, "the withering away of the state," is revolutionary for Weber, but utopian. Thus, the creation of parallel, small-scale organizations alongside of bureaucratic monoliths is the only limited, but plausible, way "to escape the influence of the existing bureaucratic apparatus" to which Weber alludes (1968, p. 224).

The dialectics of demystification

The process of rationalization has long appeared, much as Weber described it, to be progressive. We wish to consider a counterhypothesis: that the process of rationalization is dialectical in nature, that it is inherently self-destructive.

Although the word *demystification* does not appear in many modern dictionaries, it has become a favorite and frequently used term in collectivist organizations. This word perhaps more than any other distinguishes the ethos of collectivist organizations from that of bureaucratic organizations. Demystification was defined earlier as the process whereby formerly exclusive, obscure, or esoteric bodies of knowledge are simplified, explicated, and made available to the membership at large. In its essence, demystification is the opposite of specialization and professionalization. Where experts and professionals seek licenses to hoard or at least get paid for their knowledge, collectivists would give it away. Central to their purpose is the breakdown of the division of labor and pretense of expertise. In effect, demystification reinforces egalitarian, democratic control over the organization, just as the subdivision of labor enhances managerial control over the workplace (Braverman, 1974).

In their everyday practices, people in collectives are insisting that much of what passes for expertise – not all – can be opened up and taught to any interested party, short-circuiting the usual years of training and certification. At first glance, they seem to be acting in a profoundly antirational manner. On another level, however, their efforts to extend knowledge to everyone suggests that they are taking rationality most seriously. The urge to demystify the world is at the core of rationalization (Weber, 1968; Whitehead, 1925).

A dialectical conception of the process of rationalization would lead us to the hypothesis that continued extension of the logic of rationality – the demand for the demystification of experts' knowledge – will produce the transcendence of specialized knowledge, the *ultimate* demystification.

In short form, this argument might go as follows. Weber was quite correct in seeing that rationality would entail the demystification of all domains of life. Therefore, to maximize formal rationality, bureaucracies would have to be arranged hierarchically, with authority based on the technical expertise of the officeholder. Consistent with Weber's intent, this implies that the superior has come to a more demystified understanding of some relevant part of the world, and is therefore more technically competent than the subordinate. However, Weber did not follow the demystification process to its logical extreme.

The logical conclusion of the demystification process is equal knowledge: the complete diffusion of knowledge. That is, in the extreme, everyone would have the same demystified understanding of the world. There would be no need for "doctors" because everyone could doctor themselves, no need for "teachers" for everyone could teach themselves, no need for "sociologists" because everyone would possess the "sociological imagination," and so forth. The extension of the process of demystification to these *theoretical* extremes would undercut the very basis of rational authority, namely, superior knowledge. That is, if all members were equally competent in the knowledge and skills relevant to the operations of an organization, there would be no rational basis for hierarchical authority.

Although it is not plausible that the historical process of ever-expanding demystification of the world will go to such lengths as to completely eliminate the basis for the division of labor and functional specialization, it is important to note that this is the direction in which further demystification takes us. Thus, although it is standard fare in social science to predict ever-greater differentiation, specialization, and professionalization in modern society, there is reason to suspect that these processes cannot continue ad infinitum. As people come to perceive their work as being subdivided to the point of absurdity, they may recoil and begin to build bridges between subspecialties. Some may even choose the route embarked upon by the collectivist organizations described herein: demystification, functional generalization, and the diffusion of hitherto exclusive knowledge.

5. External conditions that facilitate collectivist–democratic organizations

The ability of a collectivist organization to achieve its participatory-democratic aspirations is conditioned not only by factors internal to the organization, but also by factors in its environment. Parallel to Chapter 4, this chapter argues that certain external conditions facilitate collectivist–democratic modes of organization, that their absence tends to undermine such forms, and that choices regarding these conditions generate important organizational dilemmas.

Oppositional services and values

Collectivist enterprises are usually created because their founders see some important social need that is unfilled by conventional businesses or public agencies. They perceive an opportunity to provide a social benefit at the same time they are creating an organization embodying their democratic ideals. Thus collectives often emerge from a two-pronged critique of mainstream society: a critique of the internal structure of rule-bound hierarchical organizations, and a critique of the failure of these organizations to meet social needs. Since the new collective tries to avoid direct competition with larger, more resource-rich organizations, it can hope to build its own market and niche. Alternative enterprises do best when they are able to ferret out a market that mainstream organizations cannot or will not enter because the product requires handmade or custom production, because public agencies fail to provide a required service, because mainstream businesses do not perceive the market for the alternative service, or because the service is illegal, as in the case of the abortion collective. Like any small business, collectivist firms must foresee potential markets and must pay the start-up costs of innovation. Thus, innovation and a burning sense of mission are often born of social criticism. *Both an oppositional stance vis-à-vis established institutions and the provision of qualitatively different products or services therefore tend to go hand in hand in collectivist enterprises. Both factors tend to unify and sustain democratic organization.*[1]

Our findings suggest that democratic organizations are likely to succumb to more merely cost-efficient modes of organization if they produce goods or services that are similar to or competitive with those produced by bureaucratic enterprises. The integrity of the collectivist organizational form is most readily maintained where the product or service of the organization is qualitatively different from that produced by dominant organizations.

All of the organizations in this study tried to provide services or goods that were different in quality from those provided by established institutions. The Free Clinic, for instance, was committed to preventive medicine, free medical care, understanding by patients of the healing process, and a wholistic approach to mental and physical health – principles that it assumed the "straight" medical delivery system did not share. Likewise, Freedom High assumed that its loose structure, its focus on learning outside the classroom, its attention to affective development, its highly critical perspective on social and economic institutions, and its measure of student control over the schooling process were anathema to the public school system. The *Community News* tried to select and present the news from a left perspective with the avowed purpose of liberalizing the local political climate. The Food Co-op sold food at cost, tried to carry only wholesome foods, educated its member-customers about nutrition, and supported other community-owned economic organizations, all of which distinguished it from privately owned, profit-based food stores. The Law Collective, in the cases it sought or avoided for social, political, or ethical reasons, defined itself as an alternative legal service. Similarly, the successful worker collectives studied by Sandkull (1982) all had found special market niches, providing quality goods or services not readily available elsewhere, such as a tofu factory, a natural foods bakery, a low-cost home construction and repair service, and a wholesale distributor of bulk natural foods.

Members' perceptions of being oppositional and therefore the target of outside harassment serve to solidify these groups and to justify their existence as "alternative institutions" in an otherwise bureaucratic society. This sense of opposition, buttressed by the perception of external harassment, is found generally in collectives.

An oppositional stance vis-à-vis established institutions does not permeate all cooperative organizations, however. In cases where worker-ownership has emerged as an attempt to save jobs in a plant closure situation, workers may feel grateful to the banks and government agencies for putting up the loan capital that allowed their new enterprise to get off the ground. This sense of positive identification with established institutions may inhibit, at least for a time, the development of a sense of group cohesion. Without a strong sense of group cohesion, these new groups of worker-owners may not be motivated to challenge traditional managerial prerogatives or to insist on participation rights for themselves.[2]

In many other cases cooperatives have felt discriminated against by banks, and this was part of the justification for creating the National Consumer Cooperative Bank in 1980. For example, when Hubbard & Company, a utility pole hardware manufacturer, went out of business, its 100 workers sought to buy it. The banks that held the company's debt rejected the plan, reportedly because they felt worker ownership to be unworkable. In another case of a privately held firm that was closing down, Yellow Cab of Oakland, California, its workers found that their loan applications to purchase the company were refused, whereas the offer of a private buyer was accepted (Kepp, 1981, p. 30).

By and large collectives expect little support from established institutions, and in fact may be subjected to harassment. Freedom High had a multitude of fire and building code violations charged against its storefront location. Even in locations where code violations are commonly neglected, they were often carefully enforced against urban free schools (Kozol, 1972). In another case, when the local university student government voted to grant the Food Co-op start-up money, the university administration took the unprecedented stance of trying to disallow the expenditure. The co-op was required to demonstrate to the administration that the co-op would be taking business largely from a supermarket a few miles from campus and not from the small food stores in the community adjacent to campus. One co-op founder charged "the university administration didn't like the idea of the co-op underselling local capitalist grocers and maybe putting them out of business." True or not, the university chancellor was widely known to have personal economic interests in the local community.

Feminist health centers around the country have so often felt they were the targets of harassment by the medical establishment that they have created a national network of women's health centers, WATCH (Women Acting Together to Combat Harassment) to protect themselves. In a famous case, the founder of the Los Angeles Women's Health Center, Carol Downer, was arrested and charged with practicing medicine without a license. Her defense, based on a woman's right to examine her own body, was successful in court (Reinharz, 1983, p. 46).

Usually discrimination against collectives is more subtle. The Franchise Tax Board in California refused to grant the Food Co-op the tax-exempt status it requested. Although the co-op was able to show that no member or owner received any profit or inurement from the co-op, the Tax Board maintained that the members received an indirect inurement in the form of lower food prices; hence the co-op was denied a nonprofit tax-exempt status. Board members of the co-op saw this as a form of blatant political harassment:

It [the letter of denial] was definitely written by a crew cut Bircher type who doesn't like co-ops competing with capitalist businesses.

The Food Co-op also had to pay unusually high prices to its wholesale food distributor. This is a problem faced by many food co-ops because of the relatively small volume of food they order (Giese, 1974; Zwerdling, 1975) and this is the reason co-ops are now developing in the wholesale area too. Members of the staff and board at the co-op strongly suspected that their particular wholesale distributor overcharged them because he objected to their politics. They also believed that since he knew they sold the food at cost he felt he could get by with charging them more. Similarly, workers at TRICOFIL, a worker-owned clothing manufacturer in Quebec, felt that certain large retail stores were boycotting their goods because the stores were politically hostile to worker co-ops.[3]

Whether or not charges of harassment are warranted, collectives often use opposition to mainstream institutions as a strategy. The collective's sense of mission and its internal unity are strengthened by pointing to the perceived reactionary, inept, or obsolete character of established institutions. Students and staff at Freedom High, for instance, often talked about the archaic systems and competitive values of the public school in order to positively justify the existence of their alternative. The Free Clinic did likewise with respect to the local health delivery system. Both groups ridiculed the most inadequate aspects of mainstream institutions, precisely because such aspects, used as a foil, made the alternative organization appear that much more progressive and needed.

As an illustration, the Free Clinic spent half of a staff meeting deriding "Concerned Parents," a Mormon-based group that opposed the continuation of all sex education classes in the local public school system. The Free Clinic in conjunction with Planned Parenthood had an extensive sex education speakers' program in the public high schools to protect. The ostensible purpose of the discussion at the Free Clinic's staff meeting was to choose someone to attend the Board of Education meeting who could extoll the merits of the clinic's sex education program. However, most of the time was spent simply burlesquing the antiquated attitudes of Concerned Parents. Concerned Parents made a good target for attack precisely because the issue they represented was so culturally symbolic. Lines could be clearly drawn. By focusing on this group, whether or not it represented a real threat to the clinic's sex education program, staff at the clinic enhanced their sense of unity and mission.

This illustrates the general function that an oppositional stance serves in collectivist organizations. It strengthens the groups' sense of solidarity and purpose. In the extreme, an organization may be so oppositional in the services it provides as to be illegal, as in the case cited earlier of "Jane," the abortion collective. There is little doubt from Bart's observations (1981, pp. 17–19) of this group, that the confidentiality required by such a setup helped knit the group tightly together.

If collectivist–democratic organizations benefit from an oppositional stance vis-à-vis established institutions, then we should expect that *the introduction of reforms in the dominant, target institution, along the lines that the collectivist organization pioneered, would weaken the once-oppositional organization.*

This expectation is strongly supported by our research. For instance, during Freedom High's third year of operation, the liberalization of some of the local public school programs attracted many Freedom High students back to the public system and undercut the justification for having a free school. Likewise, at the elementary school level, once the local public school opened its own "alternative school" (consisting of three classrooms), the elementary free school folded. This has indeed been the fate of many free schools around the nation, as public schools have increasingly incorporated the reforms of the free school movement. This change may represent a success for the free school movement, if not for Freedom High itself, since it signifies that the oppositional organization has now achieved the acceptance of some of its social criticisms and the institutionalization of some of its reforms.

Rape crisis centers are another illustrative case. They started in the mid-1970s very much as grass-roots collectives, based on a harsh criticism of the lack of needed shelters and other supports for women who are victimized by violence. In addition to providing a service, the centers worked together, creating a network to rally support for legislative change. By 1980, rape crisis centers were mandated in the Mental Health System Act passed by Congress, and since then many states have passed laws to fund spouse abuse and rape centers (typically through a marriage license surcharge). This means that the centers, originally a self-help alternative service with a burning sense of mission and criticism of the mainstream's insensitivity to the problem, now have been fully integrated into the publicly funded Community Mental Health Centers, be that good or bad.[4]

The converse of this principle seems to operate as well. That is, collectives may flourish because of the character of the dominant organization they oppose. The *Community News* enjoyed a more rapid expansion of its circulation than it had projected at its inception. In three years the paper grew to a paid readership of 10,000 and a circulation of 22,000 – in a time when many community newspapers were declining and folding.[5] At least in part, this success was attributable to the very conservative cast of the dominant local newspaper, which gave the *News* the opportunity to reach the large group of moderate and liberal readers in the area. The dominant newspaper did not respond, leaving the *News* with its own audience and niche.

Again, it is clear that collectivist organizations thrive where they provide a product or a service that is qualitatively different from that provided by mainstream enterprises. They must fill a social need that is, for one reason or another, neglected by conventional businesses or public agencies. An oppositional stance reinforces the collective's sense of unity and mission, and the alternative products or services that it provides may secure for it a market niche. However, should the dominant target institution change to accommodate the alternative organization's purposes, then the once-oppositional organization may find itself without a niche or a rationale for existence.

This is a dilemma for collectivist organizations. They see an unfilled social need to which they want to respond. Often they would like to have some widespread effect on society. But if they reach a mass market with their qualitatively different product or service, that (now-proven) product or service may be taken over – and often watered down – by dominant organizations, undercutting the alternative organization's basis for existence. In this way, alternative organizations may sometimes have the ironic effect of strengthening dominant organizations by absorbing the risks and costs of experimentation and innovation for them.

Supportive professional base

The collectivist organization is facilitated too by having a supportive professional base in its community. The local environment most favorable to the development of participatory-democratic organizations would combine a vulnerable target institution, which leaves significant local needs unmet, with a large and supportive professional population.

The relationship between the collectivist organization and its relevant professional community can go awry in two directions.

First, rather than support, professionals may oppose or even actively harass a collective. A feminist women's health clinic in Florida found local doctors threatening to withhold hospital privileges, intimidating the physicians who worked for the collective, and filing unfounded complaints with the local

Board of Medical Examiners. The staff members of the clinic, suspecting both sexism and economic motives (the clinic charged much lower fees than private physicians), finally filed a federal court suit charging certain private physicians with conspiracy to restrain trade in violation of the Sherman Antitrust Act (see the *Poverty Law Report* by the Southern Poverty Law Center, summer 1976, p. 6).

Second, at the opposite extreme, professionals may smother the organization with overzealous support. At the Milkwood Cooperative in England, professionals and academics seized on the idea of setting up a cooperative that would hire and train young unemployed people to repair wooden pallets, utilize experienced carpenters to train the young people, and do it all in democratically managed cooperative form. To make this possible, they received a government grant. The outside professionals and university people founded the co-op, but in time they were supposed to fade away. In reality, they became the management committee for the co-op.

The result was organizational failure. The skilled carpenters were frustrated by the dull, unimaginative work, and felt that the co-op form robbed them of the authority they needed to effectively control and train the young workers. The trainees also hated the boring work and saw the cooperative form as an invitation to malinger. The experiment lasted a total of 19 months. One researcher, with wry British understatement, summed up the experience:

Their experience, admittedly short, of working in a co-operative structure does not seem to have inspired those who worked in the enterprise with the philosophy of working co-operatively. It might be true to say that they regarded it as something of a joke, part of a game which academics play. . . . On leaving Milkwood the carpenters were unanimous in their condemnation. . . . As for furthering the cooperative cause, Milkwood cannot be said to have done the movement a service. (Rhoades, 1981, p. 36)

The overextended role of outside professionals was not the only reason for Milkwood's difficulties. Other factors included the heterogeneous work force, the dependence on outside funding, the conflicting goals of the various parties, and a dubious commitment to democracy on the part of participants. Yet Milkwood does clearly indicate the limits of professional support. Although outside professional have a valuable role to play in offering their services when requested, they cannot create co-ops out of whole cloth for others to work in. By their very nature, worker co-ops must be grass roots in origin, created by those who would work in them. Paternalistic ventures such as Milkwood, founded and managed by well-meaning outside professionals, represent a contradiction: By imposing their conception of "cooperation" on the enterprise, outsiders can only deny self-determination, the fundamental characteristic of organizational democracy.

The collectivist organizations we studied did not suffer from professional hostility, or overzealousness. They were fortunate to find in their community supportive professionals appropriate to their needs. The geographical location of these organizations, having a very attractive physical setting and climate, attracts more than its share of service workers of every profession. It is also the site of a university campus that adds greatly to the local professional population.

Professionals contributed to the maintenance of the collectivist organizations we studied in a variety of ways. For example, sympathetic professors set up a special course as a conduit through which university students could be channeled into community organizations for course credit. Without the steady supply from this course of well-educated volunteer teachers, Freedom High probably could not have existed for long. The Free Clinic recruited volunteer doctors mainly from the ranks of residents and marginally employed doctors in town. This feat would be more difficult in a city where doctors are encumbered, or blessed, by a higher ratio of patients per doctor. Another study of free clinics (Taylor, 1976) found the support of a liberal professional community important to the survival of free clinics. The Food Co-op got off the ground with seed money from a nearby university. Later, it was allowed the free use of the largest auditorium on campus for five consecutive academic quarters, and each use of the auditorium translated into a $500 to $2000 fundraiser for the co-op. A sympathetic accountant did the Food Co-op's books for no fee at tax time. The *Community News* enlisted the free talents of several professors who wrote regular columns or special features.

In short, sympathetic professionals contribute to the development of collectivist organizations in a variety of direct and indirect ways.[6] Similarly, Stern and Hammer (1978) find that professionals who are willing to donate their time and services have helped many worker-owned firms get off the ground. A collectivist organization located in a town without a base of relevant professional support, such as a free school in a town without a surplus of teachers, or a free medical clinic in a town without many doctors, is likely to find existence more tenuous.

We have made the case that collectivist organizations are facilitated by a sense of opposition toward mainstream institutions and, simultaneously, they benefit from the support of professionals who are often employed in such mainstream organizations. Thus, the last two external conditions we have posed are paradoxically related. The need to maintain an oppositional stance toward established institutions, coupled with the need to attract professional support *from* established institutions, tends to put the cooperative organization in a bind. This may produce ambivalent attitudes and inconsistent organizational behaviors. Although these two needs place the alternative organization squarely on the horns of a dilemma, they are not, in the last analysis, irreconcilable.

Consider the case of the *Community News*. The conflict was experienced by members at the paper as a desire to be "radical" (thereby pleasing oneself and one's reference group) versus a desire to be "respectable" (thereby appealing to a broader constituency). To the extent that the *News* was seen as radical in form and content, members could find personal justification and a sense of purpose in their work, but to the extent that it was seen as respectable, members believed they would attract broader community support in the form of readership and advertising. Staff members at the paper felt genuine conflicts about this:

I want the paper to be respectable. This will give us the wide circulation and success we want and will mean more money for staff. But I fear that too much respectableness could defeat our purpose of being an alternative. . . . There's a dilemma between being a daring alternative paper and having a wide constituency. I think we could be more daring.

Later in the same meeting, another staff member replied:

We've done some misleading titles that slap adversaries in the face. We've been too daring at times. . . . We need to establish more contact and possible rapport with adversaries. We should try to educate people we write about and interview, not just view them as objects of exposure.

The quest for respectability was sometimes treated at the *News* as a mere source of cooptation. In reality, it was more than that. The paper's original ambition was to reach and alter the attitudes of people who did not consider themselves "radical" and who would not be likely to read an alternative newspaper. *News* staffers hoped to forge a political coalition of all shades and types of progressives, and to use the paper to mobilize such people around progressive local issues. Hence, the achievement of the paper's original social change goals required a certain measure of respectability in the community. The *News* was started as an instrument of change, and in order to reach the unconvinced, it had to appear legitimate.

The dilemma arises, we would argue, from the paper's dual need to maintain an oppositional stance toward established institutions while it tried to attract support, readership, and advertising from those institutions.

The way in which the *Community News* experienced this dilemma was, in some respects, unique among the collectivist organizations in this study. First, the paper provided a product, not a service. As such, it was not client based. Client-based organizations can cultivate, if they wish, a rather homogeneous clientele, but it is in the very nature of a newspaper – especially one with social change goals – that it must appeal to a relatively heterogeneous population. Hence, the "respectability" issue would seem to be of more practical urgency for the *News*.

In a characteristic alternative service organization, such as the Free Clinic, the dilemma was reflected in the clinic's inconsistent posture toward its board of directors. In the early years of the Clinic, the staff sought out the most respectable, prestigious community leaders in the field of health for its board. Over time, board members came to question the less traditional services the clinic provided – they wanted to reduce the health education and counseling components – and to oppose the collectivist-egalitarian structure of the clinic, preferring instead a hierarchical structure with a director at the top. These differences led to a long series of battles between staff and board. Staff came to refer to certain members of the board as the "old guard," and to defend vehemently the oppositional practices of the clinic:

We have a choice. We can do health care the board's way, and be no different than any public health agency and be guaranteed to last forever. Or we can stick to our vision and be a true alternative and probably not last that long. . . . What makes the [Free Clinic] different than any public health bureau is our patient advocates, our staff being a collective, health ed and peer counseling, preventive medicine, our lack of professionalism. That's what I'm here for. The old guard wants us to give up just the things that make this place different than any other place to work.

These struggles finally culminated in the "old guard's" resignation from the board of directors, an event that received considerable local media coverage.

Taking the long view, a former staff member of the clinic commented:

There's no reason to have to lose those members of the board like this. It doesn't look good for the clinic and was totally unnecessary. They could have been phased into a Community Advisory Board and been innocuous there . . . but instead the staff let the old guard go along on the board, and then created a clash. They made those board members feel like their contributions were useless and unwanted for three years. That's not even true. There was a time when the staff really needed that board. . . . They made an important contribution to the clinic's acceptance in the community . . . made it seem more reliable. Now they create this clash and kick them off. It was unnecessary.

We would argue that the staff's inconsistent posture toward its board at the Free Clinic reflected essentially the same dilemma that the *Community News* faced. The clinic had to walk a tightrope. To some elements of its support base, particularly health professionals, government officials and foundations, it had to appear respectable and reliable. A prestigious board was instrumental in cultivating this image. To other elements of its support base, namely to paid staff, volunteers, and patients, it had to appear to be in opposition to mainstream medicine. It came to be extremely difficult, if not impossible, for the staff to maintain an image of struggling against "the system" when their

board consisted of shining representatives of that system. Conspicuously removing the "old guard" from the board helped to correct that imbalance, and
served to reassert the oppositional quality of the clinic. A half-year later –
and without those prestigious members of the board – the clinic found it could
still impress the County Board of Supervisors, the County Health Department, and various private foundations enough to be trusted with grants. At
the same time, it managed to convince patients and volunteers that it was
radical enough to be trusted with alternative services. Indeed, in a survey
study of this question, O'Sullivan (1977) finds that health collectives that are
more tied to mainstream institutions do *not* attract more clients, but they are
able to recruit more volunteers.

This same dilemma was reexpressed in numerous incidents at the Free
Clinic. On one occasion, the Free Clinic was offered space in a new neighborhood medical building built by the County Health Department. Such a
move offered the clinic an opportunity to leave its crowded, though colorful
and homey, quarters for a much larger and improved medical facility. Some
staff favored the move on the grounds that the new facility would make the
clinic more respectable and would attract sorely needed physicians to work at
the clinic, and its larger size would allow the clinic to serve more clients.
Others among the staff argued that any addition in clients permitted by the
larger size of the new facility would be more than offset by its barren quality
and thus it would be indistinguishable from any conventional medical setting.
Further, it was argued that because the new medical facility was across the
street from a police station:

women wanting abortions, people dropping reds, lots of people would be paranoid.
Rational or not, lots of patients wouldn't come to the [Free Clinic]. They'd be afraid
it was bugged or that they were being watched entering.

This situation put the clinic in a quandary. If the clinic moved into the new
medical building, it would have greatly improved facilities, making it more
appealing to professionals, but perhaps suspect to another necessary part of
its support base – its patients and volunteers. Again we see a case in which
the need of the Free Clinic to present an oppositional image (particularly to
its clients, volunteers, and staff) was in conflict with its need to present a
respectable image (particularly to its professional supporters). Eventually, the
clinic settled the issue by deciding not to move to the new building.

In the above example the conflict was between the desires of clients, volunteers, and staff members on the one hand, and professional supporters on
the other. In other instances, clients may line up on the side of the professionals, pushing for greater respectability and less "alternativeness." For instance,
in its early days the Free Clinic tried to appeal to three client groups – blacks,

Chicanos, and youth culture. Staff soon learned, as one of the founders of the clinic explained:

that these three groups do not interrelate too well, that we really should make a selection as to whom we were going to serve and go for that wholeheartedly. We selected the counterculture. . . . The counterculture group is very casual . . . barefoot, casual, wild colors . . . and the Chicano and the black have grown up with the image of medical care as being – if it's too casual it's second class, and they want the best because they think they've never gotten the best. They want the doctor in the white coat, everything spic and span, just right.

Thus, another clinic was opened later, one with white walls and so forth, and it attracted a tremendous minority clientele. This reserved for the Free Clinic the types of clients who would prefer its oppositional image.

When a collectivist organization is trying to broaden its constituency (of clients or customers), as the *Community News* did or the Free Clinic in its early days, customer demands may push it toward less alternativeness. For example, in her study of free clinics, Taylor (1976) found that black clients wanted "real" doctors and a clean modern clinic, and Katz (1975) discusses the same tension between alternativeness and minority community control in schools.

Not all collectivist organizations make outreach efforts to broaden the base of their clientele or customers. Freedom High appealed only to its "natural" constituency of affluent, white, hip students, as did the Free Clinic after its initial experimentation with a broader clientele. The members of the Food Co-op were also an entirely self-selected group. Thus, it appears that whether the clients of an alternative organization push it toward an oppositional stance or a harmonious stance vis-à-vis established institutions depends on the social base from which clients are drawn.

In sum, collectivist organizations are bolstered by an oppositional stance toward established institutions, but they also depend to some extent on professional support from established institutions. Sometimes these two needs are not in tension, as when the alternative attracts the support of professionals who are themselves critical of established institutions. Often, however, these two needs are in conflict. In such circumstances, the alternative must engage in a delicate balancing act, seeking creative solutions, and being careful not to ignore any element in its support base.

Social movement orientation

The preceding two conditions (opposition to target institutions, and support of professionals) refer to the relationship between the alternative organization and its "straight" environment, that is, the dominant institutions and the persons who live and work in them. However, the collectivist organization may be surrounded too by many other social movement organizations. The way in which these alternative organizations relate to one another is often crucial, as is the nature of the connection between individual organizations and the larger social movement of which each is a part.

All of the organizations in this study may be classified as social movement organizations because they are oriented toward goals of social and personal change and because participation in them is motivated by values, friendships, and material incentives, in that order (Zald and Ash, 1966, p. 329).

We hypothesize that *the more a collectivist organization remains identified with and oriented toward the broader social movement that spawned it, the less likely it is to experience goal displacement.*

There is a tendency widely reported in the literature (Zald and Ash, 1966) for the founding generation of members of social movement organizations to be attached to the wider social movement, but for the second generation of members to be much more oriented toward the goals and services of only that particular organization. Earlier we described such a transition at Freedom High. The rise of an organizationally bound attitude among the new generation of staff members leads them to see their own futures as tied to the life and success of the organization, not to the movement. Hence, they become more likely to pursue organizational maintenance as an end in itself. Members narrow their sights toward providing a good service vis-à-vis other organizations in the same arena, but they may lose the larger vision of social-historical change out of which their organization was born.

This conservatism of organizational purpose, although not unusual, does not appear to be inevitable. Organizations can maintain a movement orientation into the second generation and beyond. The broader visions of the movement can provide an ideological anchor, enabling the organization to resist displacement of goals over time. At the *Community News* for example, the second generation of staff members continued to practice advocacy journalism and to press for local social change.

The organizations in this study all began with the aim of helping to create an entire "alternative community" or "cooperative sector." The possibility of building a mutually supportive network of community-controlled organizations depends on each group maintaining a movement orientation over an organizationally bound one. Members reflect their identification with "The Movement" not only by providing support services to its people and to new movement organizations, but also by dropping out of alternative organizations they see as no longer contributing to the broader goals of the movement, and by joining other organizations that do. The latter phenomena often appear in case studies as instances of individuals getting "burned out," but our comparative study reveals a different picture. For example, many of the founders of Freedom High dropped out at the end of its second year of operation, convinced, as one of them put it, that:

providing a groovy education to upper middle-class kids isn't the most revolutionary activity in the world.

Although at the time the "burned out" interpretation was used to account for this exodus, these same people show up later as committed members of the *Community News,* the Free Clinic, and the Law Collective. Their first allegiance was to "The Movement," not to any particular organization that currently housed them.[7]

Other researchers have observed a tendency for the personnel of social movement organizations to flow back and forth among various movement organizations, government agencies, and professional schools, all of which are devoted to a single set of policy issues (McCarthy and Zald, 1973). Our own data reinforce this observation. For example, a Freedom High staff member went on to study "confluent education" in a graduate school of education, and showed up later administering a publicly financed "open classroom" project. There were also numerous instances of staff in one movement organization who later became part of other movement organizations with seemingly disparate concerns, such as one person who switched from a free school, to an ecology action organization, to a free medical clinic.

The flow of personnel from one type of movement organization to another can be understood by developing a "movements-within-a-movement" perspective. That is, at least for some participants, the free school movement, the ecology movement, the free clinic movement, and the like are all considered subsidiary to "The Movement." For such people, these submovements are unified and assume importance only in relation to the broader social movement from which they sprang. If we employ a movements-within-a-movement perspective, we take seriously the words of some of the participants that they are part of "one struggle with many fronts." When collectivist organizations are viewed as entirely unconnected organizations, the rapid ebb and flow of personnel in and out of them is thought to reflect a fickleness of commitment, or burn-out. However, to begin to see them, as many of the participants do, as subsidiary movements within an overarching movement is to recognize a basic coherence and consistency in the actions of individual participants.

Alternative organizations give evidence of an identification with broader movements in a variety of ways. Foremost, they usually provide services to other members of the "alternative community" and to other local movement organizations. People at the *Community News* sometimes sought medical attention at the Free Clinic, some of the volunteers at the Free Clinic bought their food at the Food Co-op, staff at the Law Collective sent their children to Freedom High, and so on. Since the cooperative community is an important reference group to most members of cooperative enterprises, members are often sensitive to the needs of individuals in that community. Some collectivist organizations go further. They try to provide direct support for other community-based alternative organizations. The Food Co-op, for instance, chose to deposit its assets from membership shares in a cooperatively owned credit union rather than in a privately owned bank. It likewise entered into a joint program with a nearby medical clinic to raise consciousness about nutrition. The *Community News* published a lot of feature stories on community-based organizations in town, thereby giving newly created collectivist organizations some public exposure and giving the public, or would-be clients, a chance to learn about alternative services.

The linkages at the community level between different types of collectivist enterprises do not stop with the support services they provide each other. They are also linked through shared boards of directors. As with corporations, such interlocks allow the heads (or in this case, the activists) of the constitutive organizations to be only a few "steps" from each other, thus easing communication, coordination, and collaborative action among them (Sonquist and Koenig, 1975; Whitt, 1982; Mariolis, 1975).

Consider the following illustration. One night, in the metropolitan area we studied, a group of community activists got together to launch an ad hoc ecology action organization. Its single purpose was to organize a large-scale national conference on energy. The "energy crisis" had recently become a national public event, and the conference was intended to raise public awareness of the politics of the oil-energy industry and of environmentally sound alternative sources of energy. The conference was a natural rallying point for the many environmentalist groups in town. However, bringing it off would take money – and time was short. A city council meeting was approaching in a few days and the newly formed group felt that it could win financial support from the city for the project if it could get the endorsements of respected, ongoing community and environmentalist organizations. The group brainstormed a list of 18 relevant organizations. The people present divided up the task of soliciting endorsements: "I'll call ———, he can give us the Sierra Club"; and so on. Finally the group seized on the name of a friend – Paul Q. Citizen – who, as it turned out, sat on 9 of the needed boards. One phone call to Paul is all that it took to deliver 9 of the 18 targeted endorsements. The rest was downhill. Group 10, after all, could be assured that groups 1 through 9 had already endorsed the project, and so on. The new group got the needed endorsements, it got city funding, and the conference became a reality.

As this example suggests, the number of informal, interpersonal ties among community activists is typically quite impressive. Many activists are involved in a number of community organizations at the same time, and, as pointed out earlier, many flow from one collectivist organization to another over time. Thus, when the board of directors at the Food Co-op tried to change their weekly meeting night in order to accommodate a new member, they could not do it: Virtually every other night of the week some members were obliged to attend the regular meetings of other community organizations.

On a formal level, people such as Paul Q. Citizen serve on the boards of directors of a variety of different movement organizations. Such people become pivotal for movement activity in a given locale. Unlike corporate interlocks, movement interlocks are still in a nascent state; they are developing at the community or regional level, not as often at the national level; and of course they have only a tiny sliver of the resources that corporate boards have. Even so, movement interlocks, like corporate ones, have the overriding advantage of allowing seemingly diverse organizations the possibility of effectively coordinating and uniting their action. Just as interlocks among corporate leaders help to integrate the economy by putting general corporate interests over the interests of particular organizations (Useem, 1984), the growing network of interlocks among community movement organizations reflects, and helps to create, a general movement-orientation over an organizationally bound one.

Not all signs, however, point to the prevalence of a general movement orientation in collectivist organizations. People in such organizations may also have a strong identification with the particular submovement of which they are a part, such as free schools, food co-ops, free clinics, and so on.

During the year when field observations were made of the Food Co-op, the co-op aided the creation and development of four young food co-ops within a 100-mile radius; it sent a member more than 1,500 miles away to learn firsthand about the history and operation of a successful and long-standing consumer co-op in Canada; and it sent several representatives to the inaugural meeting of the Western Region of Co-ops. The birth of the Western Region of Co-ops in 1974, dedicated to seeking solutions to common co-op problems, reflected the proliferation of food co-ops that was taking place in the West. It had counterparts in other parts of the country, and in other institutional domains, as in the free school movement and the free clinic movement. Freedom High, the *Community News,* and the Free Clinic also participated in the regional and national conferences of their respective submovements.

Of all these submovements, the free school movement was the earliest to develop. In 1967, free schools were just beginning: There were 30 in the United States. By 1973, more than 800 "outside-the-system" free schools existed, not counting the innumerable open classrooms and alternative schools within public school systems that were by then operating (*New Schools Exchange Newsletter,* 1967, 1973). As early as 1971, when there were some 350 documented free schools in the United States, 24 regional associations or networks had already been set up to act as clearinghouses of information and as placement services for interested students, parents, and teachers (Graubard, 1972). Many regional organizations produced newsletters and held conferences for free school people. Eight new periodicals of national scope were by then being published in North America, all aimed at criticizing the dominant educational system and working to create an alternative one. Freedom High staff were oriented to the larger free school movement, as was evidenced by their subscription to regional and national free school newsletters, by their attendance at regional free school conferences, and by their visits to other free schools.

The burgeoning of free clinics and feminist health clinics also turned into a well-developed submovement. The Haight-Ashbury Free Clinic in San Francisco was the first, having opened its doors in 1967. By 1971, there were 95 known free clinics in California alone.[8] Nationally, there were an estimated 340 free clinics by 1972. As with food cooperatives and free schools, free clinics created regional and national associations to help solve some of their shared problems. In 1970, the first regional association was founded in Southern California. As noted earlier, the rape crisis centers that proliferated in the mid- to late-1970s also created regional and national associations that lobbied for public monies and legislative reforms. In our own study, the Free Clinic sent representatives to the California regional conferences. The Free Clinic's identification with the free clinic movement was also demonstrated in the pride it took in rapidly filling up with its patient referrals two new neighborhood clinics in town.

The *Community News* and the Law Collective did not have such well-developed submovements with which they could identify, but in both cases such submovements were at least on the horizon. The *News* actively participated in the first national conference of alternative newspapers held in Boulder, Colorado, in 1975. At that meeting, attention began to be focused on the future possibility of sharing exceptional feature stories, articles, or columns from alternative newspapers, and even of creating an alternative wire news service. The *Community News* traded subscriptions with a large number of alternative newspapers and magazines, and regularly reviewed the contents of the alternative press for items it might want to use. Although it is clear that the *News* was oriented to the alternative media, the alternative press was not yet as plentiful or as developed as a social movement as the previously discussed submovements.

The Law Collective retained an active membership in the National Lawyers' Guild, a reform-oriented organization of lawyers founded in the 1930s. Through the guild, it supported the People's Law School, "the only radical law school in the country" (*New York Times,* October 16, 1975, p. 40). It was in touch with many other legal collectives through the guild. Despite this impressive beginning, the legal field is yet to generate the number of legal collectives needed to sustain more submovement activity.

The collectivist organizations in this study all identified with their respective subsidiary movements, but they were also more generally oriented to an overarching movement. We have introduced a "movements-within-a-movement" perspective with which to understand this dual orientation. Empirically, though, commitment to these two sides may not be equal.

A general movement orientation, as discussed earlier, has the virtue of militating against the cooptation of goals. If, however, the members of a collective are preoccupied with general movement goals to the exclusion of particular submovement or organizational goals, then they will fail to accomplish organizational ends and will be left with an organizational shell of little utility to anyone. If, on the other hand, a strong organizational orientation precludes a general movement orientation, then the organization may provide a good service vis-à-vis other organizations in the same domain, but it will probably lose its sense of social-historical purpose. Organizational maintenance as an end in itself, with its conservatizing influence, will then become a more likely prospect. Thus, the collectivist organization is faced with yet another dilemma: It must strike a delicate balance between being oriented enough toward the general movement to maintain its original sense of purpose and meaning, while being oriented enough toward particular organizational goals to be able to provide a useful service to its clients, members, or customers.

This balance is not easily maintained, and some of the organizations in this study appeared to lose their equilibrium. Freedom High, for example, was started by staff who had an overriding commitment to the larger social change movement, but their dedication to education per se was thin. In the last analysis, few of them believed a liberating education alone to be an especially vital source of societal change.

Freedom High had been politically inspired, and it was able to run for at least two years on the enthusiasm of political currents external to the school. Such enthusiasm allowed staff at the school to largely neglect its pedagogical purposes. During the first two years of its operation, the activist students who had helped found the school reported enjoying it, but, even by the end of the first year, the chorus "the school isn't academically rigorous enough" became a familiar one. It was the students who were voicing this concern. Two formerly active students, in follow-up interviews about their past experiences, said they deeply valued their experience at Freedom High, but they also assessed its major weaknesses:

I remember the fun of building a geodesic dome. Still it took a lot longer than it should have. And I enjoyed learning Chinese, for a while anyway. But the class only lasted a short while, and you can't learn Chinese in a few weeks no matter how smart you are. . . . Some of the bad . . . was the initial trauma of not learning much in the way of academics – and not being able to bring something home to my parents.

The bad thing about [Freedom High] was that we never really got anything together. Most of the stuff we started we never finished.

Another student reported that students' needs were sometimes ignored for the social-political concerns of the staff.

In short, if staff were to effectively combine the larger movement goals that guided the creation of Freedom High with an organizational orientation, they would have had to believe that high school education makes a difference, that it is at least a sensible route to social change. They were not convinced. Hence, there was little commitment to developing pedagogical skills. The school expended a good deal of effort expressing its political values (in its relationship to its environment and in generating a very high level of internal participation and democracy) but very little effort on the substance of schooling – the curriculum. As a result, the school could not progress toward distinctly educational goals. When the original staff left (largely at the end of the second year and completely by the end of the third year) it was not because the school was not effective educationally (though, in the main, it was not), but because the school as an institution was not viewed as an effective tool for social change. As one departing staff member explained:

We learned that it will be a very long time before this "new man" we of the revolution biz are always talking about can ever exist.

The first generation of staff members at Freedom High held allegiance primarily to "The Movement," not to Freedom High itself. After they left the school, some became committed members of the Law Collective, the Free Clinic, and the *Community News*. Others became involved in ecology action organizations and in organizing industrial workers in a nearby city. If we adopt a movements-within-a-movement perspective, this sort of ebb and flow of personnel in and out of seemingly disparate movement organizations takes on a new coherence. Nevertheless, we also witnessed the painful consequences that an extreme movement orientation had for Freedom High as a school.

The case of Freedom High is unusual in this respect. Members of a collectivist organization are seldom so preoccupied with general movement goals that they neglect particular organizational goals. More common is the case of the Free Clinic, where an organizational orientation comes to overwhelm a movement orientation.

From the first day of field observations at the Free Clinic, evidence of an organizationally bound orientation was apparent. After an initial introduction, one staff member boasted that the Free Clinic was probably the best free medical clinic on the entire West Coast. Another staffer disagreed: "No, the —— Clinic up in Oregon is probably better." Although people at Freedom High would not dream of rating their school vis-à-vis other free schools, this was a highly relevant consideration to staff at the Free Clinic. Where Freedom High sought out black and Chicano activist groups and other community organizations for cooperative relationships, the Free Clinic tended to look upon other medical clinics as potential competitors in an informally recognized pecking order of free clinics. Where Freedom High, the Food Co-op, and the *Community News* aggressively aided the development of other community-based organizations, members of the Free Clinic did not even consider nonmedical collectivist organizations to be a salient part of their reference group, and they felt no special obligation to the rest of the local alternative community. For instance, when the clinic needed a printer to do its formal annual report, a number of possible printers were discussed. Finally, the *Community News*, which also does outside printing jobs, was chosen, but not as a statement of support for an allied movement organization, nor as a matter of reciprocity for the several favorable and timely articles that the paper had done on the clinic. The paper was chosen simply because it was considered to be the best printer in town for the money. No mention of movement politics was ever made in the course of group discussion at the clinic.

Allegiance to organizational (in this case, medical) goals to the exclusion of broader movement goals was characteristic of the Free Clinic. In consequence, it meant that the clinic was more open to cooptation of its original social change goals, as when the Medi-Cal pamphlet was removed from circulation at the behest of an influential county official. It also meant that the clinic was less sensitive to sustaining a participatory-democratic form; for example, components meetings, the only direct input of volunteers into decision making, were suspended when some staff got too busy for them. As one staff member put it,

I wish we *did* do things so political as to endanger our financial support. But the truth is, we don't.

On the positive side, however, commitment to organizational goals over movement goals helped to ensure that a high quality and variety of medical services were provided to the clients.

In other words, both extremes – the dominance of a general movement orientation as well as the dominance of an organizationally bound one – entail important trade-offs. Some collectivist organizations are able to resolve this dilemma. They do this by skillfully integrating the particular goals of their respective organizations with the more general goals of "The Movement." This is possible when members believe that the particular goods or services that their organizations can provide, however modest they may be in terms of quantity, are nonetheless a vital tool for societal change. In the case of the Law Collective, for instance, one staff member put it this way:

Some of our early people weren't into legal work. . . . They left. All but one stayed with the movement though – in other ways, other places. Now we see doing good legal work as primary. Without it, we can't be effective politically.

In short, collectivist members must maintain an active concern for their organization if they are to provide a quality product or service, but they must maintain an identification with the general movement that first joined them if they are to contribute to its larger purposes. Some of the most successful cases of cooperative development have managed to maintain both. The Mondragon system has developed in a 25-year time span from a handful of people to more than 18,000 worker-owners in upwards of 80 cooperatives, at least partly because it found a way to respect the autonomy of the local co-op while allowing each co-op to gain the advantages of confederation. Using a similar balance, the Breman system of self-managed firms in Holland has grown from 2 enterprises with 150 workers to 12 firms with 600 workers in less than 10 years. At both Mondragon and Breman members are concerned with the well-being of their firms while also being concerned with the development of a cooperative sector (Logan, 1981; Johnson and Whyte, 1977; Rothschild-Whitt, 1981). In each, they have found practical ways to join hands with the other co-ops to buy supplies, obtain credit, develop markets, and train future workers. There is little question that confederations of this sort are to the mutual benefit of cooperatives, reflecting and helping to sustain their commitment to the goals of a larger movement.

Facilitating conditions: summary

Chapters 4 and 5 have presented, in propositional form, nine structural conditions that facilitate collectivist–democratic modes of organization. We have argued that the absence of each of them tends to undermine democratic forms, and each is shown to generate important organizational dilemmas.

Three further points are worth underscoring here. First, these are *not* definitional criteria, but *conditions* that facilitate democracy. They are not to be confused with necessary traits that would define organizational democracy (see Bernstein, 1976). Some or all of these facilitating conditions may not be present, and organizational democracy therefore suffers proportionally.

Second, many other outcomes or dependent variables could reasonably have been used instead of organizational democracy to assess these organizations, as, for example member satisfaction, organizational longevity, or quality of goods or services provided. We chose the level of organizational democracy because that is a central, defining characteristic of collectives, representing their most dearly held goal. Factors that promote a participatory-democratic form, such as a movement orientation, do not necessarily promote – and may even inhibit – the achievement of other possible organizational goals, such as the production of high-quality services or satisfied members. If the achievement of an egalitarian organization were their only priority, there would be little ambiguity, but collectivist organizations, like other organizations, often have multiple and conflicting goals. Under such circumstances, hard choices and dilemmas are inescapable.

Inescapable, but as we have also tried to show, not necessarily fatal for the collective or its goals. As is clear from our own case studies, and from the work of other researchers, some collectivist enterprises have been notably successful in building and retaining a democratic form while getting the job done very well.

Third, this list of conditions is not exhaustive. It is our hope that further studies of directly democratic organizations will uncover additional facilitating conditions. For instance, we did not examine the independent effect of democratic ideology because all of the organizations in this study contained many individuals who had strong democratic convictions. Other cooperative organizations might vary considerably on this score. We would certainly suspect that, as Bernstein (1976) and Gamson and Levin (1980) point out, variations in the level of democratic consciousness would have substantial bearing on the ability of an organization to function democratically. This issue may have special salience in employee-owned organizations where individuals have not previously developed participatory expectations and habits of

Table 5.1 *Summary of conditions and dilemmas*

Conditions	Effect of presence	Effect of absence	Organizational dilemmas
1. Provisional orientation	Militates against rigidification of rules and procedures, oligarchization, goal diffusion and organizational maintenance as an end-in-itself.	Permanence/careerist orientation promotes goal displacement (of all types), organizational maintenance, and oligarchization (especially when faced with member apathy).	If orientation is too transitory, then the organization may dissolve itself prematurely; the energy it took to build it will be needlessly wasted and useful social services ceased. If orientation is too permanent, then the organization may outlive its usefulness; it may displace its goals, rigidify its procedures and develop an oligarchy.
2. Mutual and self-criticism	As a regular and sanctioned process, criticism tends to level inequalities in influence and to curb individual assertions of power. It may also increase group morale and productivity.	Without a sanctioned process, criticisms tend to be illconsidered, totalistic, and unbound by any collective rules of fairness.	Ambivalence toward leadership: both need and resent informal leaders. Criticism levels undue influence and reasserts collective authority over individual authority, but "too much" risks losing the target of the criticism, often a valuable member.
3. Limits to size and internal growth	Deliberate limits to size and growth support familial and collectivist forms.	With unlimited growth, their personal and directly-democratic nature tends to be undone.	Large enough to obtain certain economies of scale (where relevant) but small enough to maintain collective control and sense of community.
4. Homogeneity	Common ethnic and/or cultural bonds foster group cohesion and ease consensus decision making.	Without the glue of a common background and values, groups may lack the level of trust and solidarity necessary for cooperation and consensual decisions.	The desire for homogeneity restricts the social base of the membership, making it less representative of the larger community, and in the extreme, the exclusion of "outsiders" may lead to the degeneration of the cooperative form.

5. Dependence on internal support base	Dependence on members and clients supports their participation and militates against goal displacement.	Dependence on external base of support (e.g., outside grants) tends to lower responsiveness to members and clients and to increase the likelihood of goal displacement and co-optation.	External financial support permits the organization to perform its services at less (or no) cost to clients, but it lowers participation of and responsiveness to members and clients and raises chance of goal co-optation.
6. Diffusion of knowledge and technology	If organizational technology is sophisticated then substantial knowledge diffusion is crucial to avoid monopolization of knowledge and oligarchization.	If technology is undeveloped and nonroutine, it does not lend itself to monopolization. But if technology is quite developed and concerted efforts to diffuse knowledge are not undertaken, then some individuals will be in a position to assert power and assume oligarchic control.	Where technology is developed, the processes of knowledge diffusion and demystification fortify collective control against oligarchization. But knowledge diffusion (e.g., job rotation, task sharing) may entail sacrifices in organizational efficiency and productivity.
7. Oppositional services and values	Heighten sense of purpose and solidifies group. Justifies collectivist forms and resistance to cost-efficiency criteria.	Undercuts sense of purpose. If mainstream institution is similar, undercuts justification for having an "alternative."	If stance toward established institutions is "too oppositional," then cannot get needed professional support from them. If stance is not oppositional enough, it may lose the allegiance of its members, volunteers, staff, or clients.
8. Supportive professional base	Channels human and financial resources from established organizations to alternatives; an indirect subsidy.	Lack of needed professional staff and volunteers. Loss of broad community respectability and support.	As above, most appeal to different elements in its support base. An oppositional image tends to garner the trust of volunteers, staff, clients, and members, but a respectable image tends to enlist the trust of relevant professionals.

Table 5.1 *Summary of conditions and dilemmas (cont.)*

Conditions	Effect of presence	Effect of absence	Organizational dilemmas
9. Social movement orientation	Lessens the likelihood of goal displacement, especially co-optation of goals.	Organization boundedness increases likeliness of organizational maintenance for its own sake, lowers levels of participation, and loss of original social change goals.	If oriented only to the general movement it may fail to accomplish organizational ends (i.e., providing worthwhile goods or services). If oriented only to the particular organization, it may lose its sense of social–historical purpose (conservatism of goals). Balance needed: particularistic service goals of the organization must be integrated with the general social change goals of the movement.

behavior. Zwerdling (1976) observed lack of experience with democracy as a problem at International Group Plans, a Washington, D.C., worker-run insurance company; and researchers in the New Systems of Work and Participation Program at Cornell University have also reported it at the various employee-owned workplaces they studied. Echoing the beliefs of the classical theorists of participatory democracy, the findings suggest that education for participation may indeed be an important part of any effective democratization process.

For the readers' convenience, Table 5.1 summarizes the past two chapters. It adumbrates the organizational effects of each of the proposed conditions, as well as the probable effects of their absence. The dilemmas they raise for collectivist organizations are also listed in abbreviated form.

Part III

The significance
of democratic organizations

6. Democracy and individual satisfaction

Anarchist writer Murray Bookchin once began a speech:

> You may have changes in the economy, you may have changes in who rules, you may have changes in who rules what and in who rules who, but there is no revolution without freedom, and there is no freedom without individuals controlling the conditions of their lives.[1]

Although Bookchin was not speaking of collectivist organizations per se, this quotation distills the essence of the meaning of collectivist organizations. They represent one part of a larger drive to recreate human-scale, decentralized institutions in the community and in the workplace. To the extent that they democratize organizations, they return the locus of control to the individual.

The concern of collectives with participation and democratic control makes them highly unusual as economic organizations. Profit ultimately justifies the existence of most economic organizations in a capitalist society. Corporations may speak of corporate responsibility, they may donate to philanthropic causes, and show concern for the morale of their employees, but in the end, success is judged on the basis of profit and growth. Although cooperative organizations must generate enough surplus to pay their worker-members a livable income, profit maximization is not the main point.

Benchmarks for assessing the success of capitalist organizations are well-established but for alternative organizations they are ambiguous and multifarious. Collectivist enterprises assess themselves in terms of how well they are practicing their democratic ideals, the quality of the products or services they are providing, their ability to provide alternative places of employment, the satisfaction of their members, and – most ambiguous of all – their contribution to larger societal change. The exact priority given to these different goals varies among collectivist organizations and within a single organization over time. This, of course, makes an evaluation of their success difficult. At a minimum, alternative benchmarks must be used.

So far, this work has focused on what many collective members would no doubt regard as the most central benchmark: the creation and maintenance of

145

organizational democracy. We have tried to identify structural factors that improve the chances for internal democracy. Accordingly, we have focused on the organization as our unit of analysis. In this final part of the book, however, we depart from the organizational level of analysis to look both above and below that level. We look above the organization to assess the future of collectives in general (Chapter 7) and to raise larger issues concerning the implications and social significance of democratic organizations (Chapters 7 and 8). We begin Part III by looking below the level of the organization to the level of the individual member, asking what meanings and consequences collectives hold for their members.

Democracy and worker expectations

The democratic process is valued by members of grass-roots cooperatives for its presumed connection to human happiness. People come to these organizations expecting the collectivist form to bring more autonomy, satisfaction, and meaning to their work. In this chapter we attempt to assess the extent to which collective work settings do in fact reduce work alienation and contribute to satisfaction.

Studies of work satisfaction constitute an enormous literature, and an area of continuing debate. Most of these studies have focused on either (1) occupational status (or prestige), (2) income, or (3) personal factors (e.g., values, sex, age, motivation, education) as major determinants of job satisfaction (e.g., Hall and Nougaim, 1968; Vroom, 1964). Other studies have looked at the effects of participation on job satisfaction (Blumberg, 1973; Frieden, 1980). Yet the *structural* attributes of *jobs* (e.g., the amount of control or autonomy workers have in the work situation, how interesting the job is) remain a relatively underdeveloped area of research. In a pathbreaking study, Kalleberg and Griffin (1978) demonstrate that the structural facts of *class* (i.e., whether incumbents own the means of production, control the labor power of others, or sell their own labor power) and *occupational position* (the job's placement in the technical division of labor, i.e., specific tasks performed, etc.) carry considerable power to explain variations in work satisfaction. Using a national labor force sample, Kalleberg and Griffin (1978) analyze the influence of class and occupational position on job satisfaction. They conclude that:

while occupational status exerts a net influence . . . class appears to be relatively more important as a source of inequality in job satisfaction. These results support . . . Marxian arguments about the psychological "costs" associated with membership in the working class. (Kalleberg and Griffin, 1978, p. 386)

The researchers find that both the working class and the petty bourgeoisie[2] have significantly lower job satisfaction than any other class. Workers are less satisfied because they receive relatively low financial rewards and because they work in jobs that are less intrinsically rewarding (i.e., that offer less control over the product and process of work and are less interesting). Workers would register even lower levels of satisfaction if it were not for the fact that, in these jobs that provide little control and interest, workers tend to scale down what they expect from the jobs, and lower expectations mean less active dissatisfaction (Kalleberg and Griffin, 1978, pp. 389–390). The petty bourgeoisie expect more, and are relatively low in satisfaction because:

[they] both attain and value intrinsic rewards to a greater extent than do workers, and such a valuation enhances satisfaction for this group. . . . They obtain less income than employers and top managers, however, and this depresses their level of job satisfaction. Overall, then, the petty bourgeoisie appear to balance their levels of rewards and values and report levels of satisfaction comparable to those observed for the working class. (Kalleberg and Griffin, 1978, p. 391)

No systematic studies of work satisfaction exist for cooperatives or collectives. The above findings do contain, however, several implications for what levels of work satisfaction we should expect to find in them. We argue that the structural dimension of work is particularly relevant to an assessment of work in cooperatives. As we detailed in Chapter 3, special structural features define the cooperative form, and also are the prime reason members are attracted to the democratic organization in the first place. Moreover – as we will shortly see – class factors are the appropriate dimension for assessing Marxian expectations concerning alienation.

The class position of co-op members does not fit neatly into the classification of Kalleberg and Griffin, nor into any other with which we are acquainted. Members own the means of production, they do not sell their labor power to others, and they do not directly control the work of others. They are thus similar to the petty bourgeoisie. Yet, there is a crucial difference. They are not individual entrepreneurs, but members of a *collectivity* having influence over the work of all members. Their position thus has elements of the small employer, too. Consequently, we maintain that worker-owners occupy an ambiguous class position, different from both the petty bourgeoisie and small employers because of the unique collective element. No studies have been done on the consequences of the emergent, special class position occupied by cooperators or worker-owners, a promising area for future research.

Given the structural similarities between cooperators and the petty bourgeoisie and between cooperators and small employers, we would suppose, on the one hand, that cooperative members would experience similar levels of satisfaction. On the other hand, there are two important complicating factors that make prediction difficult. First, as a result of their values and the self-selection process, cooperators are likely to have extremely high job expectations, certainly higher than conventional workers and probably higher than the petty bourgeoisie. This would depress actual satisfaction levels. Second, collectivism in the workplace is a unique element in cooperators' experience. According to the limited research that now exists, this element should have a positive effect on satisfaction (see Blumberg, 1973; Frieden, 1980).

We do not have the data to systematically test these ideas, but we can provide some suggestive evidence. We begin not with cooperatives but with related organizations that hold out the promise of ownership and greater voice to workers.

The worker-owned firms that have arisen since 1975 using the Employee Stock Ownership Plan (ESOP) provisions in statutes of that year illustrate our point. Many of these firms emerged as urgent and often last-ditch efforts to save jobs in the face of plant shutdowns. Other types of transfers of ownership to workers have taken place at the initiative of a retiring owner of a closely held firm, who preferred, for a variety of reasons, to sell through an ESOP to his employees rather than find and sell to an outside buyer. Some ESOPs extend minority ownership to workers, whereas others extend majority ownership. In all of these types of cases, though, ESOPs represent *conversions* to worker ownership from conventional ownership, and for that reason, even in cases where they are majority worker-owned, they are very different from grass-roots collectives. The collectives are started from scratch, and are thus in a position to gather up worker–owner–members who specifically believe in the democratic process, whereas ESOP conversions to worker ownership contain the employees who happened to work in the previous conventional firm. By examining ESOP firms, therefore, we can see how the coming of worker ownership alone – without any special, preexisting participatory ideologies – affects workers' job satisfaction.

Researchers at the New Systems of Work and Participation Program at Cornell University have studied many cases of worker buy-outs of firms that otherwise would have been shut down. At the inception of many of these firms, workers cooperate closely with management and community leaders in an attempt to save their firm and their job. During this start-up phase, workers and leaders convince themselves that it is worth the risk to buy the firm, an *espirit de corps* develops among participants, and hopes run high. Workers, when asked, say they expect that ownership will bring them a greater say in the firm. Management expects that ownership will induce workers to comply more effectively with their directives. Neither side is likely to consider any concrete changes in the style of management or methods of decision making that would bring organizational procedures in line with the new form of ownership. The old ways continue to be followed. Attention is given instead to the more pressing matters of finance, marketing, production, and so forth. As a result, several months into the new venture, the spirit of cooperation wanes. Denied an avenue for greater voice in company affairs, workers begin to feel that their ownership is without meaning. In cases where workers have held a majority ownership position, but where they do not gain effective representation and their known preferences are explicitly contradicted by management as in the case of the Vermont Asbestos Group, they are likely to become frustrated and sell their shares to private investors.

Thus, in such buy-out situations, the anticipation of the coming ownership appears to inculcate in workers a sense of "rights" to democratic participation.[3] If the newly formed worker-owned firm does not deliver any substantial participation opportunities, these raised expectations then are dashed. The transformation to worker ownership does not match workers' initial high hopes. They still have no control. In the end, this may leave workers feeling worse than before about their workplace and may render industrial relations more tense.

We do not mean to suggest that worker ownership in the absence of a high degree of worker participation is of no social benefit. It may still save or create jobs. And ongoing research indicates that workers in these sorts of ESOPs do report a greater degree of interest in the financial success of the firm, they are glad to have the ESOP, they do plan to stay with the firm longer, and they do report more pride in their work.[4] However, on measures of job satisfaction, perceived influence, or better industrial relations, the responses appear more equivocal.

Taken together, the many recent case studies of worker-owned (ESOP) firms strongly indicate that the less participation accompanies ownership, the less effective is ownership by itself in improving the quality of people's work lives. Studies by Hammer and Stern (1980) and by Long (1979) show that there is no significant difference between owners and nonowners with regard to the preferred distribution of power in the firm. In fact, according to Hammer and Stern, the more shares workers own, the more they are willing to defer to managerial decision making. French and Rosenstein (1981) in a survey of another ESOP firm find that, among blue-collar and clerical workers, the number of shares owned is insignificant in predicting the desire for influence. These results are based on firms in which workers did have voting rights, profit sharing, and rights to certain information. In other ESOP firms, where workers do not have rights to voting, profits, or information, and where workers were not involved in the initiation of the ESOP, ownership may not only fail to improve job satisfaction, it may actually diminish it. At Crosby Valve, workers came to see little in the ownership plan besides a bonus at retirement. One study concludes that the objective limitations on participation at Crosby caused the workers to become "cynical about ownership rather than causing them to desire or demand any right to control" (Kruse, 1981, p. 115).

Not all ESOPs are without worker participation. Many firms have developed substantial avenues for workers to participate in decision making, and in these cases we anticipate that the combination of ownership and influence will have salutary effects upon workers.

To summarize, worker ownership by itself does not seem able to generate added worker allegiance or satisfaction. In certain circumstances, ownership by itself does appear to raise workers' expectations that they will have more say, or will be treated with greater respect, but in instances where it does not deliver on this promise, it disappoints. Its fuller potential is realized only when ownership is coupled with added opportunities for employee involvement in decision making and control.

This empirical finding underscores the importance of worker participation, but it does not imply that ownership is unimportant. "Quality of Work Life" (QWL) projects try to develop employee participation in the firm, while not extending ownership to workers. Their record reveals numerous cases in which the QWL project was curtailed when management decided that the program had gone far enough in the sharing of power. It then becomes evident to all concerned that any participation program that is called into being by management can be called to a halt by management.

This is not true in situations in which workers are owners of the firm. Worker ownership provides the *legal foundation* and ultimately the *motivation* for worker participation. It provides the legal foundation because voting and other participation rights can be tied to equity ownership, and then managers cannot unilaterally terminate participation. It is a motivator for the workers because they now have a claim to any productivity gains deriving from participation.

Grass-roots collectives, in contrast to ESOP and QWL firms, have a fundamental commitment to democratic participation. Though they are often cooperatively owned, democratic *control* is the defining characteristic, not a mere adjunct to ownership. Because they are started from scratch, co-ops attract and recruit people who want specifically to build democratic workplaces. Thus self-selection is a powerful filter, and co-ops do not contain the broad cross section of the working population that ESOPs have. Also, because they are created as new organizations, they can be developed at a deliberate pace, not in extremis as organizations that need to preserve jobs in a community. Where ESOPs often reproduce earlier styles of management and methods of decision making, co-ops inherit little from the past and are free to experiment with new forms of organization.

Less alienation, more stress

With both worker ownership and democratic control, can co-ops offer a more satisfying work life? From a Marxian standpoint, work in cooperatives should be more satisfying than in capitalist enterprises. Marx argued that under capitalism workers are not able to control either the process or the product of their labor. Since they must work as hired labor, in a workplace owned and controlled by others, their labor power is not freely given, they are unable to influence the disposition (i.e., selling, trading, storing, giving away) of the final product, and their labor merely serves to enrich an opposing class. Under such conditions, work is inherently exploitative, coercive, and alienating for the worker. In Marx's words, from *The Economic and Philosophical Manuscripts:*

His work is not voluntary but imposed, *Forced labour.* It is not the satisfaction of a need, but only a *means* for satisfying other needs. Its alien character is clearly shown by the fact that as soon as there is no physical or other compulsion it is avoided like the plague. Finally, the alienated character of work for the worker appears in the fact that it is not his work but work for someone else, that in work he does not belong to himself but to another person. . . . It is another's activity, and a loss of his own spontaneity. (Quoted in Bottomore, 1964, pp. 169–170)

As an example, in the never-ending search for profits, capitalists impose a rigid division of labor upon the workers:

[A]s soon as the division of labour begins, each man has a particular, exclusive sphere of activity, which is forced upon him and from which he cannot escape. He is a hunter, a fisherman, a shepherd, or a critical critic, and must remain so if he does not want to lose his means of livelihood. (*The German Ideology,* from Bottomore, 1964, p. 97)

Marx's essential thesis was that a communist society would free workers from this condition of exploitation, alienation, and rigidified work roles. Surveying the achievements of workers' cooperatives in the mid-nineteenth century, Marx wrote:

By deed, instead of by argument, they [worker co-ops] have shown that production . . . may be carried on without the existence of a class of masters employing a class of hands . . . [and that] hired labor is but a transitory and inferior form, destined to disappear before associated labor plying its toil with a willing hand, a ready mind, and a joyous heart. (Quoted in Avineri, 1968, pp. 179–180)

It follows then, from a Marxian perspective, that where workers *do* have control over the conditions of their labor, as in a collective, work should be freely motivated, less objectively alienating, and more subjectively satisfying.

Our observations of the contemporary cooperatives, however, lend only partial support to the Marxian expectations. We argue that although collectivist workplaces *do* lower alienation, providing engaging and meaningful work to their worker-owners, expectations also are much higher, and the picture is rather mixed in terms of overall satisfaction.

Following extensive field observation in each of our collectives, written surveys were conducted in three of the groups: the Food Co-op, the Free Clinic, and the *Community News*. In contrast to the findings of Kalleberg and Griffin (1978), occupational position (as indexed by organizational membership) appeared to have no effect here. The three organizations differed little in overall response patterns, so all data have been aggregated. Staff members at each of the organizations were asked, "In general, how satisfying do you find your work at ———— to be?" Of those responding, 38 percent declared it to be "the most satisfying thing I've ever done;" 46 percent indicated that it was "very satisfying;" for 16 percent it was "fairly satisfying;" and none reported "very little satisfaction" or "not at all satisfying." Although we do not have directly comparable data, these responses seem to indicate very high levels of satisfaction compared with responses in conventional organizations (HEW, 1973) and certainly much higher than for the categories of workers and petty bourgeoisie reported by Kalleberg and Griffin (1978). The collectivist structure of the organization may account for this greater level of satisfaction among cooperators compared with that of their nearest class equivalents.

A more detailed question in our survey tried to pinpoint the organizational features with which co-op members were most or least satisfied. Of 21 listed dimensions, the ranking listed in Table 6.1 emerged (in descending order).

Table 6.1 indicates that the organizational qualities with which virtually all members are satisfied (75 percent or more) concern the overall mission and service of the organization, the autonomy it offers, and the defining attributes of the collectivist form, such as equality and collective ownership. Similarly, in the Mondragon cooperatives in Spain, surveys of worker-members show that members rate autonomy more highly than money (Logan, 1981, p. 17). Attributes of work life with which relatively few members are satisfied (50 percent or less) relate to the organization's efficiency, job pressures, money, and job security – the very things that bureaucracies are considered good at providing. Virtually no one (8 percent) feels that the operations of the organization go smoothly. This indicates that members' subjective impressions of

Table 6.1 *Satisfaction of co-op members*

Dimension	Percentage satisfied with it
Feeling of doing something worthwhile	92
Collective ownership of the workplace	92
Freedom from supervision	90
Chance to help individuals	88
Accounting to coworkers	83
Equality with coworkers	82
Appreciation from clients	82
Changing the community	73
Recognition from coworkers	73
Learning for future career	70
Opportunity to be creative	67
Opportunity to do own thing	64
Room for spontaneity	64
Sense of community	64
Chance to change society	54
Money	50
Job security	50
Freedom from high pressure	42
Efficient decision making	42
Provide high-quality product or service	33
Smooth operations	8

what their collectives are good at or not good at are consistent with the structural features and constraints of collectivist-democratic organizations we set forth in Chapter 3. *Here psychology accurately reflects organizational structure.*

One source of dissatisfaction is harder to interpret. Members gave a low ranking to the quality of goods and services provided by their organizations. Only one-third of the members were satisfied with the quality of the product or service. As our impression is that all organizations were in fact producing high quality services, this statement may simply reflect the high, near-perfectionist standards of respondents, or it might reflect members' frustration about providing quality services in what they may feel is an inefficient manner.

Other studies also have discovered positive psychological benefits of collectivism. In one of the few social psychological studies of a collectivist organization, Schlesinger and Bart (1982) find that the women in "Jane" reported a deep sense of satisfaction with what they were accomplishing. The researchers attribute this to the broadened skills and competencies that developed as a result of the multifaceted jobs in the organization. Self-confidence went up and people developed a desire to learn more and to participate more. The extensive work by Menachem Rosner on the democratic general assemblies and industrial plants that make up the kibbutzim system in Israel demonstrates that a taste of participation does lead to the desire for more, and thus supports the notions of the classical theorists of participatory democracy: J. J. Rousseau, J. S. Mill and G. D. H. Cole. Having studied the directly democratic assemblies both in the community and in the workplace of the kibbutz, Rosner is able to separate the effects of participation in the community general assembly from participation in the plant assemblies. Overall, Leviatan and Rosner (1980) find that mental health and reduced alienation are more related to involvement in the *community* assembly than in the plant assembly. Rosner (1981, pp. 17–25) finds that attendance at the community assembly meetings correlates positively with members' sense of commitment, satisfaction, and influence. In the plant assembly, on the other hand, satisfaction and influence correlate negatively with attendance at the meetings. In other words, those who come to community meetings are satisfied; those who come to plant meetings are not. This is because members feel that the kibbutz community assembly has considerable influence on outcomes important to them, whereas the plant assembly is not perceived to have enough influence. This study underscores the psychological benefits of participatory democracy at the community level.

Another way to appreciate the effect of cooperative organizations on the individual is to compare, within a society, similar organizations with different ownership forms. There are only three types of ownership available in our society: private, governmental, or cooperative. Garbage collection is one of the very few industries in the United States in which examples of all three can be found. In a study of private, municipal, and cooperative garbage collection firms, researchers were able to compare the effects of each form of ownership. Overall, the cooperative firms, by allowing their worker-owners to feel like "partners" rather than "garbagemen," and by permitting them to pursue many business tasks (such as collecting accounts in addition to picking up garbage) bring pride of ownership and a sense of dignity to this usually stigmatized job (Perry, 1978). Russell, Hochner, and Perry (1979, p. 339) find that worker-owners show a statistically higher level of satisfaction than nonowning workers in the cooperative firms.

Not all research findings are favorable to workplace democracy. The garbage collection co-ops were started more than 50 years ago and today contain both worker-owners and nonmembers who have been hired to help out. Comparing the attitudes of these two groups, Hochner (1981) finds that those members of the cooperatives who perceive their organizations to be democratic are no more satisfied than members who do not. On the other hand, hired help who see their workplaces as more democratic are more satisfied with their work. Moreover, adding to job complexity has little effect on worker-owner's job satisfaction, but job complexity and higher pay do boost the hired workers' job satisfaction.

Another anomalous set of findings comes from Yugoslavia, where Obradovic (1970) finds that members of the workers' councils in self-managed firms are more alienated than nonmembers. In the United States, worker ownership has also brought some surprising findings regarding the individual. Although one might expect worker ownership to raise commitment to the firm and thereby reduce absenteeism, for example, the latter has not happened. In one employee-owned firm studied by Hammer, Landau, and Stern (1981), the number of "voluntary" absences (elective time off) went down following the conversion to employee ownership, but the number of "involuntary" absences (due to illness, for example) went *up*. Overall, the absenteeism rate did not change. Finally, Norwegian social scientist Frederik Engelstad, (personal communication), comparing a family-owned newspaper with a collectively owned paper in Norway, concludes that the collective did raise commitment and lower alienation among its members, but that it also raised their stress levels and the rate of eventual "burn-out."

How can one make sense of the mixed picture that these findings present?

People in collectives, at least in the United States, are usually very different from their counterparts in private firms or government agencies. First, collective members are a self-selected group who have sought out and have taken great pains to develop a very unconventional form of ownership and control in their work organizations. The boldness of this move suggests that they have an unusually high sense of efficacy. Such a sense of mastery, or belief in one's own ability to effectively control one's life, was evident in all of the five collectives we studied. Of those members who answered two items on the survey intended to measure sense of personal efficacy, more than 80 percent reported they "strongly agree" or "agree." Second, as noted, members of collectives want and expect a great deal from their work. Most of them have come to these organizations for idealistic reasons. They have a strong sense of mission, they yearn for work that is worthwhile, autonomous, and integrated in its execution. In short, they are, and expect to remain, highly involved in their work. *All* of our respondents answered "fairly great" or "very great" to an item on our questionnaire, "How big an effect would you say that your involvement in —————— has on your life at the moment?" In addition to lofty standards for work institutions, people in collectives tend to be critical of society and of the institutions that comprise it. It is out of this critical spirit that their desire to change society comes.

For all of these reasons, we conclude that member–worker–owners of collectives are not easily pleased. The great expectations they bring to their work (and the atypical inducements to which they are responding) tend to counteract somewhat the overall – but still very high – levels of satisfaction they apparently derive from their work. Therefore one must be careful in interpreting satisfaction statements of cooperators and in comparing them to similar statements from conventional organizations.

Worker expectations help us better understand the puzzling findings of Hochner and Russell. The hired (non-owning) workers in the garbage collection co-ops showed a boost in their satisfaction levels when their workplaces allowed for more democracy, more multifaceted jobs, or more pay. This was not true for the worker-owners. It is likely that for the hired help (for whom this is a conventional wage-labor exchange) very little is *expected* of a garbage collection job, and thus if they get to attend a few meetings with management or receive more interesting job duties or more pay, then they are happy.

For the worker-owners, expectations are higher, and so added increments of these benefits become background factors that are accepted but do not add to satisfaction (Hochner, 1981). Similarly, Obradovic's finding that members of the workers' councils in Yugoslavia are more alienated than nonmembers may be a case of unfulfilled hopes.

High expectations and the sense of mission in collectives may lead to more intense, engaging work, but engagement exacts a price: stress. Because work in collectives is freely chosen, and because it is relatively autonomous and equitable, we, like Marx, would expect members to show little alienation. However, contra-Marx, we are led to conclude that the very features that define and give meaning to collectivist work also generate personal stress.[5]

Three structural features of collectivist organization in particular cause personal stress: collective authority, de-differentiation, and familial interpersonal relations. First, collective authority often leaves nebulous the question of what is the appropriate exercise of individual judgment. An individual may need to make an immediate job-related judgment, but feel unsure whether it is rightly an individual decision or a group decision that must wait for the next group meeting. In bureaucracies, because authority resides in individual positions, rights and responsibilities can be more clearly delineated than in collectives. Thus, the individual in a collective may feel uncertain as to whether a decision should be delayed until the next group meeting, or acted upon, and thus run the risk of group criticism for overstepping unspoken bounds of personal authority.

Second, the effort to reduce specialization in collectives and give people a broader array of jobs to do introduces an additional form of role ambiguity. Instead of having one job, the individual may be expected to do several different tasks. The person may not know what the priority is at any given time. If one is part of a team that has been assigned to a certain task, then it may not be clear which team members are to do what. In a bureaucracy where specialization is respected and jobs are narrow, everyone (in theory) knows what they are supposed to be doing, and expectations are limited. This may be boring, but role expectations are at least clear.

The price of the stimulation and freedom implied in broad job roles is that jobs are more taxing and the organization is less predictable. Blurry, ill-defined jobs tend to make people anxious: There is always more one *could* be doing, and what one should be doing is not necessarily clear. Gamson (1981) has described the same problem in the Ann Arbor collectives she studied. The strong sense of purpose among participants only makes this problem worse. Because members are working for a cause, they are driven to take on an overload of work, leading to the familiar phenomenon of "burn-out."

This explains why Engelstad (personal communication) discovered that although the collectively owned publishing house in Norway provided less alienating work, it raised the levels of stress. Swidler finds the same pattern in her study of collectively run free schools. Because teachers did not hold legal-rational authority, they had to draw on their own reserves of charm and skills to engage the students: "[T]hey must fuel their teaching with their private lives. This process is exhausting, and the more successful teachers are at it, the more worn out they become" (Swidler, 1979, p. 71).

The demystification of knowledge and job rotation in collectives give members an opportunity to widen their competencies, and this builds self-esteem. On the other side of the picture, though, job rotations sometimes produce a mismatch – as in the case of Ann, the photographer – in which a person does not want, or is not adept at, the new job.

The desire for demystification in these groups makes illegitimate most claims to special expertise. Those who are, or could be, excellent in a job have no incentive to highly develop their skills, because they are unlikely to receive extra rewards for outstanding work and they might even be criticized as "elitist." There is thus an incentive to downplay one's skills. In the words of one woman who had been a member of a collectivist band:

At the beginning even though the skill levels were hopelessly unequal, the fact that you thought there was a commitment to learning things made everything seem possible. . . . It later began to be apparent that there was not this commitment; instead there was "militant amateurism." . . . In the case of the [alternative music band] one woman in the movement seriously advanced the idea that we should not put our names on the record because that would separate us from all our sisters who couldn't be on the record and weren't playing in bands. For a long time we never played on a stage because that would elevate us symbolically above The People. (Wenig, 1982/ 1983, p. 18)

Third, the small size and egalitarian nature of these groups and the close, personal relationships that knit them together, while aiding satisfaction, also ironically contribute to stress. Having peers in a position where they are obligated to evaluate the collective's activity means that job performance will be judged not by a boss (who in a bureaucracy one can shrug off as a fool or worse), but by people whom one knows well and cares about. This makes people work harder, but family-style performance appraisals are more anxiety laden. As we have seen in earlier examples, criticism from peers carries more sting.

A self-selection factor, too, operates in cooperatives: Co-ops often attract idealists, people who demand a strong sense of purpose from their work. Such people are probably also more prone to guilt than most. This disposes them to overburden themselves with extra responsibilities and tasks. Coupled with the aforementioned structural factors, the individual self-selection factor therefore compounds stress. In short, having a cause one believes in makes work more meaningful, and building a cooperative with close friends provides social satisfaction and a sense of community, but these same things raise the anxiety associated with possible failure and with performance evaluations. Extending ownership and control in the workplace integrates work into people's lives, making work more central to their psyches. People care more, and they take on more work. They experience stress, impairing overall levels of satisfaction. We argue that this is not a failure of particular collectivist organizations or of the individuals in them. Rather, it is part and parcel of the way collectives do things. It is the consequence of collective authority, equality, personal relations, and de-differentiation.

Collectives appear to have a difficult time dealing with this dilemma. Recognizing the unusual intensity of collectivist work, some collectives try to implement practical ways to give members an occasional respite from these stresses. The Free Clinic, for example, initiated "mental health days," giving members the right to choose a certain number of days off explicitly to renew themselves. That workers need a certain amount of time off is illustrated by one of the worker buy-out cases studied at Cornell. There, as noted, researchers found that following the conversion to employee ownership, the overall absenteeism rate did not change, but the rate of "voluntary" absenteeism went down, whereas "involuntary" absenteeism increased (Hammer, Landau, and Stern, 1981). It seems workers change the excuses they give for being absent. For example, they say they are ill rather than they want time off. This alteration in the justifications people give for being absent may well be a response to changes in the informal culture of the workplace. With worker ownership come new group norms and attitudes that support maximum effort and allegiance. In this context, workers may feel compelled to come up with better excuses for their absences, absences that remain important to them. The data from this study then suggest that the extension of ownership to workers may not reduce the need for time off, and if our argument regarding stress is correct, it may actually increase the need.

As we have seen, collectivists expect a high level of both personal fulfillment and social utility from their work. They construct organizations designed to achieve these ends, and in practice they seem to succeed fairly well. There are positive psychological benefits deriving from collectivism, such as a generally strong sense of work satisfaction, broadened competencies, and raised self-esteem. With them, however, comes an undesirable side-effect: personal stress. Individuals will, of course, react in a variety of ways to this stress, but a substantial level of stress does appear to be endemic to collectivist organizations. Our observations lead us to suppose that in order to capture the other benefits of cooperation, many people in cooperatives decide that it is a cost worth bearing.

7. The future of cooperation

The question remains: How will cooperatives fare in the United States, and how significant a sector of the economy will they become? Will they remain relatively marginal, deviant forms of organization, rising and falling in waves as they have in earlier periods of American history? Or does the current burgeoning of cooperatives signal the beginning of a larger and more permanent cooperative sector?

We believe the future of the cooperative form of organization will depend on three main factors: whether they can be competitive in a market economy, and if so, in what specific niches; what the average life span of individual cooperatives turns out to be; and what role the state takes vis-à-vis cooperative enterprises.

Economic performance

The definitive study of the economic performance of cooperatives has yet to be done. There have been, however, a few economic studies of more limited scope that bear on this question.

The issue of how to properly measure economic performance is complex. In ordinary capitalist firms, profitability is usually used as the yardstick of success. When this yardstick is applied in the context of producer cooperatives, the results can be misleading for two reasons. First, members of cooperatives can manipulate the profit level down or up by deciding to pay themselves higher or lower wages. Abell and Mahoney (1981) have therefore argued that residual profit bears no necessary relationship to the economic viability of a cooperative enterprise, and urge instead the use of value-added per unit of labor as a better measure of economic performance. Second, although grass-roots collectives strive to earn enough surplus to provide each worker-member with a livable income, profit maximization is not their primary aim. Thus, profit becomes merely a limiting factor, with some level being necessary for survival. To evaluate collectives solely on the basis of profit would be to use the wrong criterion.

160

Nevertheless, the ability of a collective to generate an economic surplus by having revenues exceed costs by at least a moderate amount is important to the viability of the organization and to the attainment of its members' individual and collective goals. The issue of economic performance therefore is relevant to the future of collectives.

Some writers have argued that cooperative firms will perform worse than their privately owned counterparts in a capitalist society. Vanek (1977), an economist of self-managed firms, contends that cooperatives rely heavily on internally generated savings, that they give limited returns to share capital, and that they show a preference for consumption. The net result, argues Vanek, is that cooperatives typically will underinvest and will therefore have an unreasonably low capital-to-labor ratio. Empirical studies of worker-owned firms in countries such as Sweden do reveal a tendency to put additional earnings into higher wages rather than investment (Lindkvist and Svensson, 1981). On the other hand, studies of cooperatives in developing countries such as India, Peru, and Senegal do not support the Vanek hypothesis of high consumption and low savings (Abell and Mahoney, 1981). Moreover, in the Spanish Mondragon cooperatives, profits are credited to individual worker's accounts in a system-wide cooperative bank, leaving these collective savings to be plowed back into the co-op firms. Far from being cash-starved, Mondragon is able to retain some 85 percent of the profits for reinvestment (Johnson and Whyte, 1977). The Vanek thesis of overconsumption and underinvestment does not appear inescapable.

Others argue that co-ops, operating in a capitalist context, suffer discrimination, which impairs their ability to obtain bank credit, enter new markets, bring about advantageous relationships with suppliers, and so forth.

Co-ops do suffer from outside prejudice against the cooperative form, and there are many corroborating anecdotal accounts. However, systematic documentation of economic discrimination does not exist and would be difficult to demonstrate. If a bank declines to advance a loan to a co-op, it might be a case of pure prejudice, or it might be simply the bank's assessment of the perceived financial risk. It is no doubt easier for large, established businesses to obtain loans and to penetrate new markets, and it is possible that co-ops suffer only the same handicaps as small businesses in general. This issue is not clear.

Although we agree that external prejudice on political or ideological grounds does exist, its extent may be overstated by both theorists and participants in the field. As discussed in Chapter 5, participants in co-ops achieve a heightened sense of worth and unity from seeing themselves in opposition to mainstream institutions. Since they receive a secondary gain from the perception of external slights and from the interpretation that these are prejudicial in nature, we might expect a bias in this direction. As an explanation for economic problems, we maintain that this factor is overshadowed by others. Since some evidence suggests that capital starvation is not the main reason for co-op failures (Abell and Mahoney, 1981, pp. 13–14), the bank prejudice hypothesis should recede in importance.

Of greater consequence, we suggest, are the structural biases contained in the patterns of economic concentration and in the laws of taxation and incorporation. Of importance too, is the lack of active support of co-ops on the part of the state (to be discussed later). For people outside co-ops, lack of knowledge and indifference may be a more ubiquitous problem than active hostility toward co-ops. For example, very few attorneys know anything about the rather obscure body of co-op law, and therefore co-ops often are greatly disadvantaged in finding relevant legal forms, instituting effective accounting procedures, and claiming appropriate tax entitlements.

The Webbs (1920) in an early and influential critique of cooperatives, took the view that co-ops were destined to underperform in comparison with their capitalist counterparts, not so much because of underinvestment or a hostile environment, as ineffective management. In the Webbs' view, the one-person-one-vote principle encumbers good management, slowing down decision-making processes and blocking technological innovation in the organization.

The Webbs' argument, although it has been echoed by many since, has not been subjected to empirical testing. We question, for example, the argument's implicit assumption that "good management" in a privately owned hierarchical firm is the same as "good management" in a democratic cooperative. If the characteristics outlined in Chapter 3 are in fact desired and typical in collectives and anathema in pyramidal bureaucracies, then there is no reason to expect that such a transference is possible. To the extent that the values, goals, and processes of the organization are different, principles and procedures that would constitute good management should be different. For this reason, claims that cooperatives entail "bad management" require careful scrutiny. Further, the Webbs' argument was published in 1920 when management entailed less specialized functions than it does today. The subsequent specialization of management functions makes it important to be more precise as to which functions of management might be deficient in co-ops and which might be strong.

Few systematic studies have compared the management outcomes of co-ops and those of conventional enterprises (certainly an important subject for future research). One exception is the work of Jones (1980). In a study of British footwear cooperatives, he finds that they *are* able to introduce technological change. In fact, the more participatory they are, the more technological innovations they introduce. Jones's data are confined mostly to the shoe industry, however, and he uses a number of indirect measures of relevant variables.

Our own observations convince us that co-op members are generally quite good at personnel management – related skills such as group process and human relations. They are also fairly perceptive and judicious in the choice of personnel who will be dedicated and hard working. Letting go of people when circumstances warrant it (in recessionary times or when an individual does not work out) is a difficult problem for many cooperatives. This is probably an inherent problem of co-ops. As a legal entity, the co-op form allows workers to become owner-members. Thus termination is usually reluctantly done and emotionally painful in these family-like groups. Collectives sometimes choose to build in future flexibility in the labor force by not extending ownership to new members, but of course this dilutes the co-op form and produces a two-tiered system of owners and hired help. Alternatively, members may decide in a recessionary period to cut time and pay for everyone by a certain percentage rather than lay off anyone. In either case, because of their broader ownership structure, co-ops are faced with personnel management issues that are thornier than those in ordinary firms.

In terms of financial management, Abell and others have found worse returns to capital in co-ops. Abell (1981) had argued this is the single most fundamental problem of co-op management. Partly, this may be a matter of skills that may be learned, since the members of the co-ops Abell studied (in the Third World) were barely numerate, much less literate. In response to a similarly perceived failing in co-ops in the United States, the New School for Democratic Management established a national program to teach financial and general management skills to cooperators.

Another set of skills, related to the above but analytically separable, are entrepreneurial in nature. It may be that the disadvantages of cooperatives with respect to returns to capital derive from a lack of entrepreneurial talent. This could be a built-in disadvantage of cooperation. As Abell and Mahoney (1981, p. 19) put it:

Consider a potential entrepreneur (assumed self-interested) with either his own capital or access to loan capital and what he believes to be a marketable idea. Why should he choose to establish an IPC [Industrial Producer Co-op] when he faces (a) limited returns to his capital, (b) no guarantee of control of the enterprise, and (c) a situation where the benefits of his idea become a bounded public good within the cooperative? Surely he will rather be attracted to a partnership or traditional private firm.

In short, entrepreneurs in a capitalist society have little incentive to share with others the fruits of their ideas or control over the production process. We believe, with Abell and Mahoney, it is this lack of attractiveness for individual entrepreneurs that contributes to the relatively low historical frequency of co-operative formation.

Some present-day cooperatives come about because the head of a private firm wants to transform it into a cooperative or democratic enterprise for essentially moral or religious reasons.[1] Other instances of worker ownership come out of the urgency of communities that stand to lose jobs because of local plant shutdowns. In these cases, some form of cooperation or employee-ownership may be tried as the solution of last resort. On the other hand, grass-roots cooperatives tend to be created spontaneously by groups of people who are homogeneous in values and who bring relatively equal levels of capital and skills to the enterprise, as in our cases. Through the development of a co-op, as in the examples of the plywood and garbage collection enterprises, members can syndicate the financial risk, pull together the labor and the skills of many, build a community, and earn a livelihood. Conspicuously absent from the history of cooperatives is the solo entrepreneur who, armed with a fresh idea and the capital to make it work, gathers up a group of people to implement the idea and makes them into a co-op. Co-ops provide no incentives for the *individual* entrepreneur.

Workers' ownership and cooperation can bring certain economic advantages, particularly enhanced worker commitment. Worker stakes in the ownership of the firm and worker voice in decision making do appear to promote workers' sense of allegiance and commitment to the firm and to strengthen bonds of solidarity among the work force. For instance, in the early stages of worker buy-outs of failing firms, workers – drawing from their years of observation and experience on the shop floor – often come forward with constructive suggestions for cutting down on waste and improving quality. The move to worker ownership also causes a change in the culture of the factory. Informal norms disapproving of waste and voluntary absence begin to take root. Turnover declines, as might be expected, when employees have a financial stake in the firm. Under such conditions there is less need for supervision, and the costs of surveillance decrease.[2] The result of these processes is higher labor productivity.

Closely related to improvement in worker commitment is a strengthening of the bonds that hold the group together and contribute to its morale. In some instances, as in the case of threatened job loss, solidarity comes from the perception of a common enemy and a common circumstance. Similarly, labor-management conflicts such as lockouts or strikes sometimes precipitate the creation of a workers' cooperative. For example, the *Citizen's Voice,* a co-op newspaper in Wilkes-Barre, Pennsylvania, arose out of a conflict with the *Times-Leader* and its new conglomerate owner, Capital Cities Communication, Inc. It was this conflict with Capital Cities that helped to unite an otherwise diverse group of workers represented by four separate unions (Keil, 1982). In other instances, workers may be bound together by ethnic and kinship ties, as was the case in many of the nineteenth-century co-ops and in the garbage collection and plywood co-ops of the 1920s. Sometimes, too, cohesion derives from the common religious, cultural, or value background of the participants, as in the case of the Israeli kibbutzim, the Mondragon co-ops, some of the co-ops Abell studied in Senegal, the Breman enterprises in Holland, and others. In many cases, of course, solidarity arises from the combination of these elements. In the contemporary collectives that are the subject of this work, members are bound by common values – though they are not religious or ethnic in origin – and by their oppositional stance toward dominant institutional arrangements.

Worker solidarity, like commitment, is of significance beyond the gains in worker satisfaction and morale that it may bring. One research team has found in its study of cooperatives in developing countries that high solidarity goes with various measures of economic success, just as low solidarity goes with economic failure (Abell and Mahoney, 1981, p. 14). This team posits that cooperatives rely on their solidarity and commitment advantages to achieve their economic performance; if these are lacking, the result is more diseconomies than in a conventional enterprise. As is apparent from the organizational features outlined in Chapter 3, a collective orientation depends on mutual trust. Internal conflict is especially disruptive precisely because of the consensual basis and personal relations that characterize these groups. Thus, compared with conventional firms, higher levels of worker commitment and solidarity are often observed in cooperative enterprises – but by the same token, they are also more necessary.

Research concerning the economic performance of worker-owned firms has begun to accumulate, and much of it shows good performance. Studies of worker-owned firms that have emerged out of impending plant closures reveal a number of cases – such as Bates Fabrics in Lewiston, Maine, and Saratoga Knitting Mills in Saratoga, New York – in which corporate earnings after the conversion are far higher than before. A survey of 30 worker-owned firms found, when controlling for size and industry, that worker-owned firms show a level of profit higher than similar conventional firms. Further, the most important single determinant of profitability is the percentage of the company's equity owned by the nonsalaried employees. As this percentage goes up, so do the company's profits (ISR, 1977, pp. 2–3).[3] Another study currently in progress by Tannenbaum and associates indicates that employee-owned firms are neither more nor less profitable than conventional firms, but the employee-owned firms do stay in business longer (reported in Rosen et al., 1986, p. 2).

Except in the case of ESOPs, few studies have examined the economic performance of worker cooperatives. For those co-ops that have been studied, the results look generally positive. The kibbutz industries, probably the most studied cooperative system in the world, show high levels of profit per worker, high labor productivity, and a healthy return on capital investment compared with that of privately held companies in Israel (Melman, 1971, pp. 203–220; Barkai, 1977). Looking at Italian producer cooperatives, Jones (1981) finds that workers' capital stakes promote productivity in some industries, but hurt it in others. In comparing British footwear cooperatives and conventional firms in the footwear industry, he finds no difference in productivity. When examining American producer cooperatives historically, Jones finds some industries (such as plywood) in which labor productivity surpasses that of conventional enterprises, and other industries (such as barrel making) in which the cooperatives have performed worse (1980, pp. 144–145). Overall, the picture presented by Jones is a mixed one, in which the relative performance of worker co-ops depends on the industry in which they are located.

Virtually no economic studies have considered contemporary grass-roots co-ops. Much information does exist, however, on some of the cooperatives that were established during the 1920s and are still in operation today, notably the plywood and garbage collection co-ops. In these, an impressive record of performance has been demonstrated.

A study of the 15 plywood cooperatives in the Pacific Northwest finds that they average 20 to 30 percent higher productivity than conventional plywood firms (Berman, 1967, p. 189). Commensurate with this productivity, salaries in these worker-owned firms are 25 percent higher than those in privately owned plywood firms. When the Internal Revenue Service challenged some of the cooperatives for paying salaries higher than the industry average and sought to tax the excess as corporate income, the cooperatives successfully demonstrated that the higher wages were justified on the basis of productivity 25 to 60 percent greater than the plywood industry average.

The refuse collection cooperatives in San Francisco have consistently outperformed their counterparts. They provide higher-quality services at lower prices than the refuse collection firms of any other major city in the United States. At the same time, worker-owners in the cooperatives are paid an average annual income that is far higher than that paid to employees of the private refuse collection firms, which in turn is higher than wages paid to municipal garbage collection workers (Russell, 1982a). Workers in the privately owned firms are paid an average of 25 percent more than in the municipal firms, and worker-owners in the cooperatives receive 83 percent more.

In sum, a systematic study that controls for firm size, industry, and internal structure is needed before we can draw firm conclusions about the economic performance of co-ops. In the light of the available evidence, we are led to provisionally conclude that worker ownership and democratic management bring effectively higher levels of worker commitment and solidarity, and this often can be turned into a labor productivity and profitability advantage. But this economic advantage is precarious in cases where mechanisms are not established to give workers more voice in company affairs. Instances of worker ownership without avenues for democratic participation run the risk of losing the morale and therefore the economic advantage that would otherwise be inherent in this organizational form. This danger can be seen in the declining economic fortunes of several employee-owned firms (such as South Bend Lathe and the Library Bureau in Herkimer, New York) that appear to have paid insufficient attention to the participation implications of broadened ownership. In an overview of the economic research on producer cooperatives, Jones (1980, p. 147) concludes that co-ops without democratic majority control perform worse economically than those with democratic control. Likewise, Olivarius finds in a survey of 400 producer cooperatives in the United Kingdom a strong correlation between economic vitality and the degree to which decision-making procedures are democratic.[4]

The state

The degree to which the governmental machinery of the state fosters the development of cooperatives varies greatly across societies. Logically, government can take four stances toward co-ops: It may attempt to repress them, it may be indifferent and inactive, it may encourage or facilitate private cooperatives, or it may directly set up co-ops. The future strength of the co-op sector in the United States, as anywhere, will depend not only on how well co-op values fit with values in the rest of society and on how economically competitive they can be, but also on the action (or inaction) of government. It is therefore difficult to predict the future course of a cooperative sector without knowing which groups will hold political power and what their biases may be.

The U.S. government over the decades has maintained a largely indifferent stance toward co-ops, with the notable exception of the farm co-ops that did receive significant supportive legislation in the 1930s and now represent a strong part of the agricultural economy. Nonfarm producer cooperatives, however, have been neglected. The U.S. government has shown no cognizance of worker co-ops and has taken no role in their formation. The hundreds or thousands of producer cooperatives formed during the 1970s are grass roots in origin and, given their predilection for independence and self-sufficiency, might not be receptive to state overtures even if they were forthcoming. Indeed, they likely would be suspicious that outside intervention would undermine local autonomy and control.

In this country, co-ops have for the most part been created and operated on the basis of self-initiative, with periodic help from related social movements. This is not the case in many other parts of the world. In other countries, co-op development often has been fostered by the state and supported by other major institutions such as labor unions, political parties, and private business. It is instructive to look at examples of what other nations have done to encourage cooperative enterprise, and what resulting benefits have accrued to the state.

We examine cooperative development, especially the state's role in such development, by focusing on the important cases of France, Italy, Spain, Portugal, Poland, and China. Our strategy here is to draw attention to some important examples of cooperative development around the world that are lesser known. We also wish to help bring to light a valuable recent research literature, much of which is relatively inaccessible because it is as yet unpublished or appears in publications that are not widely circulated.[5] We try to draw out of these cross-national experiences some general lessons for the United States.

Western Europe contains a surprising number of co-ops. Though the co-op movement was severely reduced during the facist period in Europe, since 1945 worker cooperatives in France have grown to more than 600 (Thornley, n.d., p. 5). In Italy, the cooperative sector has 400,000 workers (Jones, 1981, p. 6) in some 3,000 co-ops (Derrick, 1981, p. 3) and accounts for 7 percent of the gross national revenue (Thornley). In Britain co-ops declined after the war, but have spread since 1975 with the support of about 40 local Cooperative Development Agencies (CDAs). Today there are approximately 500 co-ops in the United Kingdom (Jones, 1981, p. 6; Derrick, 1981, p. 3; Cornforth, 1983). The CDAs generally derive their funds from labor-controlled city councils.

Support for cooperatives in France goes back to 1884, when a government agency was established to provide advice to co-ops; by 1938 it had capital to loan to co-ops. In recent years the governments of France, Italy, and Britain have awarded an increasing number of contracts to cooperative enterprises because of their reputation for reliability, quality, and low cost, and private business is beginning to subcontract particular jobs to co-ops for essentially the same reasons. In Italy, the Ministry of Works and Social Services was empowered in 1971 to develop cooperatives and to set up courses to train co-op leaders. The government in Italy also has set up an agency to provide loans to co-ops through the Banca d'Italia. As in France, loans are given at favorable (i.e., subsidized) interest rates and expert advice is made available to cooperatives.

Another major underpinning of the cooperatives sector in Italy and in France has been the development over the years of cooperative federations. Italy has three such federations and France has one. These are private, self-help organizations, though taken together they have garnered the support of five of the political parties in Italy. They function to provide business expertise to co-op participants. In addition, during the 1970s consortia (Consorzi) have developed in Italy to serve centralized functions for the co-ops: acquiring raw materials, marketing finished goods, negotiating for loans and contracts, and providing consultation. The federations also play a key role in promoting and setting up new co-ops. Thornley estimates that 60 percent of new Italian co-ops are set up with federation help. Sometimes the government, private business, and labor unions call upon the federations to form worker cooperatives out of failing firms (Thornley, n.d., p. 18). In Britain there are also self-help cooperative organizations (such as the International Common Ownership Movement) intended to promote co-ops, but these have relatively meager resources compared with those in France and Italy.

Hegland (1981) reports at least 130 "alternative institutions" in Denmark, much like their grass-roots counterparts in the United States. A study of worker-owned enterprises in Sweden (Lindkvist and Svensson, 1981) located 60 such companies encompassing 2,000 workers in industrial production. In addition, the study found many co-ops in the service sector, such as architectural firms, legal coops, and engineering firms quite like those reported in this study. The authors report that, as in the United States, the Swedish cooperatives are of three types: "paternalistic" firms in which ownership is transferred from a private owner to the workers for philanthropic or idealistic reasons; "defensive" firms in which worker ownership is used as a strategy to save jobs when a plant is faced with a shutdown; and "offensive" cases in which cooperative firms are started from scratch. All three types have been expanding since the Swedish industrial minister decided to support worker-owned firms with monetary grants.

Comparing data on worker participation for Western Europe, the Stephenses (1982) argue that the strength of labor union organization and of labor party (or socialist party) incumbency in office determine the extent to which shop-floor democracy will be realized. The degree to which a country's labor force is unionized and the resulting political power of labor appear to have direct effects on the passage of legislation favorable to workers' participation and on the development of all kinds of workers' cooperatives. Although this may not be a complete explanation for the different types and degrees of worker participation in Western Europe, liberal government policies supported by labor, often in coalition with other parties, have had a great deal to do with the spread of workers' participation or cooperation in Western Europe. In contrast, in other countries we see that workers' cooperatives have developed in spite of the policies of the nation-state, or in other cases, because of revolutionary changes in who holds state power.

One of the most extensive networks of workers' cooperatives, involving more than 20,000 worker-owners, exists today in Spain. This system, dating from 1956, developed in spite of decades of fascist rule under Franco. To understand the widespread development of cooperatives under such oppressive circumstances, we must look at the particular politics and history of the region. Mondragon, where this development has occurred, is in the Basque region of northern Spain, a region that has a long history of intense separatist and anarchist sentiments and bitter memories of the devastation of the Spanish Civil War. It is in this context that the Basque Nationalist Party, affiliated with the Basque trade union movement, first proposed the establishment of a cooperative economy in 1933. In addition to the political support provided by the regional party and trade unions, an important cultural underpinning was the rural Basque tradition of offering one's labor for community service (Logan, 1981, p. 8). Moreover, the solidarity required for workers' cooperation derives in the Basque region, as indeed we have argued it does everywhere, from the homogeneity of the participants – in this case cultural, political, and religious in origin – and from the perception of a common enemy.

As in Italy and France, federative activity has played an important role in the Mondragon system. From the beginning, Mondragon's leaders saw the need for auxiliary institutions to support the cooperative development. Today a cooperative bank, school, child care center, and technical innovation center support the co-ops' financial, ideological, social, and technological needs.

Portugal, after five decades of fascist rule, is another country that illustrates how quickly grass-roots cooperatives can develop when given the opportunity. By 1978, Portugal had 511 agricultural co-ops with some 42,000 worker-members, and an estimated 1,200 industrial co-ops with some 59,000 members. In a detailed examination, Hammond (1981) has shown that the Portuguese revolution of 1974–75 set the stage for this flowering of grass-roots cooperatives. Although the new state leadership that resulted from the revolution was centralist and socialist in orientation, it did allow local worker control efforts to develop. In this context, decentralized neighborhood committees were formed, landless farm workers took over plantations and turned them into co-ops, state-chosen union leaders were thrown out and replaced by democratically elected ones, and workers took over industrial plants (Hammond, 1981). Thus, worker control of the factories was part of a broader movement for democratic control of all institutions. The revolution had ushered in a climate of freedom and self-determination, and this new *zeitgeist* favored the development of workers' cooperatives as well as these other forms of popular control. The revolutionary (but centralized) state did not pursue workers' control as a policy, but did accept it, and the police did defend the new worker co-ops, and the nationalized bank gave them credit.

In late 1975, a right-wing military coup took place, purging the revolutionaries from positions of power. After this date, no more factory occupations took place. Since the counterrevolution, many of the agricultural co-ops and some of the industrial co-ops have been forcibly dismantled by the government and returned to their original owners, with the aid of the military to quell worker resistance. Other co-ops have been allowed to continue to exist, probably because they are able to provide employment in a deteriorating economy (Hammond, 1981).

To summarize, we have seen in the nations of Western Europe that the more liberal capitalist states (i.e., those supported by labor parties) tend to produce legislation and policies that favor worker participation. In Mondragon, even without state support, co-ops can still develop extensively at the grass-roots level if there is enough local and regional support. Portugal demonstrates the implications for the birth and demise of co-ops, even at the grass-roots level, of revolutions and counterrevolutions in state power.

Next we turn to Eastern Europe, to see how a centralized socialist state may respond to worker cooperatives.

Providing rare information concerning cooperative development inside Poland, Kowalak (1981) reports that the first worker cooperative dates back to 1873, but that co-ops were a negligible part of the economy until the end of World War II. Following the war, many small and medium-sized factories were turned over to cooperatively organized groups of workers. In some cases this was done because the factories were partly ruined by the war; in other cases the owners feared expropriation, and so they handed over their plants and joined the co-op. Since 1945, cooperatives have gradually come to be seen as an effective and relatively inexpensive way to diminish unemployment. They have been used to create job opportunities, especially for those who would otherwise find it difficult to enter the work force: women with young children, disabled persons, pensioners, university students, and others. A 1961 Polish law recognized and defined the rights of co-ops. By 1979, 203,000 disabled persons were employed in the worker co-ops. All together, the cooperatives employ about 800,000 people, representing 6.7 percent of the work force in Poland (Kowalak, 1981, pp. 3–4). Reports indicate that from 1965 to 1975 the cooperative enterprises had higher rates of growth and productivity than the state industrial enterprises (Kowalak, 1981, p. 19).

Since 1975 the Polish cooperatives have become more centralized. First, there were many mergers of co-ops, presumably to bring economies of scale. Such mergers, however, have led to a large organization incompatible with democracy. In addition, the central and regional state-sponsored unions (to which the co-ops must belong) have begun to usurp the cooperatives' power by making important decisions concerning credit, investment, supply, and marketing. As decisions are increasingly being taken by "persons situated above the enterprise," the autonomy and power of the local cooperatives is dwindling, and the feelings of dissatisfaction and alienation that plague conventional enterprises are beginning to spread in the cooperative enterprises. As a result of this centralization of power in Poland, the productivity advantages that the cooperatives once had have now ended (Kowalak, 1981, pp. 16–19).

At the time of the presentation of his paper (May 1981), Professor Kowalak envisioned good prospects for the development of worker cooperatives in Poland, since this was one of Solidarity's (the independent trade union) chief aims. With the subsequent reassertion of state authority and the suppression of Solidarity, there is now little information available on the status of cooperatives in Poland.

In Poland the state was quick to grasp the job-creation potential of cooperatives and promoted them in order to stimulate national economic recovery. In time, however, as workers' power grew, the state was not content with autonomous co-ops, and it pushed decision making to progressively higher levels of the system. In short, the Polish state wanted to capture the economic benefits of cooperation, but it wanted to control the organizations. Since cooperation implies the right of workers to control the process of production and the surplus, this usurpation of power by the state produced an internal crisis in the co-ops and detracted from members' motivation to work, a contradiction that many state socialist societies may face in their treatment of co-ops.

Moving outside of the Soviet bloc to yet another type of socialist state, we see in China some similarities to Poland in the treatment of cooperatives. In a detailed analysis, Lockett (1981) shows that the first interest in establishing cooperatives in China surfaced in 1919 with a student-based movement; then during the 1920s and 1930s credit and producer co-ops were brought into existence by radical intellectuals, international relief agencies, missionaries, and peasants. Reports indicate that the credit co-ops lasted some time, but the producer co-ops were often repressed by the state. During the two decades that preceded the Chinese revolution, the development of cooperatives in China was intricately tied to the evolving struggle between the two main contending political parties: the Khoumentang (KMT) and the Chinese Communist Party (CCP). The KMT, in search of a "third way" that was neither capitalist nor communist, decided to promote cooperatives. During the 1930s, the KMT set up thousands of credit, agricultural, and producer cooperatives. Later, however, as the co-ops began to pose an economic challenge to the urban and rural property owners who represented the base of political support for the KMT, the KMT withdrew its support of the cooperatives, and in fact became antagonistic toward them. The Communist Party, on the other hand, started from a position of suspicion toward the co-ops, and gradually came to embrace them during the 1940s, urging a position of more popular control of the co-ops and more profit sharing than the KMT had allowed.

With the revolution in 1949 and the ascendancy of the CCP, cooperativization of the economy accelerated (Lockett, 1981). By 1955, about 10 percent of the handicraft work force was involved in producer cooperatives. This amounted to some 850,000 persons. During the first 12 days of 1956, however, the government attempted to convert by fiat most of the remaining handicraft enterprises to a cooperative form. Suddenly there were 3.7 million persons in approximately 100,000 handicraft cooperatives. The party found, however, that by so directly and speedily trying to set up co-ops or to intervene in privately owned enterprises to turn them into co-ops, it encountered resistance and created organizational problems. The party then turned to more indirect means of control over the economy, including tax incentives, control over wages and work conditions, prices, and contracts for purchase of products. During the period of the Great Leap Forward there was another wave of new cooperative formation, this one largely the result of local initiative – often by unemployed women – to create employment in a difficult time.

Since 1958, the distinction between cooperative enterprises (those owned and run by the workers in them) and collective enterprises (owned and run by a locality) has become blurred, and evidence concerning magnitudes is scarce and often unreliable. The line between cooperatives and collectives has become particularly blurred because the government has placed controls on wages, work conditions, and surplus in the co-ops and has appointed managers in them (Lockett, 1981). This effectively removes from cooperative members the control they would normally expect to have over the process and product of their labor, and reduces the usual motivation for working in a co-op. In fact, it brings into question to what extent enterprises called "cooperatives" in China during this period can be considered cooperatives as that term is generally understood elsewhere.

According to a 1973 study (reported in Lockett, 1981), labor productivity was 3.2 times higher in the state industrial sector than in the cooperative sector, although the state achieved this productivity advantage on the basis of 5 times more capital per worker. In other words, co-ops have demonstrated their usefulness in China as enterprises that can create jobs with less capital.

Since around 1976 and the break with the Cultural Revolution, several changes in economic policy in China have tended to favor the development of co-ops. First, the CCP leadership has looked to co-ops as a means of creating relatively inexpensive jobs for the millions of unemployed urban youth. Second, the turn toward more consumer goods and lighter industry favors cooperative development. Third, there has been a tendency to try to loosen the reigns of control over the co-ops and the collectives and to allow them to elect their own managers and to retain more of their surplus. Recent newspaper articles have praised cooperatives' superior flexibility and job-creation potential, especially in small-scale production, in subcontracting for the larger state enterprises, and in services. This reflects a positive change in party attitudes toward co-ops, but the fundamental contradiction between the requirements of a centrally planned economy and the desire of workers in cooperatives for autonomy has not been resolved. Some members of the CCP view the cooperatives as less socialistic; others want to develop out of the mixture of cooperatives, collectives, and state enterprises some new type of social property (Lockett, 1981).

The minimal involvement of the state in cooperative development in the United States stands in marked contrast to the cases described above. As noted in Chapter 1, this country has experienced five successive waves of grass-roots cooperative formation in its history – waves that occurred without government support or repression. Cooperatives, consistent with their anarchistic roots and their values of self-sufficiency, generally have not sought state aid.

Today, however, some forms of government recognition and advancement of co-ops are emerging in the United States. In 1979 a National Consumer Cooperative Bank, modeled on the successful farm cooperative bank of decades earlier, was passed into law by Congress and signed by President Jimmy Carter. The bank itself, however, was the product of consumer activism, and as the name suggests, was intended to aid consumer co-ops. As an afterthought, a clause was put into the legislation allowing up to 10 percent of its funds to be loaned to producer co-ops. To date only a handful of worker co-ops have received loan support from the bank. With this small exception, the government has done nothing to assist producer co-ops.

In the mid-1970s, however, the federal government did begin to give considerable support to Employee Stock Ownership Plans (ESOPs), a new form of property that in effect broadens ownership to include the workers in an enterprise. By establishing a legal form, special tax incentives, and a financing mechanism (out of future pretax earnings), the government has provided strong incentives for these sorts of transfers to worker ownership. A recent study by Rosen et. al. (1986, p. 1) locates eight thousand ESOPs, involving some 7 to 8% of the national workforce. In an estimated 10% of these ESOP firms, workers hold or will come to hold, a majority of the voting stock, but in most of these firms workers hold between 15% and 40% of the stock.

Since 1974, Congress has passed 16 laws to encourage employee ownership, and 13 states have passed 16 laws to do the same (Rosen, 1986, p. 2). Why has the U.S. government become involved in promoting ESOPs? It is always difficult to infer motivations from actions, especially collective actions such as an act of Congress, but some common themes emerge in the speeches and writing of political leaders. ESOP legislation has been politically unusual in that it has received broad bipartisan support from conservatives as well as liberals. It appears to be a phenomenon into which different people read different virtues. To the conservative, it is "People's Capitalism": a chance to revitalize our capitalist economy by broadening its ownership base. To the liberal, employee ownership means a fairer distribution of future wealth and the potential for greater worker control in the production process. To both, employee ownership offers a way to save jobs in plants that might otherwise be shut down by their corporate owners. Additionally, the connection between workers having an ownership stake in their firms and worker motivation and productivity has not been lost on policy makers. Some have argued that worker participation schemes appear to grow in times of declining corporate profits and productivity (Heckscher, 1980).

Labor unions, on the other hand, started out lukewarm to ESOPs. Naturally, trade unionists want to preserve jobs wherever possible, but they are concerned about the role trade unions would have in worker-owned organizations. Moreover, they are concerned about the financial risk to workers in the minority of ESOP cases in which the former pension plan is exchanged for shares of company stock because this practice eliminates the diversification that one might seek in a long-term pension investment. In addition, those ESOPs that have emerged out of plant closings have often entailed wage cuts in exchange for stock, and union leaders have feared that this might have a contagion effect, depressing wages in a whole industry. Finally, many of the early ESOPs (1975–80) were initiated by management and gave workers little say in company affairs. Since 1980, however, studies show a change in trade unionists' attitudes toward worker ownership. Several new cases of worker ownership have been spearheaded by local unions and contain ample measures to ensure a voice for workers in voting rights, shop-floor participation, representation on the board of directors, access to financial information, and appointment of managers. These cases have received widespread attention in the mass media and especially in union circles. Consequently, some unions in the United States are beginning to view the ESOP as a flexible instrument that can be shaped to benefit workers, communities and unions, if they can be involved in its planning and development.[6] Even with this change in union attitudes, the extent of labor union organization in the economy is much less in the United States than in Europe, and there are no labor parties. As a result, trade unions in the United States have not been nearly as vigorous or effective in pushing for national policies encouraging workers' cooperation or participation, as they have in Europe.

Although it is within the realm of state power to encourage workers' cooperation, any prediction for the United States would have to depend on who holds state power. In a context of high unemployment, worker cooperatives offer a policy option that has barely even been examined. Evidence from nations as diverse as Italy, Spain, Poland, and China demonstrates that jobs can be created in a cooperative sector more inexpensively (with less spent on a per-job basis) than in conventional firms. This is the major reason why governments in those countries have embarked on programs to encourage worker cooperatives, and it is the chief benefit that has accrued to them. Similar potential exists in the United States. Recently, it has been shown that ESOP firms where the employees own a majority of the stock generate three times more net new jobs per year than comparable conventional firms (Rosen, 1986, p. 2).

A program of workers' ownership, or cooperativization, would have as a political asset the perception that it is a third route, neither capitalist nor socialist. As we have seen, this could mean a broader base of political and popular support for such a program. On the other hand, although both socialist and capitalist countries have found good reasons to support economic development through a program of workers' cooperation, albeit of different types, they have both faced a dilemma with it as well. Both capitalist and socialist societies want to capture the economic benefits of cooperation, but they want to control it. For the capitalist country, an economically vital cooperative sector would compete against private enterprise; for the socialist country, it would compete against state enterprise. Because worker cooperatives are neither fish nor fowl, they can make both sides edgy. At the same time, they cannot be rejected easily by either side. We have seen most clearly in the cases of Poland and China that government efforts to deny local members control of the co-ops (by moving important decisions to the state apparatus) has had a deleterious effect on motivation and performance in the co-ops. Similarly, efforts in the United States to reduce or eliminate local member control in employee-owned firms (by not granting voting rights and other avenues for worker voice) can be expected to have the same consequence.

In the last analysis, the role of the state in promoting cooperatives is limited. The experience with worker co-ops in Spain, Portugal, Italy, Poland, China, and elsewhere suggests that their democratic character can be preserved only if they are grass-roots formations. Once co-ops exist, the state can effectively facilitate them, if it wishes, through the provision of loan capital, purchasing contracts for goods or services, seed grants, technical advice, or tax incentives. The co-ops themselves can be expected to build self-help federations to provide support services for each other. Democratic control is an inherent feature of workers' cooperation, of whatever form, and this means that external agencies such as governments, or banks, or labor unions can restrict the autonomy of the enterprise or its members only at the peril of losing many of the benefits of the cooperative form.

Life span

Another factor that will greatly affect the future growth of the cooperative sector is the average life span that individual cooperatives may expect. Logically, cooperatives may terminate in two ways: They may cease to exist, or they may be transformed into a nondemocratic form of organization, thereby losing their defining cooperative character. Experience teaches that the processes by which cooperatives (or more generally, democratic organizations) tend to die or to degenerate can be inhibited or speeded up by specific choices that their members make at critical junctures.

Earlier in this book we made the case that a provisional or transitory orientation follows from participant commitment to higher goals, and that such an orientation was characteristic of the particular population of people in our collectives. A provisional orientation generally is not characteristic of people with greater family or financial responsibilities. Certainly, members of the plywood and garbage collection co-ops of the 1920s wanted their co-op enterprises to last, and worker-owners in the contemporary wave of ESOPs equally desire organizational stability. Organizational continuation is important, both for individual job security and for the goods and services the organization provides to the community, and thus relatively few people are in a position to be unconcerned with organizational longevity.

The data on how well cooperatives meet this need for stability are seriously limited. Systematic research comparing the longevity of worker cooperatives and that of comparable small businesses has not been done. Only a few scraps of data are available. Jones (1979) found in his study of nineteenth century worker cooperatives a median duration of somewhat less than 10 years, although longevity varied widely between industries. More than half of the co-operatives dating from the 1920s and 1930s, particularly in the plywood industry and in the refuse collection industry, are still in operation today. Of the contemporary wave of grass-roots collectives, still less is known. One effort to make phone calls to all of the collectives listed in the 1976 San Francisco Bay Area Collective Directory found that almost one-third of the previously listed collectives had disconnected phone numbers by 1981 (Kepp, 1981, p. 31). If it is assumed that all those collectives with disconnected numbers had gone out of business, this information would indicate only a 33⅓ percent rate of dissolution over five years. This compares with an 80 percent rate of dissolution over five years for conventional small businesses in the United States, according to figures from the Small Business Administration. Although many participants in and observers of the contemporary collectives mythologize a short life span, we are aware of no general data that support this belief, and in fact what little data exist suggest that collectives are doing a good deal better than conventionally owned small businesses.

These figures on longevity do not say what specific causes may lead to the demise of cooperatives. The death of a co-op can mask a number of different phenomena.

Many co-op failures are essentially economic in origin. They are market failures. In this respect they are no different from their small business counterparts. In the view of Beatrice Webb (1921, p. 229),

So long as the co-operative society . . . constitutes only one among other forms of production and distribution . . . the co-operative society has to maintain itself in continual rivalry with capitalist enterprise. . . . Except in so far as it can effect a genuine improvement or economy in management, every step by which it departs from the competitive standard set by its capitalist rivals results in lowering the margin between cost and price. Any wide departure, whether in the way of higher wages, shorter hours, more favourable conditions of employment, or failing to take advantage of the best terms of obtaining raw materials or of employing the most efficient processes, means failure to serve the customers on the same terms as the capitalist trader. Thus the co-operative society, if it is to continue to exist and make headway against capitalist enterprise, cannot go beyond the currently prevailing conditions of employment.

There is, no doubt, some truth to these assertions, especially where co-ops exist in a relatively unregulated market economy. On the other hand, we join others in arguing that to the extent that worker cooperatives democratize ownership and control of the workplace, they have demonstrable advantages in terms of labor motivation, productivity, lowered waste, and higher quality. Ultimately, this often lessens the need for and cost of management supervision. Cooperatives often do best where they are providing services or goods that are not available from capitalist enterprises. For this reason, some of the contemporary co-ops have turned to customized or hard-crafted goods, and others have pioneered alternative services, such as wholistic health care, legal services for the poor, feminist counseling, or conservation and ecology-related consulting. The cooperative's oppositional ideology allows it to fill a specialized niche: to serve specific social needs that generally go unattended by conventional businesses. By providing qualitatively different goods or services, the cooperative may reduce its direct competition with capitalist enterprises.

In other circumstances, not contemplated by the Webbs, cooperatives may disband, not out of economic failure, but because they choose to do so. Some worker cooperatives in the nineteenth and twentieth centuries were formed as a result of a strike or work lockout. In these cases, the cooperative was conceived by participants as a temporary solution to put pressure on the previous employer, and the voluntary termination of the cooperative signaled not its failure but its success in convincing the employer to take the workers back under more favorable terms.

Some of the contemporary co-ops decide to dissolve, despite the fact that they are economically viable, because members do not want to see certain alterations made in the form or purpose of the organization. As discussed earlier, Free Clinic members considered this line of action, but ultimately rejected it. Where changes appear imminent and where members are at odds with the original purposes for which they joined the organization, their commitments to higher goals may win out. In such cases, they may purposefully disband the organization, an unlikely event in bureaucratic organizations.

Still other processes, having little to do with economic failure or purposeful dissolution, may lead to the demise of cooperatives. As Whyte (1978) points out, cooperatives have often faced a "catch-22 situation: over a period of years they were doomed to lose this form of ownership either because they failed or because they were successful." Cooperatives may be killed by their very success. Several causes for this have been observed. Individuals generally start a cooperative as equal partners, but with the passage of time and the success of the firm, they see that it is not in their economic self-interest to let new members in, since the creation of new shares will only dilute the equity of the previous members. If more workers are needed to meet the demand of growing production and sales, cooperative members learn that they can often make more money by hiring additional help and expropriating the surplus value of others, rather than by extending full ownership rights to new workers. As a result (unless there is a proviso in the original charter of the co-op permitting new workers the right to membership after some probationary period, or unless the co-op is exceptionally committed to democracy for idealistic reasons), there is a tendency over time for cooperatives to hire more help and to extend fewer memberships. This leads to a serious deterioration in the cooperative form, producing a two-class system of owners and nonowners.

In addition to this strong economic incentive, cooperatives often have ethnic or cultural bonds that lead them in a similar direction (Russell, 1984, 1985). Such ties are an enormous aid in the formation stage of the co-op, helping the group to work together smoothly, but on the other side of ethnic/kinship/friendship solidarity is the possibility that it may lead to the exclusion of "outsiders," people who are seen to be different. In the end, the Italian immigrants who founded the garbage collection co-ops in San Francisco in the 1920s, like the Soviet Jewish immigrants who started the taxi co-ops in Los Angeles 50 years later, resisted the entrance of other minority group members into their co-ops, producing a sharp line of demarcation between members and hired help, the "ins" and the "outs" (Russell, 1984, 1985). This is an example of the solidarity that can be created by a "clan" structure (Ouchi, 1980).

Finally, degeneration of the cooperative form may be hastened by the influence of the outside environment. Even where cooperatives seek seclusion from the environment, communal autarky is a practical impossibility. In his study of the kibbutzim system, Ben-Ner (1982) argues that communes gradually adapt their values and their form of organization to the environment, even though adaptation may be antithetical to collectivist values and principles of organization. Using a novel empirical approach, Ben-Ner looks at "revealed preferences" implicit in kibbutzim choices for collective consumption versus private consumption. He computes a ratio of collective to private consumption in different kibbutzim in 1955 and 1965, and the data indicate a strong decommunalization of values (Ben-Ner, 1982, pp. 27–30). In order to do business with dominant economic enterprises, communes must, according to Ben-Ner, develop structures and values that are isomorphic with surrounding institutions. We would add that outside inequality forces cooperatives to pay members more unequally than they might otherwise desire in order to attract and retain highly skilled personnel. Similarly, outside record-keeping requirements may foist off the same need on reluctant collectives. These adaptations to the environment (i.e., isomorphism) may help the cooperative to survive, but they may also lead to the degeneration of the cooperative form.[7] Organizational theorists have argued that the tendency toward isomorphism is a fact of all organizational life, but that it varies with the environment of the organization (Emery and Trist, 1965; Aldrich, 1979).

These processes of developing a closely knit "in-group" that resists taking in outsiders, of hiring help rather than offering full membership, and of gradually adapting to the values and the ways of the outside environment, are unplanned, natural, perhaps even imperceptible. But taken together, they weaken the fabric of the collective. With fewer members and fewer shares, the price of the shares is bid up. And with the decommunalization of cooperative values, emotions will no longer hold the cooperative together. Ultimately, the cooperative may lose its integrity as a cooperative, and members may become more open to private investor offers for the purchase of shares.

The *Real Paper,* for example, was ultimately defeated by its own economic success. After 2½ years of operation, this newspaper had built up an impressive circulation and was turning a substantial profit. This made it attractive to private investors who offered $325,000 for the paper. Like the *Community News* in this study, the *Real Paper* was collectively owned by its staff members. For those staffers who were fatigued, disillusioned, or otherwise ready to move on, the $325,000 proved irresistible. Hence, what began as a staff-owned and controlled alternative paper became, by virtue of its financial success, a privately owned enterprise (Kopkind, 1974, 1975). Similarly, Bernstein (1975) describes a cooperative plywood factory where pressures to sell out to a large corporation mounted for a variety of reasons, not the least of which was the attractiveness to the workers of getting big money for their share of the stock (between $20,000 and $40,000 apiece). Again, the very financial success of the cooperative enterprise makes it that much more enticing to sell into private hands, thereby eliminating altogether the collectivist basis of the organization.

To end here on a negative note would be deceptive. The point of this section has been to show the various ways in which co-ops come to an end, either by ceasing to exist or by changing into something else. Many co-ops do not die early deaths, but continue to function as effective and democratic organizations over a period of many years. Overall, as was previously noted, co-ops appear to survive considerably better than conventional small businesses, an impressive testimony to their viability. Mere survival of an organization says nothing, of course, about whether internal democracy has been preserved, but organizational democracy can be made to work indefinitely if members are committed to the principle, if they are knowledgeable about the organizational conditions that foster its development, and if they are wiling to work at creating, maintaining, and occasionally renewing direct democracy in the workplace. To paraphrase Menachem Rosner, there are no permanent achievements. Democracy requires permanent struggle.

The proliferation and success of cooperatives depends not only on the struggle for democracy within the collectivity, but also on social forces beyond the organization's control. The future of cooperatives will hinge on the extent to which cooperatives receive state and other major institutional support, compete effectively in the marketplace, and develop the organizational capability for long-term, democratic survival.

8. Overview and conclusions

Organizations come and go. Cooperatives, in particular, have risen and fallen in at least four previous waves in American history. Only history can tell how long the current movement will last, whether it will burgeon into a substantial and lasting sector of the economy, or whether it will become a forgotten experiment.

The master trend of the twentieth century has not been toward greater democratization of organizations – quite the contrary. It has been toward growing concentration both in the economy and in government institutions, with fewer and fewer economic units having control over an increasing share of the assets. Trends of this magnitude, however, often set into motion social forces that oppose them, countertrends that eddy against the main current. The desire for self-determination is such a countertrend. As the autonomy of the individual diminishes in ever-larger organizations, and as control becomes increasingly remote, some individuals recoil. Joining with others, they try to build communities, families, and workplaces that offer autonomy and control. What all of the examples discussed in this book have in common is this simple, but profound, desire for self-initiated, self-paced, self-controlled work. Given, too, the necessity and desire for meaningful group life, individual freedom becomes a value to be maximized within the context of local, collective control.

Today, the drive for workplace democracy has forms of expression that were unknown a short time ago. In the United States there are small grassroots collectives in virtually every community, "quality of work life" efforts in many *Fortune* 500 corporations, and worker-owned ESOPs in scores of formerly private industrial plants. Similar trends exist in Europe, in addition to the legislated workers' councils and workers' representatives on boards of directors in many European nations. The breadth of the drive for workplace democracy today is indicated by its international scope. The constituency, too, is broad and various. The people involved in, for instance, quality-of-work-life programs are different from the people involved in co-ops or in ESOPs. Each group has its own conferences, newsletters, and networks.

183

They are each in a sense participants in separate submovements with little articulation between them, but they are responding to the same human need for voice, for some measure of control, and the same organizational need for flexibility and innovation. Democratic control gives the organization the benefits of experience and knowledge from all levels of the organization; it gives the individual the chance to be heard. The many faces that workplace democratization has assumed this past decade and the international appeal of this movement suggest that this is not a passing fad, but an enduring historical evolution.

The recent growth of democratic forms in the workplace comes as a counterpoint to the time-honored sociological belief in the inevitability of oligarchy, a belief so widespread that it led Alvin Gouldner (1955, p. 507) to comment that social scientists have become in this respect "morticians, all too eager to bury men's hopes." This book takes seriously the evidence for the fragility of democratic systems, but does not present simply another case study in which democracy yields to oligarchy and abandons its original goals. Instead, we observed grass-roots democratic organizations in order to tease out the generic organizational features of democracy and the specific conditions that aid or impede the struggle for democratic control. By taking this conditional approach, we hope both to contribute to an empirically grounded theory of organizational democracy and to support by systematic investigation people's aspirations for self-managed work.

The larger political meaning of this set of organizational phenomena will reside, we believe, in the ability or inability of new forms to demonstrate that democratically managed organizations can "work." They must show that they can accomplish the tasks that need doing in this or any society (education, health care, production, etc.) without recourse to hierarchical authority relations. To the extent that they manage to do this, they provide a concrete model of what cooperative relations to production can look like.

American values and organizational democracy

The American public may be more receptive to these new ideas and forms of organization than is generally recognized. A poll by Hart Associates asked Americans which of three types of economic systems they would prefer to work in: Only 8 percent preferred work in a government agency, and only 20 percent chose the private investor–owned company, the now dominant form. The majority, 66 percent, preferred to work in companies owned and controlled by their employees (Rifkin, 1977, pp. 45–57). In addition, Hart found that only 17 percent of the public would keep the economic system as it is, while 37 percent would make "minor adjustments," and 41 percent favored "making a major adjustment to try things which have not been tried before." Recent Yankelovich polls show sharply declining levels of confidence in many American institutions and occupational groups.

These polls would seem to reflect substantial changes in public attitudes. They suggest an increasingly prevalent questioning of established institutions and an openness to alternative ways of organizing work. But delegitimation alone does not ensure change, particularly if it is replaced by cynicism. This is where concrete alternative models play a role. In the absence of any international models that have gained widespread acceptance in America, domestic models of democratically controlled institutions are being created. In their very form of operation, democratic workplaces serve an educative function: They begin to convince participants (and clients and onlookers) that "workers do not need bosses to get work done" (Vocations for Social Change, 1976), that hierarchical authority structures and their corresponding stratification systems may not be necessary incentives to get people to do their jobs, and that labor and capital need not be separated.

Although some members in the collectives we observed did set out to build a model, an exemplar organization, that would demonstrate a better way to organize work, countercultural visions always take root among a minority. Is there any evidence that the collectivist values found in the co-ops are diffusing throughout our society?

It is reasonable to suppose that most ordinary people are not as value-driven as co-op members. Indeed, most scholars have presumed that people turn to cooperatives or ESOPs for practical, economistic reasons, though there have been relatively few empirical studies of the actual motives of participants. A case study of a mid-1970s worker buy-out of a firm scheduled for shutdown found job-saving motives to be foremost among both blue-collar and white-collar employees (Hammer and Stern, 1980). Examining historical materials on cooperatives in the United States from 1880 to 1935, Shirom (1972) concludes they were formed by members chiefly as a defensive measure to save jobs or to avoid downward mobility, and secondarily, to achieve entrepreneurial ambitions. Totally lacking in America, he argues, were collectivist ideals, although such ideals occasionally were found among European cooperators. Greenberg, picking up Shirom's argument in a recent study of the plywood co-ops, finds that members of the cooperatives (started in the 1920s) joined the firms primarily for economistic reasons. Over time, the experience of being in the co-op reinforces in the members their original individualistic, petit-bourgeois values (Greenberg, 1981).

This view contrasts markedly with the communal and egalitarian values we found in our study. As we argued in Chapter 1, we see participation in collectivist organizations as motivated by a *coalescence* of material and ideal interests. Participation provides a means of livelihood consistent with members' values, where conventional work situations are distasteful or not available to members. Even in conventional work settings, we expect that values favorable to cooperation are more widespread in our society than is supposed by the economistic view.

Hochner and his associates are studying a case unfolding at present wherein A & P, a national supermarket chain, closed most of its stores in Philadelphia. This put 2,000 employees out of work, but A & P agreed, in a unique contract with the United Food and Commercial Workers union, to reemploy many of these people in new "Super Fresh" markets, which would have a QWL program to involve employees in decision making. Other employees would be allowed to purchase closed A & P stores and run them independently. The Super Fresh stores and the "O&O" stores (meaning worker owned and operated) opened in late 1982 and early 1983. Because the former A & P workers have an unusual set of options open to them, the researchers are in a position to analyze differences between those workers who choose worker ownership and those who don't. Hochner and Granrose (1986) find that those workers who pledge money for worker ownership (a worker must pledge $5,000 to become a member of an O&O) *are* more interested in avoiding unemployment, and *are* more entrepreneurial than nonpledgers. However, they *also* have more collectivist/participatory values than nonpledgers. The strength of the latter factor was contrary to the researchers' initial hypotheses and came as a surprise. Hochner and Granrose (1986) conclude that "the level of collective idealism expressed by these workers points to a greater interest in workplace reform than is generally recognized among American workers."

The finding of such values among grocery workers suggests that the countercultural belief in autonomy and self-determination of the 1970s has spread far. Further evidence comes from a just-completed reanalysis of the Hart public opinion survey (Zipp, Luebke, and Landerman, 1984). The researchers find the social base of support for workplace democracy to include nearly *all* segments of the society, especially blue-collar workers and professional/technical workers. The only class that does not support the redistribution of power in the workplace are managers and owners. Further, affluence does not much diminish blue-collar workers' support of democracy. Union membership has no significant effect, and there are no significant differences by race or party, although liberals are more in favor. Young persons and females are somewhat more likely to support democratization than middle-aged persons and males. On the basis of the evidence, the authors conclude that workplace democracy is an issue that cuts across important political cleavages in the United States. Where most surveys of political-economic attitudes in this country have focused on traditional welfare state items, using these to draw conclusions about working class conservatism, Zipp and his associates argue that political attitudes are multidimensional and that quite different conclusions are warranted on issues of workers' control.

The findings of Zipp et al. are reinforced by a recent reanalysis of the 1977 Quality of Employment Survey national probability sample of working Americans. Excluding owners and managers from their analysis, the researchers find that support for workplace participation is stronger among women than among men and stronger among nonwhites than among whites (Fenwick and Olson, 1984). Somewhat at odds with the Zipp findings, however, Fenwick and Olson find that support for workplace participation increases with education, but declines with age, occupational status, and income. Also, contrary to Zipp et al., they find that union members favor participation substantially more than nonunion workers (1984, pp. 17–18).

Finally, comparing a sample of United States workers in Indianapolis and a sample in Sweden, Haas (1980) finds both groups of workers to be extremely supportive of workplace democracy, but only the Swedes favor having a "final say" in work-related decisions.

Although the collectivist values in small grass-roots co-ops cannot, on the face of it, be assumed to be shared by broader segments of society, the above studies indicate that the counterculture may have been a leading indicator of value shifts in America. Today, even before workplace democracy has received sustained public discussion, it apparently holds natural attraction for broad segments of the working population. The current backlash against big business and big government may well speak of a desire to enhance individual autonomy and grass-roots collective control.

The desire for grass-roots, democratically controlled organizations is not limited to the American counterculture nor, indeed, to twentieth century industrial workers. In times of social upheaval, locally initiated alternative institutions have played an important role.

In revolutionary periods, alternative work organizations are required, not only for their propagandistic functions, but also to provide needed human services and products in a time when mainstream institutions are disrupted. Roberta Ash (1972, pp. 75–78) documents the vital role played by locally organized alternative institutions during the American Revolution. Dual structures, such as the Committees of Correspondence and the Minutemen, were crucial to the Revolution's success. In times of general strikes, ad hoc worker-established cooperatives are frequently organized (again, at the local level) to provide essential services to the population (Brecher, 1972). Likewise, the "soviets" played a necessary role in revolutionary Russia, providing decentralized and effective alternative industrial, political, and social structures. Later, after consolidating his power, Lenin abandoned the soviets in favor of a more centralized model of social organization (Gurley, 1976). During the Spanish Civil War, self-managed workers' committees collectivized both industry and agriculture until they were militarily defeated (Guerin, 1970, pp. 114–143). Throughout American history workers' cooperatives have risen in times of social protest and subsided during quieter times, persistently reasserting the desire of working people to control directly the process and end products of their work. In recent revolutionary actions in Portugal, as we saw, worker cooperatives sprang up in agriculture and in industry to control production, until their development was halted by a military coup. In Poland, too, local control and self-management in the economy were a major demand of Solidarity until the movement was repressed.

It is clear that collectivist, alternative structures have been important historically. Yet, the organizations studied here are very different from the Russian soviets, the Portuguese collectives, or the alternative structures discussed by Ash. The kinds of alternative organizations discussed by Ash and Brecher were born in revolutionary times and were therefore more self-consciously and immediately revolutionary in purpose. Few of the contemporary cooperatives would claim revolutionary goals.

We must leave to history the question of what social impact the current wave of alternative institutional development in the United States will have. So far, collectivist organizations have attracted only a rather limited social base of clientele and worker-owners, and they have remained predominantly, though not entirely, in the service sector of the economy. Whether they can spread in significant ways to other segments of the economy and attract a wider social base remains to be seen.

Important, some of the ideas and lessons from the experimentation with democratic management in the collectives over the past 15 years are being applied, albeit in somewhat watered-down fashion, to the more recent developments of worker-ownership using the ESOP form and to QWL in conventional firms. However, there has been considerable reinventing of the wheel. It is not necessary to argue that the organizational practices and values of the collectives are being directly appropriated, without due credit, by some of the ESOP and worker participation programs. Indeed, we believe one of the major weaknesses of the workplace democracy movement is that most people in the ESOP and QWL movements have little awareness of collectives, or of each other's experiences. In our opinion, each movement could learn much from the achievements and difficulties of the other two (Rothschild-Whitt, 1983). Each of these three movements appears to represent different constituencies' responses to the same spirit of the times: a growing desire by individuals to control fundamental aspects of their work lives, and a growing realization of the need for organizations that can sustain commitment, innovation, and flexibility. The grass-roots collectives may have been the earliest and purest expression of this *zeitgeist,* but what began as oppositional values and practices are now on their way to such broad acceptance in the business world and among the public at large that the collectives are perhaps in danger of losing some of their oppositional flavor.[1]

Work and play

The basic contradiction within democratic organizations is between the logic of substantive rationality, in which the democratic process is of value in itself, and instrumental rationality, which is directed toward a product. All organizations are concerted actions toward some end and, as such, must be instrumental. One may begin by making shoes because one gets pleasure from the act of creating them. But what begins as a vehicle for self-expression must also sell on a market. It is impossible to live in a market economy, dominated by exchange-for-profit maximization, and not be touched by this concern.

As sites of production, co-ops exist in a world of markets. Otherwise, they could be purely playful enterprises. In a sense, collectivist organizations may be said to be developing a coalescence of work and play in their dual commitment to process and product. Concern for product is forced upon them by the necessity of exchange in a market. Concern for process is of their own creation and is at odds with commercial values.

People have had different reasons for introducing greater participation in the workplace. In QWL it is to improve productivity and the quality of product in order to better compete for markets. It is assumed that drawing information from the widest group of employees and involving them will add to the organization's know-how and to members' commitment and satisfaction. In co-ops, the purpose of democratic control over the organization is to ensure that the product or service will be in line with one's own values, that the distribution of surplus will be more egalitarian, and that the process of work will be, in and of itself, autonomous and therefore "fun."

To oppose formal rationality principles with substantive rationality principles is perhaps only an academic and bulky way of contrasting organizational practices that are intended to achieve something in the marketplace with organizational practices that are undertaken because they are directly gratifying for the people involved. Possibly the collectivist organization can arise only where technological capacity is great enough to free most from toil. We can hunt in the morning, fish in the afternoon, and talk philosophy at night only when we have the technological capacity to easily sustain material existence. When work is relatively free from the press of necessity it becomes self-expressive, playful activity.

The mechanical-industrial age vastly increased humankind's capacity to reproduce material existence. Now we appear to be moving into an electronic age that vastly again increases our capacity in this respect and also alters the nature of work, from transforming things to creating and disseminating new values, services, and knowledge. This transformation perhaps will give us more freedom to merge work with play.

This is, we believe, the fundamental meaning of the organizational paradigm defined and analyzed in this book. After 50 years' elaboration and specification of the behavior and theory of bureaucracy, the experience of the grass-roots collectives suggest a wholly new model of organization that must be assessed against its alternative values and aspirations.

Awareness that the world's resources are limited and shrinking suggests that we are moving away from gargantuan size and rapid growth rates as yardsticks of success, to a concern with the social utility and quality of products or services. The move from the mechanical age of moving parts to the electronic age of integrated systems will lead us to seek organic forms of organization to replace mechanistic ones. The greater difficulty and complexity of problems faced by organizations will come to require the gathering of information from wider sectors of the organization, especially those involved in the direct production or provision of services, in turn calling for cross-department communication and collaborative relations. Ultimately, in a world of limited resources and complex questions, values and priorities assume more importance. And so democracy comes to the fore.

The pioneering experiments in alternate forms of organization may be deviant in our society, but we hold that the major shifts in our society will make them more "normal" over time. The exact forms that future organizations will take in modern society are not predictable, but we believe that the organic, collaborative, and democratic forms with which these alternatives are experimenting presage parallel changes in other organizations, which will come perhaps long after the current wave of co-ops comes and goes. It is thus important to observe these naturally occurring experiments now, to see what we can learn from them about the structures and processes of democratic management.

We have developed an empirically grounded theory of organizational democracy. The essential feature of such organizations, from the Weberian perspective, is that authority is collectively held. From the Marxian perspective they are important because they alter the social relations to production, dissolving at the organizational level the antithesis between capital and labor. Those who work also manage. The upshot of both is that the organization derives its logic and its unity from substantive values. Such values can come to the fore and be implemented only if there is democratic control of the process and product of labor. These organizations signal a shift from production for exchange value to production for use value, from a market calculus to a social utility calculus.

The major contribution of collectivist organizations to both social science and to social change is, as we see it, their development and practice of a new model of organization. We have tried to identify the organizational properties that characterize this model, the constraints on its practical realization, and the conditions enhancing members' potential for democratic control of the organization. We have pursued a dialectical analysis of organizational democracy, examining the contradictory forces within this form or acting upon it, and the potentials for reconciling such forces and synthesizing a viable form of democratic management. As a result, we have continually turned our attention to the dilemmas that collectivist organizations face in their everyday efforts to get the job done, while still retaining their democratic form.

The essence of play is that it does not have an instrumental end in mind: In itself it brings gratification. It is a triumph of process over goals. However, in our society a clear line of demarcation separates work from play. We are told not to "confuse" the two, that they are opposites. Collectivist organizations see them as related. In a sense, although they don't put it this way, members are trying to integrate the world of work with the sentiments of play. By putting process before product, they are trying to find a place for expressive impulses in an arena ordinarily reserved for instrumental activity. Of course it might be argued that even the most formalized bureaucracy cannot eliminate all traces of human emotion and expression, but the point is that these are regarded as inappropriate or misplaced in the bureaucracy. In the collectivist organization they are cultivated and sought. They are part of the way that the organization *accomplishes* its business.

Notes

Introduction

1 Our definition is similar to that used by Rob Paton in a study of worker cooperatives in England (1978, p. 2).
2 The term *producers' cooperative* is used in the legislative clauses of the National Consumer Cooperative Bank statute. For this reason it is now beginning to be picked up by some participants in the co-ops, but it is still a minority expression.

Chapter 1

1 For an analysis of how organizations that reject authority find functional alternatives to authority that allow them to maintain social control, see Swidler (1979).
2 For a fuller examination of the history of anarchist ideas and movements, see: Guerin, 1970; Woodcock, 1962; Krimerman and Perry, 1966; Benello and Roussopoulous, 1972; Bookchin, 1980.
3 Our synonymous use of the terms *authority* and *domination* (*Herrschaft*) is consistent with the interpretation of Reinhard Bendix (1962, pp. 290–292) and the translation of Weber by Roth and Wittich (Weber, 1968, p. 946), but it differs substantially from the translation by Henderson and Parsons (Weber, 1947, p. 152).

Chapter 2

1 The mean age of the general membership at the Food Co-op is 21 years, and only 8.5 percent of its membership 24 or older. The staff and board members of the co-op (who are much more likely to identify with the New Left) show a mean age of 24.5 years. At the Free Clinic the mean age is 27.5 years, and at the *Community News* it is 24.5 years.
2 If, as our evidence indicates, there is considerable continuity between activists of the 1970s and those of the 1960s, then the New Left is alive and active, albeit with an altered political direction and strategy. This does not imply that it always will be. Like others, we have argued that conditions of affluence render traditional work and accumulation values obsolete and incoherent, especially to those who are young enough and lucky enough to have grown up with the assumption of affluence. The reintroduction of conditions of apparent scarcity has caught such people unprepared. Thus, political energy may smolder and collective action may be dispersed as individuals seek to secure their personal futures. If the line of argument here is basically correct, then the appearance of scarcity can be expected to have a conservatizing influence.

Chapter 3

1 The organizational structures and processes of alternative service organizations bear considerable, though certainly not complete, resemblance to collectivist organizations in contemporary China. For specific points of comparison see Martin King Whyte (1973) and Bettleheim (1974).

2 As organizations grow beyond a certain size they are likely to find purely consensual processes of decision making inadequate, and may turn to direct voting systems. Other complex, but nevertheless democratic, work organizations may sustain direct democracy at the shop-floor level, while relying on elected representative systems at higher levels of the organization (see Edelstein and Warner, 1976).

3 Actually, Weber did recognize the possibility of directly democratic organization, but he dealt with this only incidentally as a marginal case (1968, pp. 948–952, 289–292). Although Weber's three types of legitimate domination were meant to be comprehensive, both in time and in substance, it is difficult, as Mommsen points out (1974, pp. 72–94), to find an appropriate place for modern plebiscitarian democracy in Weber's scheme. Weber did come to advocate the "plebiscitarian leader-democracy," but this was a special version of charismatic domination (Mommsen, 1974, p. 113). He did not support "democracies without leadership" (*fuhererlose Demokratien*), which try to minimize the domination of the few over the many, because organization without *Herrschaft* appeared utopian to him (1974, p. 87). Thus it is difficult to identify the acephalous organizations of this study with any of Weber's three types of authority.

4 Research in the San Francisco Bay area found that free school teachers have higher degrees from more prestigious universities than their public school counterparts (McCauley, 1971, p. 148).

5 Industrial organizations in China have implemented similar changes in the division of labor. These were considered an essential part of transforming the social relations of production. Their means for reducing the separation of intellectual work from manual work were similar to those used by the alternative work organizations reported in this paper: team work, internal education, and role rotation. For specific points of comparison see Bettleheim (1974) and Whyte (1973).

6 The eight dimensions put forth here are clearly interrelated. However, there is evidence from bureaucracies that these dimensions may be somewhat independent (Hall, 1963). That is, an organization may be highly collectivist on one dimension but not so on another, and the interrelationships between these variables may be elusive. For instance, of seven propositions offered by Hage (1965) in an axiomatic theory of organizations, six could be supported by the organizations in this study. One, however, that higher complexity produces lower centralization, was contradicted by the evidence of this study, although it has received empirical support in studies of social service bureaucracies (Hage, 1965; Hage and Aiken, 1970). Hage suggests that relationships in organizational theory may be curvilinear: When organizations approach extreme scores, the extant relationships may no longer hold or may actually be reversed. This is an important limitation to bear in mind, especially as we begin to consider organizations such as the ones in this study, which are by design extreme on all eight continua proposed in this model.

Menachem Rosner, a scholar of the Israeli kibbutzim, has argued on both theoretical and empirical grounds that the dimensions of collectivist democracy are internally cohesive (1983). In an empirical test of the internal consistency of this sort of model, Leslie Brown (1984) found that 8 out of 18 food co-ops met her criterion of having at least 8 out of her 12 characteristics of participatory democracy. In an original research proposal to the National Science Foundation, Etzkowitz and Cuzzort (1983) suggest that an alternative organization may reject hierarchical authority in favor of egalitarian decision making, while at the same time accepting the formalization of rules. This implies that the dimensions of the model presented in this chapter do not necessarily have to go together. They maintain that their model, "Type X," may have advantages over collectivist democracy.

7 The result of this effort was a two-tiered structure: The paper is incorporated as a general corporation and a trust, which owns all the stock in the paper. Each six months of full-time work is worth one voting share in the trust. This grants ultimate control of the paper to the staff, past and present. Immediate control is exercised by the Board of Directors of the corporation, which consists of the currently working staff. As a member of the paper said, "[T]he structure is neither graceful nor simple, but it . . . guarantees that the working staff will maintain editorial control, and makes it nearly impossible ever to sell the paper."

8 See, for example, the abortive attempt to raise capital for employee ownership at Kasanof's Bakery (*Boston Phoenix*, April 26,1977).

9 Organization-environment relations are always reciprocal. In part, the low wages, hard work, and intense personal involvement that make collectivist organizations seem so costly may be due to costs imposed by the environment. Conversely, collectivist organizations rely on goods and services produced by the surrounding bureaucratic organizations, e.g., light bulbs, fast food chains.

10 Swidler (1976) vividly describes the extent to which members of a free school will ransack their private lives to locate sources of glamour that will enhance their sense of worth and influence in the group.

11 Mansbridge (1976) observes that even the most genuinely democratic organization will accept some measure of inequality of influence in order to retain individual liberties.

Chapter 4

1 "Charismatic" individuals are not entirely absent from alternative institutions, of course. Swidler (1979) aptly describes the use of "charisma," or more broadly, of personal appeal, as a means of social control in free high schools. Charismatic authority – complete with hierarchical leadership and privileges based on rank – was evidenced in many of the successful, long-lived nineteenth-century communes examined by Kanter (1972a, pp. 117–120). However, such formalized authority would be anathema to the organizations in our study.

2 Organizations that are homogeneous in this sense probably register substantial agreement over organizational goals (or what Thompson and Tuden [1959] call "preferences about outcomes"), but register considerable disagreement about how to get there ("beliefs about causation"). In such cases, Thompson and Tuden predict that organizations will reach decisions by majority judgment. A collegium type of organization, they maintain, is best suited for solving judgmental problems. This would require all members to participate in each decision, route pertinent information about causation to each member, give each member equal influence over the final choice, require fidelity to the group's preference structure, and designate as ultimate choice the judgment of the majority. On all but the last point they correctly describe collectivist work organizations. Further, as they point out, the social science literature does not contain models of this type of organization as it does for bureaucracy (Thompson and Tuden, 1959, p. 200).

3 The effect of level of compensation, or more broadly, of the level of financial resources, on the collectivist organization requires further study. On the one hand, there is evidence from the work of Kanter (1972a, pp. 78–80) that an austere life-style contributed to commitment in nineteenth-century communes, whereas affluence diminished it. Likewise, Duberman (1972) found that economic precariousness helped to knit the community together and to

generate commitment at Black Mountain, a forerunner (1933–56) of the free school movement. People in the cooperative organizations we observed seemed to believe that a low level of financial gain would help to avert careerism. Still another possibility is that limited financial resources encourage innovation, by forcing the organization to imagine new ways of fulfilling their organizational needs that are not so costly as conventional means. What is needed is a systematic comparison of relatively poor cooperatives with quite prosperous ones, several of which have developed over the last few years, to investigate the effects of affluence on cooperative organizations.

4 The meager pay and demanding work schedule at the *Community News* bring to mind the sort of self-exploitation that owners of small businesses often practice (Galbraith, 1973). In some ways, the economic marginality of alternative enterprises is not unlike that of any small enterprise. Both seem to impose heavy doses of self-exploitation. In fact, the social change goals of collectivist organizations may provide a much stronger ideological justification for self-sacrifice than do the private profit goals of the small entrepreneur.

5 Similarly, Eisenstadt (1959) argues that direct dependence of the organization on its members and clients is a condition that facilitates the debureaucratization process. However, Eisenstadt is concerned with the debureaucratization of already bureaucratic organizations, whereas this work focuses on new organizations that have resisted bureaucratization from their inception.

6 Researchers in the New Systems of Work and Participation Program at the School of Industrial and Labor Relations, Cornell University, have investigated cases of employee-ownership: Robert Stern and Tove Hammer have studied the Library Bureau at Herkimer, New York; Janette Johannesen has examined the Vermont Asbestos Group; and Michael Gurdon the Saratoga Knitting Mill in Saratoga Springs, New York. In each of these cases, the role of the banks in limiting the participatory rights of the worker-owners has been in evidence (Rothschild-Whitt, 1979b).

7 This was reported in the *Los Angeles Times,* January 26, 1975, pt. 5, p. 5. Drawing on inherited wealth and on the profits of some countercultural enterprises, some young wealthy activists are committing their philanthropy to radical social change efforts. These radical sources of financial support are still relatively rare, and their impact on the receiving organization may be unlike that of conventional agencies of external funding.

8 Personal communication with Sandy Morgan, Department of Anthropology, University of North Carolina, Chapel Hill, 1980.

9 Though this sort of eagerness may be widespread, especially in the beginning stages of alternative organizations, it is not without exception. The Food Co-op, for instance, was offered a $6,500 grant from the student body government of a nearby university. Although this money was critical in allowing the co-op to buy the food refrigeration equipment it needed before the story could be legally opened, it did not grasp it eagerly. The co-op seriously debated the strings that might be attached to the grant and its effect on the future development of the co-op, before deciding to accept it. Sarason (1972) and Kozol (1972) have also noted the rarity of this kind of careful anticipation of future organizational problems in alternative institutions.

10 For an interesting analysis of the impact that advances in technology may have on cooperative forms of organization, see Russell, Hochner, and Perry (1977). Here the introduction of new packer trucks and centralized billing procedures in garbage collection cooperatives in San Francisco has reduced the number and complexity of jobs, carrying with it less task sharing and more division of labor. In a historical overview of this issue, Braverman (1974) shows how increasing differentiation and specialization in our society have degraded work, making jobs less wholistic, less skilled, and less equal.

11 Although the sharing of information, and therefore of influence, is value-based in collectives, it may also arise as a structural need in more conventional organizations. In a study of Children's Center, a psychiatric facility for children, Blau and Alba (1982) show that although this organization did not set out as a matter of policy or ideology to be collectivist in nature, certain units did evolve in a participatory-democratic direction. This happened because the complexity of role relations in the organization promoted interunit communication. The researchers found that individual staff members gained more influence in decision making to the extent that the *unit* they were part of was integrated into organization-wide communication networks. In other words, to the extent that individuals had access, through their units, to the information and contacts possessed by higher levels of the organization, they had more influence. The Blau and Alba research indicates that some of the general characteristics of collectivist democracy, as discussed in Chapter 3 (especially knowledge diffusion) may evolve in ordinary service bureaucracies. This is so because people's jobs require negotiating a complex network of role relations, for which they need rather broad information and contacts.

12 The Law Collective contributed to the development of the Peoples College of Law in Los Angeles. Established under the auspices of the National Lawyers Guild, Peoples College was described by the *New York Times* (October 16, 1975, p. 40) as "the only radical law school in the country." Peoples College was unique in many ways. It was run primarily by its students, had free child care, was guided by an activist philosophy, and offered courses on topics rarely considered in conventional law schools (e.g., on legal aspects of tenant-landlord relationships, police brutality, racism, immigration).

13 For a good review of this growing body of literature, with special reference to Third World countries, see Vail (1975). For industrialized society, Rueschemeyer (1977) has shown that traditional efficiency arguments for differentiation may be seriously flawed. Melman (1969), Stein (1974), and Frieden (1980) have addressed the issue of efficiency as it relates to cooperative enterprises.

Chapter 5

1 In positing an oppositional relationship between the alternative organization and its environment, this condition assumes that the society in which the alternative exists is predominantly capitalist and bureaucratic. Hence, this condition would not be expected to hold in a socialist–collectivist society.

2 This line of reasoning fits well the data from a number of case studies of worker-owned firms—Vermont Asbestos Group; Saratoga Knitting Mill; and the Library Bureau in Herkimer, New York—that were conducted at the New System of Work and Participation Program, School of Industrial and Labor Relations, Cornell University.

3 *Canadians for a Democratic Workplace Newsletter,* vol. 1, no. 4 (1977), p. 7.

4 It is not clear that the publicly funded centers will provide better services than did the grass-roots organizations. In fact, the opposite might be the case. A recent study (Forman and Wadsworth, 1983) finds that many federally funded community mental health centers provide few, if any, rape-related services, despite the mandate to do so.

5 There are more than 300 "straight" community newspapers in the Los Angeles metropolitan area. Unlike the *Community News,* they are privately owned, they see their purpose as covering traditional community news (e.g., civic clubs, high school football, PTA), and what national news they do contain is simply from the established wire services. They do not do the sort of original investigation, analysis, and comment that characterizes the *News.* All of these papers face financial hardships owing to the rapidly rising costs of

newsprint and advertising cutbacks by retailers in times of recession. But in a time when the readership of these traditional community newspapers is declining, that of the *Community News* is growing. (*Los Angeles Times,* 22 June 1975, pt. I, pp. 1, 25–28).

6 For illuminating discussions of the structural bases of this sort of intellectual and professional support for social change efforts, see Flacks (1971) and Zald and McCarthy (1975).

7 It is no doubt true that many individuals do get "burned out" by their experiences in alternative institutions. Emotional drain and exhaustion may be built into the structure of collectivist organizations, as Swidler (1976) vividly describes in free schools. What we are stressing here is that these individuals often resurface in other equally committed contexts.

8 For further details, see the *Socio-Economic Report* put out by the Bureau of Research and Planning, California Medical Association, October 1971.

Chapter 6

1 Delivered at the Caucus for a New Political Science, Brown University, November 8, 1975.

2 Starting with a basic schema developed by Wright (1976), Kalleberg and Griffin (1978, p. 380) categorize class as follows: "(1) the *petty bourgeoisie,* who own the means of production but do not control the labor power of others, (2) *small employers,* who own both the means of production and control the work activity of not more than 50 employees, (3) the *working class,* who, having neither ownership nor managerial functions, simply sell their labor power in the market . . . (4) the *managerial class,* who, while denied ownership roles, do control the labor power of others . . . [and (5) the *bourgeoisie*] who own production facilities and employ more than 50 persons." Lacking a large enough sample, they do not examine the job satisfaction of the last category.

3 Although worker expectations appear to rise when workers buy out firms to avoid a shutdown, expectations do not necessarily rise in other ESOPs. For example, when a founder sets up an ESOP for estate planning/financial reasons – depending on how the ESOP is described to the workers – employees may see the ESOP as merely a retirement benefit, a good profit-sharing tool, an indication of management's good-heartedness, or a tax dodge for the company (Katherine Klien, personal communication, 1983).

4 Based on personal communication with Katherine Klein of the National Center for Employee Ownership (1983).

5 Personal stress, particularly at high levels, is generally considered unpleasant, and most people seek to avoid it. However, not all stress is undesirable. All organizations must create some level of stress in their members. Psychologists have proposed that there is probably some *optimum* level of stress, below which little motivation or activity exists, and above which severe disorganization sets in. We are here considering disruptive levels of stress.

Chapter 7

1 See, for example, the cases of the IGP insurance firm in Washington, D.C., and of Breman enterprises in Holland (Rothschild-Whitt, 1981).

2 A study by Keith Bradley of the London School of Economics concludes that the economic performance of the Mondragon co-ops is better than that of local competing companies, partly because workers are more motivated and need less supervision (cited in Logan, 1981, p. 9).

3 For a detailed review of the research on workplace democracy and productivity, see Frieden (1980).

4 Personal communication with Ann Olivarius, Oxford University, 1982.

5 For these reasons and because of limitations of space, we do not examine in this section

the cases of Yugoslavia and Israel, two of the best-known and most extensively studied examples of cooperative development. Interested readers should consult, for example, Obradovic and Dunn (1976), Arzensek (1983), Rus (1970), Leviatan and Rosner (1980), Rosner (1983).

6 For a detailed analysis of the ways owners and managers have shaped ESOPs versus the ways workers would fashion them, and for an assessment of the recent union-initiated cases of Rath in Iowa, Hyatt-Clark in New Jersey, and the "O&Os" in Philadelphia, see Rothschild-Whitt (1984).

7 Contrarily, Holleb and Abrams (1975) have argued that collectives must forsake their early structure of personal relationships, autonomy in work, undifferentiated tasks, and commitment to ideology and must develop hierarchies, and formalized interaction and lose their ideological commitment before they can develop into "consensual democracies." The latter they view as a "stable compromise between the values and rewards of communalism and the necessities of existing in the real world" (1975, p. 149). Although Holleb and Abrams regard this as a positive process through which collectives should grow, there is no evidence in our study or any other that we know of to suggest that collectives can substantially bureaucratize and then revert back to some more mature form of democracy. The "real world" to which Holleb and Abrams want collectives to adapt is, of course, a capitalist–bureaucratic world in which the dominant institutions, social relations, and attitudes are in the main antithetical to collectivist principles of organization. With Ben-Ner, we would argue that the more cooperatives or communes decommunalize their values and organizational structures, the weaker and less able to resist environmental influences they become.

Chapter 8

1 It has been estimated that one-third of the *Fortune* 500 firms are developing worker participation programs (Walton, 1979), and a study by the New York Stock Exchange (1982) speaks admiringly of such efforts. A recent QWL conference (1981) attracted 1,500 participants, with many corporations sending a contingent of 10 or 15 people as representatives. In the sessions of the meeting, the corporate presenters spoke of the "new," "innovative," and even "revolutionary" ideas they are implementing in their firms. Virtually all of these ideas were in fact modest versions of participatory democracy. None of the corporate presenters gave any indication of awareness of cooperatives, and none seemed to have considered the possible importance of worker ownership in motivating the participation they desired.

In a very different context, Rothschild-Whitt spoke about the experiences of collectives in the United States at an international conference in Brussels. She found scholars, particularly those from Eastern Europe and the Soviet Union, to be incredulous at the idea that a movement toward worker ownership of any kind could be unfolding in the United States. How could such a thing gain support, they asked, in the heartland of capitalism? Americans, more familiar with the value Americans have long placed on autonomous work, on democratic decision making, on self-reliance, and on ownership, should be much less surprised.

References

Abell, Peter. 1981. "A Note on the Theory of Democratic Organization." *Sociology,* 15:262–264.

Abell, Peter, and Nicholas Mahoney. 1981. "The Social and Economic Potential of Small-Scale Industrial Producer Cooperatives in Developing Countries." Prepared for the Overseas Development Administration, London.

Aldrich, Howard. 1979. *Organizations and Environments.* Englewood Cliffs, N.J.: Prentice-Hall.

Aldrich, Howard, and Robert Stern. 1978. "Social Structure and the Creation of Producers' Cooperatives." Paper presented at the Ninth World Congress of Sociology, Uppsala, Sweden, August.

Appelbaum, Richard. 1976. "City Size and Urban Life." *Urban Affairs Quarterly,* December, pp. 139–170.

Argyris, Chris. 1974. "Alternative Schools: A Behavioral Analysis." *Teachers College Record,* 75:429–452.

Arzensek, Vlado. 1983. "Problems of Yugoslav Self-Management." *International Yearbook of Organizational Democracy,* 1:303–313.

Ash, Roberta. 1972. *Social Movements in America.* Chicago: Markam.

Avineri, Shlomo. 1968. *The Social and Political Thought of Karl Marx.* Cambridge: Cambridge University Press.

Bales, Robert F. 1950. *Interaction Process Analysis.* Chicago: University of Chicago Press.

Barkai, H. 1977. *Growth Patterns of the Kibbutz Economy.* Amsterdam: North Holland.

Bart, Pauline. 1981. "Seizing the Means of Reproduction: An Illegal Feminist Abortion Collective." Chicago Circle, School of Medicine, University of Illinois. Photocopy.

Bates, F. C. 1970. "Power Behavior and Decentralization." In *Power in Organizations,* ed. Mayer Zald, pp. 175–176. Nashville, Tenn.: Vanderbilt University Press.

Bendix, Reinhard. 1962. *Max Weber: An Intellectual Portrait.* Garden City, N.Y.: Anchor Books.

Benello, C. George, and Dimitrios Roussopoulos, eds. 1972. *The Case for Participatory Democracy.* New York: Viking Press.

Ben-Ner, Avner. 1982. "Changing Values and Preferences in Communal Organizations: Econometric Evidence from the Experience of the Israeli Kibbutz." In *Participatory and Self-Managed Firms: Evaluating Economic Performance,* ed. Derek Jones and Jan Svejnar. Lexington, Mass.: Lexington Books.

Bennis, Warren, and Philip Slater. 1968. *The Temporary Society.* New York: Harper & Row.

Berman, Katrina. 1967. *Worker-Owner Plywood Companies: An Economic Analysis.* Pullman, Wash.: Washington State University Press.

Bernstein, Paul. 1976. "Necessary Elements for Effective Worker Participation in Decision Making." *Journal of Economic Issues,* 10:490–522.

Bettleheim, Charles. 1974. *Cultural Revolution and Industrial Organization in China*. New York: Monthly Review Press.

Biggart, Nicole. 1977. "The Creative-Destructive Process of Organizational Change: The Case of the Post Office." *Administrative Science Quarterly*, 22:410–426.

Blau, Judith, and Richard Alba. 1982. "Empowering Nets of Participation." *Administrative Science Quarterly*, 27:363–379.

Blau, Peter. 1970. "Decentralization in Bureaucracies." In *Power in Organizations*, ed. Mayer Zald, pp. 150–174. Nashville, Tenn.: Vanderbilt University Press.

Blau, Peter, and W. Richard Scott. 1962. *Formal Organizations*. San Francisco: Chandler.

Bluestone, Barry, and Bennett Harrison. 1980. "Why Corporations Close Profitable Plants." *Working Papers for a New Society*, 8:15–23.

Blumberg, Paul. 1973. *Industrial Democracy: The Sociology of Participation*. New York: Schocken Books.

Bookchin, Murray. 1980. *Post-Scarcity Anarchism*. Palo Alto, Calif.: Ramparts Press.

Bottomore, T. B., ed. 1964. *Karl Marx: Selected Writings in Sociology and Social Philosophy*. New York: McGraw-Hill.

Bowles, Samuel, and Herbert Gintis. 1976. *Schooling in Capitalist America*. New York: Basic Books.

Braverman, Harry. 1974. *Labor and Monopoly Capital: The Degradation of Work in the Twentieth Century*. New York: Monthly Review Press.

Brecher, Jeremy. 1972. *Strike!* San Francisco: Straight Arrow Books; distributed by World Publishing Co., New York.

Brown, Leslie. 1984. "Patterns of Organizational Democracy: New Wave Food Coops and the Challenge of Congruence." Sociology Department, University of Minnesota. Photocopy.

Buber, Martin. 1960. *Paths in Utopia*. Boston: Beacon Press.

Calhoun, C. J. 1980. "Democracy, Autocracy, and Intermediate Associations in Organizations: Flexibility or Unrestrained Change?" *Sociology*, 14:345–361.

Cavan, Sherri. 1972. *Hippies of the Haight*. St. Louis: New Critics Press.

Chickering, Arthur W. 1972. "How Many Make Too Many?" In *The Case for Participatory Democracy*, ed. Benello and Rossopoulos. New York: Viking Press, pp. 213–227.

Cicourel, Aaron. 1964. *Method and Measurement in Sociology*. New York: The Free Press of Glencoe.

Coleman, James. 1970. "Social Inventions." *Social Forces*, 49:163–173.

Cornforth, Chris. 1983. "Experiences in the UK." Cooperatives Research Unit, Open University, Milton Keyes, England. Photocopy.

Crain, Joyce. 1978. "A Survey of U.S. Producer Cooperatives: Summary of the Initial Phase." Center for Economic Studies, Palo Alto, Calif. Photocopy.

Crozier, Michael. 1984. *The Bureaucratic Phenomenon*. Chicago: University of Chicago Press.

Derrick, Paul. 1981. "Industrial Cooperatives and Legislation." Paper presented at First International Conference on Producer Cooperatives, Copenhagen, Denmark, June.

Duberman, Martin. 1972. *Black Mountain: An Exploration in Community*, New York: E. P. Dutton.

Eckstein, Alexander. 1977. *China's Economic Revolution*. New York: Cambridge University Press.

Edelstein, J. David. 1967. "An Organizational Theory of Union Democracy." *American Sociological Review*, 32:19–31.

Edelstein, J. David, and Malcolm Warner. 1976. *Comparative Union Democracy: Organization and Opposition in British and American Unions*. New York: Wiley.

Eisenstadt, S. N. 1959. "Bureaucracy, Bureaucratization, and Debureaucratization." *Administrative Science Quarterly,* 4:302–320.

Elden, J. Maxwell. 1976. *Democracy at Work for a More Participatory Politics: Worker Self-Management Leads to Political Efficacy.* Ph.D. diss., University of California, Los Angeles.

Ellul, Jacques. 1964. *The Technological Society.* New York: Alfred A. Knopf.

Emery, F.E., and E.L. Trist. 1965. "The Causal Texture of Organizational Environments." *Human Relations,* 18:21–32.

Engels, Friedrich. 1959. "On Authority." In *Marx and Engels: Basic Writings on Politics and Philosophy,* ed. Lewis Fever. Garden City, N.Y.: Anchor Books.

Etzioni, Amitai. 1961. *A Comparative Analysis of Complex Organizations.* New York: The Free Press of Glencoe.

Etzkowitz, Henry, and Ray Cuzzort. 1983. "Organizational Succession and Emergent Forms." Research proposal submitted to the National Science Foundation.

Etzkowitz, Henry, and Laurin Raiken. 1982. "The Transformation of Artists' Organizations: A Case Study." New York University. Photocopy.

Etzkowitz, Henry, and Gerald Schaflander. 1978. "Fight for the Sun." Department of Sociology, State University of New York, Purchase, New York. Photocopy.

Fenwick, Rudy, and Jon Olson. 1984. "Contested Terrain or Created Consensus: Why Workers Want Participation in Workplace Decision-Making." Paper presented at the annual meetings of the American Sociological Association, San Antonio, Tex.

Flacks, Richard. 1967. "The Liberated Generation: An Exploration of the Roots of Student Protest." *Journal of Social Issues,* 23:52–75.

    1971. "Revolt of the Young Intelligentsia: Revolutionary Class Consciousness in Post-Scarcity America." In *The New American Revolution,* ed. Roderick Aya and Norman Miller. New York: The Free Press.

Forman, B.D., and J.C. Wadsworth. 1983. "Delivery of Rape-Related Services in CMHCs: An Initial Study." *Journal of Community Psychology,* 11:236–240.

French, J. Lawrence, and Joseph Rosenstein. 1981. "Employee Stock Ownership and Managerial Authority: A Case Study in Texas." Paper presented at the annual meeting of the Southwestern Sociological Association, March.

Frieden, Karl. 1980. *Workplace Democracy and Productivity.* Washington, D.C.: National Center for Economic Alternatives.

Galbraith, John Kenneth. 1973. *Economics and the Public Purpose.* Boston: Houghton Mifflin.

Gamson, Zelda. 1981. "Problems of Collectivist-Democratic Workplaces." Paper presented at Harvard University, June.

Gamson, Zelda, and Henry Levin. 1980. "Obstacles to the Survival of Democratic Workplaces." Center for Economic Studies, Palo Alto, Calif. Photocopy.

Gardner, Richard. 1976. *Alternative America.* Privately published.

Geise, Paula. 1974. "How the 'Political' Co-ops Were Destroyed." *North Country Anvil,* October-November, pp. 26–30.

Gillespie, David. 1981. "Adaptation and the Preservation of Collectivist-Democratic Organization." Department of Sociology, Michigan State University. Photocopy.

Glaser, Barney, and Anselm Strauss. 1967. *The Discovery of Grounded Theory: Strategies for Qualitative Research.* Chicago: Aldine.

Goodman, Richard, and Lawrence Goodman. 1976. "Some Management Issues in Temporary Systems: A Study of Professional Development and Manpower – The Theater Case." *Administrative Science Quarterly,* 21:494–501.

Gouldner, Alvin. 1954. *Patterns of Industrial Bureaucracy.* Glencoe, Ill.: The Free Press.

1955. "Metaphysical Pathos and the Theory of Bureaucracy." *American Political Science Review,* 49:496–507.

Graubard, Allen. 1972. *Free the Children.* New York: Pantheon Books.

Greenberg, Edward. 1981. "Industrial Self-Management and Political Attitudes." *The American Political Science Review,* 75:29–42.

Guerin, Daniel. 1970. *Anarchism: From Theory to Practice.* New York: Monthly Review Press.

Gurley, John G. 1976. *Challengers to Capitalism: Marx, Lenin, and Mao.* San Francisco: San Francisco Book Co.

Gusfield, Joseph. 1955. "Social Structure and Moral Reform: A Study of Women's Christian Temperance Union." *American Journal of Sociology,* 61:211–232.

Gyllenhammar, Pehr. 1977. *People at Work.* Addison-Wesley.

Haas, Ain. 1980. "Workers' Views on Self-Management: A Comparative Study of the U.S. and Sweden." In *Classes, Class Conflict, and the State,* ed. Maurice Zeitlin, pp. 276–295. Cambridge, Mass.: Winthrop.

Hage, Jerald. 1965. "An Axiomatic Theory of Organizations." *Administrative Science Quarterly,* 10:289–320.

Hage, Jerald, and Michael Aiken. 1970. *Social Change in Complex Organizations.* New York: Random House.

Hall, D., and K. Nougaim. 1968. "An Examination of Maslow's Need Hierarchy in an Organizational Setting." *Organizational Behavior and Human Performance,* 3:12–35.

Hall, John. 1978. *The Ways Out.* London: Routledge and Kegan Paul.

Hall, Richard. 1963. "The Concept of Bureaucracy: An Empirical Assessment." *American Journal of Sociology,* 69:32–40.

Hammer, Tove, and Robert Stern. 1980. "Employee Ownership: Implications for the Organizational Distribution of Power." *Academy of Management Journal,* 23:78–100.

Hammer, Tove, Jacqueline Landau, and Robert Stern. 1981. "Absenteeism When Workers Have a Voice: The Case of Employee Ownership." New York State School of Industrial and Labor Relations, Cornell University. Photocopy.

Hammond, John. 1981. "Worker Control in Portugal: The Revolution and Today." City University of New York. Photocopy.

Heckscher, Charles. 1980. "Worker Participation and Management Control." *Journal of Social Reconstruction,* 1:77–102.

Hegland, Tore. 1981. "Social Experiments and Education for Social Living." Aalborg University Center, Denmark. Photocopy.

Helfgot, Joseph. 1974. "Professional Reform Organizations and the Symbolic Representation of the Poor." *American Sociological Review,* 39:475–491.

Hendricks, Wendell. 1973. "On the Growing Edge." *Friends Journal,* June.

Henry, Jules. 1965. *Culture against Man.* New York: Vintage Books.

Hinton, William. 1966. *Fanshen: A Documentary of Revolution in a Chinese Village.* New York: Vintage Books.

Hochner, Arthur. 1981. "The Mentality of Worker Ownership: Reflections on Some Anomalous Findings." Paper presented at the First International Conference on Producer Cooperatives, Copenhagen, Denmark.

Hochner, Arthur, and Cherlyn Granrose. 1986. "Sources of Motivation to Choose Employee Ownership as an Alternative to Job Loss." *Academy of Management Journal.*

Holleb, Gordon, and Walter Abrams. 1975. *Alternatives in Community Mental Health.* Boston: Beacon Press.

Ingham, G. K. 1970. *Size of Industrial Organization and Worker Behavior.* Cambridge: Cambridge University Press.

Institute for Social Research, University of Michigan (ISR). 1977. *Employee Ownership*. Technical Assistance Project, Economic Development Administration. Washington, D.C.: U.S. Department of Commerce.

Jackall, Robert. 1976. "Workers' Self-Management and the Meaning of Work: A Study of Briarpatch Cooperative Auto Shop." Center for Economic Studies, Palo Alto, Calif. Photocopy.

Jackall, Robert, and Joyce Crain. 1984. "The Shape of the Small Worker Cooperative Movement." In *Worker Cooperatives in America*, ed. R. Jackall and W. M. Levin. Berkeley, Calif.: University of California Press.

Jenkins, J. Craig. 1977. "Radical Transformations of Organizational Goals." *Administrative Science Quarterly*, 22:568–586.

Johnson, Ana Gutierrez, and William Foote Whyte. 1977. "The Mondragon System of Worker Production Cooperatives." *Industrial and Labor Relations Review*, 31:18–30.

Jones, Derek. 1979. "Producer Cooperatives in the U.S." Department of Economics, Hamilton College. Photocopy.

1980. "Producer Cooperatives in Industrialized Western Economies." *British Journal of Industrial Relations*, 18:141–154.

1981. "Italian Producer Cooperatives, 1975–1978: Productivity and Organizational Structure." Paper presented at the First International Conference on Producer Cooperatives, Copenhagen, Denmark, June.

Kalleberg, Arne, and Larry Griffin. 1978. "Positional Sources of Inequality in Job Satisfaction." *Sociology of Work and Occupations*, 5:371–401.

Kanter, Rosabeth Moss. 1972a. *Commitment and Community*. Cambridge: Harvard University Press.

1972b. "The Organization Child: Experience Management in a Nursery School." *Sociology of Education*, 45:186–211.

1977. *Men and Women of the Corporation*. New York: Basic Books.

Kanter, Rosabeth M., and Louis Zurcher, Jr. 1973. "Alternative Institutions." A special issue of *The Journal of Applied Behavioral Science, 9*.

Katz, Michael. 1975. *Class, Bureaucracy, and Schools: The Illusion of Educational Change in America*. New York: Praeger.

Kaye, Michael. 1972. *The Teacher Was the Sea: The Story of Pacific High School*. New York: Links Books.

Keil, Thomas J. 1982. "Extraorganizational Factors in the Emergence and Stabilization of a Producer Cooperative." Paper presented at the International Sociological Association meetings, Mexico City.

Keith, Pam. 1978. "Individual and Organizational Correlates of a Temporary System." *The Journal of Applied Behavioral Science*, 14:195–203.

Keniston, Kenneth. 1968. *Young Radicals*. New York: Harcourt, Brace, and World.

Kepp, Michael. 1981. "The Berkeley Collectives: An Outside Perspective." *Communities*, 47:29–31.

Kopkind, Andrew. 1974. "Hip Deep in Capitalism: Alternative Media in Boston." *Working Papers for a New Society*, Spring, pp. 14–23. See also follow-up comment by Bernstein in *Working Papers for a New Society*, Summer 1975, pp. 2–3.

Kowalak, Tadeusz. 1981. "Work Co-operatives in Poland." Paper presented at the First International Conference on Producer Cooperatives, Copenhagen, June.

Kozol, Jonathan. 1972. *Free Schools*. Boston: Houghton-Mifflin.

Krimmerman, Leonard, and Lewis Perry, eds. 1966. *Patterns of Anarchy*. Garden City, N.Y.: Doubleday.

Kropotkin, Peter. 1902. *Mutual Aid: A Factor in Evolution*. London: McClure, Phillips.

Kruse, Douglas. 1981. "The Effects of Worker Ownership Upon Participation Desire: An ESOP Case Study." Honors B.A. thesis. Economics Department, Harvard College, Cambridge, Mass.

Lawson, Ronald. 1981. "He Who Pays the Piper: The Consequences of Their Income Sources for Social Movement Organizations." Urban Studies Department, Queens College, New York. Photocopy.

Leavitt, H. J. 1964. *Managerial Psychology.* Chicago: University of Chicago Press.

Levitan, Uri, and Menachem Rosner. 1980. *Work and Organization in Kibbutz Industry.* Norwood, Pa.: Norwood Editions.

Lindenfeld, Frank. 1982. "Problems of Power in a Free School." In *Workplace Democracy and Social Change.* Boston: Porter Sargent.

Lindkvist, Lars, and Claes Svensson. 1981. "Worker-Owned Companies in Sweden." Paper presented at the First International Conference on Producer Cooperatives, Copenhagen, Denmark, June.

Lipset, S. M., Martin Trow, and James Coleman. 1962. *Union Democracy.* New York: Anchor Books.

Litwak, Eugene. 1961. "Models of Bureaucracy Which Permit Conflict." *American Journal of Sociology,* September, pp. 177–184.

Lockett, Martin. 1981. "Producer Cooperatives in China: 1919–1981." Paper presented at the First International Conference on Producer Cooperatives, Copenhagen, Denmark, June.

Logan, Christopher. 1981. "Adapting the Mondragon Experience." Paper presented at the First International Conference on Producer Cooperatives, Copenhagen, June.

Long, Richard. 1979. "Desires for and Patterns of Worker Participation after Conversion to Employee Ownership." *Academy of Management Journal,* 22:611–617.

Mansbridge, Jane. 1973a. "Town Meeting Democracy." *Working Papers for a New Society,* 1:5–15.

    1973b. "Time, Emotion, and Inequality: Three Problems of Participatory Groups." *Journal of Applied Behavioral Science,* 9:351–368.

    1977. "Acceptable Inequalities." *British Journal of Political Science,* 7:321–336.

    1980. *Beyond Adversary Democracy.* New York: Basic Books.

    1982. "Fears of Conflict in Face-to-Face Democracies." In *Workplace Democracy and Social Change.* Boston: Porter Sargent.

Marcuse, Herbert. 1962. *Eros and Civilization.* New York: Vintage Books.

Mariolis, Peter. 1975. "Interlocking Directorates and Control of Corporations: The Theory of Bank Control." *Social Science Quarterly,* 56:425–439.

Marx, Karl. 1938. *Critique of the Gotha Program.* New York: International.

    1967. *Capital.* 3 vols. (A, B, C). New York: International.

Maslow, Abraham. 1954. *Motivation and Personality.* New York: Harper & Row.

McCarthy, John, and Mayer Zald. 1973. *The Trend of Social Movements in America: Professionalization and Resource Mobilization.* Morristown, N.Y.: General Learning Press.

McCauley, Brian. 1971. *Evaluation and Authority in Radical Alternative Schools and Public Schools.* Ph.D. diss., Stanford University.

Melman, Seymour. 1969. "Industrial Efficiency under Managerial vs. Cooperative Decision Making: A Comparative Study of Manufacturing Enterprises in Israel." *Studies in Comparative Development.* Beverly Hills: Sage.

    1971. "Industrial Efficiency under Managerial versus Cooperative Decision-Making." In *Self-Governing Socialism,* ed. B. Horvat et al.: International Arts and Science Press, pp. 203–220.

Merton, Robert. 1957. *Social Theory and Social Structure.* Glencoe, Ill.: The Free Press.

1964. "Anomie, Anomia, and Social Interaction: Contexts of Deviant Behavior." In *Anomie and Deviant Behavior*, ed. Marshal Clinard, pp. 213–242. New York: The Free Press of Glencoe.

Messinger, Sheldon. 1955. "Organizational Transformation: A Case Study of Declining Social Movement." *American Sociological Review*, 20:3–10.

Michels, Robert. 1962. *Political Parties: A Sociological Study of the Oligarchical Tendencies of Modern Democracy*. New York: The Free Press.

Milgram, Stanley. 1973. *Obedience to Authority: An Experimental View*. New York: Harper & Row.

Mills, C. Wright. 1959. *The Sociological Imagination*. New York: Oxford University Press.

Milofsky, Carl, and Frank Romo. 1981. "The Structure of Funding Arenas for Community Self-Help Organizations." Institute for Social and Policy Studies, Yale University. Photocopy.

Moberg, David. 1979. "Experimenting with the Future: Alternative Institutions and American Socialism." In *Co-ops, Communes and Collectives*, ed. John Case and Rosemary Taylor, pp. 274–311. New York: Pantheon Books.

Molotch, Harvey. 1976. "The City as a Growth Machine: Toward a Political Economy of Place." *American Journal of Sociology*, 82:309–332.

Mommsen, Wolfgang. 1974. *The Age of Bureaucracy: Perspectives on the Political Sociology of Max Weber*. New York: Harper & Row.

Mouzelis, Nicos. 1968. *Organization and Bureaucracy: An Analysis of Modern Theories*. Chicago: Aldine.

Nagy, Michael. 1980. Personal communication (letter), Department of Sociology, Concord College, Athens, W.Va.

New York Stock Exchange. 1982. *People and Productivity: A Challenge to Corporate America*.

Obradovic, Josip. 1970. "Participation and Work Attitudes in Yugoslavia." *Industrial Relations*, 9:161–169.

Obradovic, Josip, and William N. Dunn, eds. 1976, *Workers Self-Management and Organizational Power in Yugoslavia*. Pittsburgh: University of Pittsburgh.

Olson, Mancur. 1971. *The Logic of Collective Action: Public Goods and the Theory of Groups*. Cambridge, Mass.: Harvard University Press.

O'Sullivan, E. 1977. "International Cooperation: How Effective for Grassroots Organizations?" *Group and Organizational Studies*, 2:347–358.

Ouchi, William G. 1980. "Markets, Bureaucracies and Clans," *Administrative Science Quarterly*, 25:129–141.

Palisi, Bartolomeo. 1970. "Some Suggestions about the Transitory-Permanence Dimension of Organizations." *British Journal of Sociology*, June, pp. 200–206.

Pateman, Carole. 1970. *Participation and Democratic Theory*. Cambridge: Cambridge University Press, 1970.

Paton, Rob. 1978. *Some Problems in Co-operative Organization*. Co-operatives Research Monograph 3. Milton Keynes, England: The Open University.

Perrow, Charles. 1970. *Organizational Analysis: A Sociological View*. Belmont, Calif.: Wadsworth.

1976. "Control in Organizations: The Centralized-Decentralized Bureaucracy." Paper presented at the annual meeting of the American Sociological Association.

Perry, Stewart E. 1978. *San Francisco Scavengers*. Berkeley: University of California Press.

Quinn, Robert, and Graham Staines. 1977. *The 1977 Quality of Employment Survey*. Ann Arbor, Mich.: University of Michigan, Survey Research Center.

Reinharz, Shulamit. 1984. "Alternative Settings and Social Change." In *Psychology and Community Change*, ed. K. Heller, R. Price, S. Reinharz, S. Riger, and A. Wandersman. Homewood, Ill.: Dorsey Press.

Rhoades, Rosemary. 1981. "Milkwood Cooperative, Ltd." Cooperative Research Unit, Case Study no. 4. Milton Keynes, England: The Open University.

Rifkin, Jeremy. 1977. *Own Your Own Job*. New York: Bantam Books.

Rosen, Corey, Katherine Klein, and Karen Young. 1986. *Employee Ownership in America: The Equity Solution*. Lexington, Mass.: Lexington Books.

Rosner, Menachem. 1983. "Participatory Political and Organizational Democracy and the Experience of the Israeli Kibbutz." *International Yearbook of Organizational Democracy*, 1:455–484. Chichester: John Wiley & Sons.

Rosner, Menachem, and Joseph Blasi. 1981. "Theories of Participatory Democracy and the Kibbutz." In *Festschrift Volume for Professor S.N. Eisenstadt*, ed. Erik Cohen et al. Boulder, Colo.: Westview Press.

Rothschild-Whitt, Joyce. 1976a. "Problems of Democracy." *Working Papers for a New Society*, 4:41–45.

1976b. "Conditions Facilitating Participatory-Democratic Organizations." *Sociological Inquiry*, 46:75–86.

1979a. "The Collectivist Organization: An Alternative to Rational-Bureaucratic Models." *American Sociological Review*, 44:509–527.

1979b. "Worker Ownership and Control in the U.S." School of Industrial and Labor Relations, Cornell University. Photocopy.

1981. "There's More Than One Way to Run a Democratic Enterprise: Self-Management from the Netherlands." *Sociology of Work and Occupations*, 8:201–223.

1983. "Worker Ownership in Relation to Control: A Typology of Work Reform." *International Yearbook of Organizational Democracy*, 1:389–406.

1984. "Worker Ownership: Collective Response to an Elite-Generated Crisis." *Research on Social Movements, Conflict and Change*, 6:99–118.

Rueschmeyer, Detrich. 1977. "Structural Differentiation, Efficiency, and Power." *American Journal of Sociology*, 83 (July):1–25.

Rus, Veljko. 1970. "Influence Structure in Yugoslav Enterprise." *Industrial Relations*, 9:148–160.

Russell, Raymond. 1982a. "Rewards of Participation in the Worker-Owned Firm." In *Workplace Democracy and Social Change*, ed. F. Lindenfeld and J. Rothschild-Whitt, pp. 109–124. Boston: Porter Sargent.

1984. "The Role of Culture and Ethnicity in the Degeneration of Democratic Firms." *Economic and Industrial Democracy*, 5:73–96.

1985. *Sharing Ownership in the Workplace*. Albany: State University of New York Press.

Russell, Raymond, Art Hochner, and Stewart Perry. 1977. "San Francisco's Scavengers Run Their Own Firm." *Working Papers for a New Society*, 5:30–36.

1979. "Participation, Influence and Worker-Ownership." *Industrial Relations*, 18:330–341.

Sale, Kirkpatrick. 1980. *Human Scale*. New York: Coward, McCann & Geoghegan.

Sandkull, Bengt. 1982. "Managing the Democratization Process in Work Cooperatives." University of Linkoping, Sweden. Photocopy.

Sarason, Seymour. 1972. *The Creation of Settings and the Future Societies*. San Francisco: Jossey-Bass.

Satow, Roberta. 1975. "Value-Rational Authority and Professional Organizations: Weber's Missing Type." *Administrative Science Quarterly*, 20:526–531.

Scaff, Lawrence. 1981. "Max Weber and Robert Michels." *American Journal of Sociology*, 86:1269–1286.

Schlesinger, Melinda, and Pauline Bart. 1982. "Collective Work and Self-Identity: Working in a Feminist Illegal Abortion Collective." In *Workplace Democracy and Social Change*, ed. F. Lindenfeld and J. Rothschild-Whitt, pp. 139–153. Boston: Porter Sargent.

Schumacher, E. F. 1973. *Small Is Beautiful: Economics As If People Mattered*. New York: Harper & Row.

Schumpeter, Joseph. 1942. *Capitalism, Socialism, and Democracy*. New York: Harper and Brothers.

Scott, W. Richard. 1981. *Organizations: Rational, Natural, and Open Systems*. Englewood Cliffs, N.J.: Prentice-Hall.

—— 1949. *TVA and the Grass Roots*. Berkeley: University of California Press.

Shirom, Arie. 1972. "The Industrial Relations System of Industrial Cooperatives in the U.S., 1880–1935." *Labor History*, 13:533–551.

Sills, David. 1957. *The Volunteers*. New York: The Free Press.

Simmons, John, and William Mares. 1983. *Working Together: Participation from the Shop Floor to the Boardroom*. New York: Knopf.

Simpson, Richard. 1972. "Beyond Rational Bureaucracy: Changing Values and Social Integration in Post-Industrial Society." *Social Forces*, 51:1–6.

Sonquist, John, and Thomas Koenig. 1975. "Interlocking Directorates in the Top U.S. Corporations: A Graph Theory Approach." *Insurgent Sociologist*, 5:196–229.

Stein, Barry. 1974. *Industrial Efficiency and Community Enterprise*. Cambridge: Center for Community Economic Development.

Stephens, Evelyne, and John Stephens. 1982. "The Labor Movement, Political Power, and Workers' Participation in Western Europe." In *Political Power and Social Theory*, Vol. 3, pp. 215–249. Greenwich, Conn.: JAI Press.

Stern, Robert, and Tove Hammer. 1978. "Buying Your Job: Factors Affecting the Success or Failure of Employee Acquisition Attempts." *Human Relations*, 31:1101–1117.

Sullivan, Teresa. 1978. *Marginal Workers, Marginal Jobs: The Underutilization of American Workers*. Austin: University of Texas Press.

Swidler, Ann. 1976. "Teaching in a Free School." *Working Papers for a New Society*, 4:30–34.

—— 1979. *Organization without Authority: Dilemmas of Social Control in Free Schools*. Cambridge, Mass.: Harvard University Press.

Taylor, Rosemary. 1976. "Free Medicine." *Working Papers for a New Society*, 4:21–23, 83–94.

Terkel, Studs. 1975. *Working*. New York: Avon.

Thompson, James D., and Arthur Tuden. 1959. "Strategies, Structures, and Processes of Organizational Decision." Chap. 12 of *Comparative Studies in Administration*, ed. James Thompson. Pittsburgh: University of Pittsburgh Press, 1959.

Thornley, Jenny. n.d. "The Product Dilemma for Workers' Co-operatives in Britain, France and Italy." Co-operatives Research Occasional Paper no. 1. Milton Keynes, England: Co-operatives Research Unit, The Open University.

Thurow, Lester. 1980. *The Zero-Sum Society: Distribution and Possibilities for Economic Change*. New York: Penguin Books.

Toffler, Alvin. 1970. *Future Shock*. New York: Random House.

Torbert, William. 1973. "An Experimental Selection Process for a Collaborative Organization." *Journal of Applied Behavioral Science*, 9:331–350.

Useem, Michael. 1984. *The Inner Circle*. New York: Oxford University Press.

U.S. Department of Health, Education, and Welfare (HEW). 1973. *Work in America*. Cambridge, Mass.: MIT Press.

Vail, David. 1975. "The Case for Rural Industry: Economic Factors Favoring Small Scale,

Decentralized, Labor-Intensive Manufacturing." Institute on Science, Technology, and Development, Cornell University. Photocopy.

Vanek, Juroslav. 1977. "Some Fundamental Considerations in Financing and Form of Ownership under Labour Management." In *The Labour Managed Economy*. Ithaca, N.Y.: Cornell University Press.

Vocations for Social Change. 1976. *No Bosses Here: A Manual on Working Collectively*. Cambridge, Mass.: Vocations for Social Change.

Vroom, V. 1964. *Work and Motivation*. New York: John Wiley.

Walton, Richard. 1979. "Work Innovations in the United States." *Harvard Business Review* (July-August):88–98.

Ward, Colin. 1966. "The Organization of Anarchy." In *Patterns of Anarchy*, ed. Leonard Krimerman and Lewis Perry, pp. 386–396. Garden City, N.Y.: Anchor Books.

1972. "The Anarchist Contribution." In *The Case for Participatory Democracy*, ed. C. George Benello and Dimitrios Roussopoulos, pp. 283–294. New York: Viking Press.

Webb, Beatrice. 1921. "The Co-operative Movement of Great Britain and Its Recent Developments." *International Labour Review*, November, pp. 227–256.

Webb, Eugene. 1970. "Unconventionality, Triangulation, and Inference." In *Sociological Methods*, ed. Norman Denzin. Chicago: Aldine.

Webb, Sidney, and Beatrice Webb. 1920. *A Constitution for the Socialist Commonwealth of Great Britain*. London: Longmans.

Weber, Max. 1946. *From Max Weber: Essays in Sociology*. Trans. and ed. Hans Gerth and C. Wright Mills. New York: Oxford University Press.

1947. *The Theory of Social and Economic Organization*. Trans. A. M. Henderson and Talcott Parsons. Glencoe, Ill.: The Free Press.

1954. *Max Weber on Law in Economy and Society*. Cambridge, Mass.: Harvard University Press.

1968. *Economy and Society*. Ed. Guenther Roth and Claus Wittich. New York: Bedminster Press.

Wenig, M. 1982/83. "Still Serving that Dream: An Interview with Virginia Blaisdell." *Communities*, 56:15–22.

Whitehead, Alfred North. 1925. *Science and the Modern World*. New York: Macmillan.

Whitt, J. Allen. 1982. *Urban Elites and Mass Transportation: The Dialectics of Power*, Princeton: Princeton University Press.

Whyte, Martin King. 1973. "Bureaucracy and Modernization in China: The Maoist Critique." *American Sociological Review*, 38:149–163.

Whyte, William Foote. 1978. *Congressional Record*. House of Representatives. Washington, D.C.: Government Printing Office, June 19.

1979. "On Making the Most of Participant Observation." *The American Sociologist*, 14:56–66.

Woodcock, George. 1962. *Anarchism: A History of Libertarian Ideas and Movements*. New York: World.

Wright, E. 1976. "Class Boundaries in Advanced Capitalist Societies." *New Left Review*, 98:3–41.

Zablocki, Benjamin. 1971. *The Joyful Community: An Account of the Bruderhof*. Baltimore: Penguin Books.

Zald, Mayer, and Roberta Ash. 1966. "Social Movement Organizations: Growth, Decay, and Change." *Social Forces*, 44:327–341.

Zald, Mayer, and John McCarthy. 1975. "Organizational Intellectuals and the Criticism of Society." *Social Service Review*, 49:344–362.

Zeitlin, Maurice. 1970. *Revolutionary Politics and the Cuban Working Class*. New York: Harper & Row.

Zipp, John, Paul Luebke, and Richard Landerman. 1984. "The Social Bases of Support for Workplace Democracy." Washington University, St. Louis, Mo. Photocopy.

Zwerdling, Daniel. 1975. "Shopping Around: Nonprofit Food." *Working Papers for a New Society,* 3:21–31.

1976. "The Day the Workers Took Over." *New Times,* December 10, pp. 38–45.

1979. "The Uncertain Revival of Food Cooperatives." In *Co-ops, Communes and Collectives,* ed. John Case and Rosemary Taylor, pp. 89–111. New York: Pantheon Books.

Index

213

Other books in the Arnold and Caroline Rose Monograph Series of the American Sociological Association